FREE DVD FREE FREE DVD

Essential Test Tips DVD from Trivium Test Prep

Dear Customer,

Thank you for purchasing from Cirrus Test Prep! Whether you're looking to join the military, get into college, or advance your career, we're honored to be a part of your journey.

To show our appreciation (and to help you relieve a little of that test-prep stress), we're offering a **FREE** *Praxis Essential Test Tips DVD** by Cirrus Test Prep. Our DVD includes 35 test preparation strategies that will help keep you calm and collected before and during your big exam. All we ask is that you email us your feedback and describe your experience with our product. Amazing, awful, or just so-so: we want to hear what you have to say!

To receive your **FREE** *Praxis Essential Test Tips DVD*, please email us at 5star@cirrustestprep.com. Include "Free 5 Star" in the subject line and the following information in your email:

1. The title of the product you purchased.

2. Your rating from 1 – 5 (with 5 being the best).

3. Your feedback about the product, including how our materials helped you meet your goals and ways in which we can improve our products.

4. Your full name and shipping address so we can send your **FREE** *Praxis Essential Test Tips DVD*.

If you have any questions or concerns please feel free to contact us directly at 5star@cirrustestprep.com.

Thank you, and good luck with your studies!

* Please note that the free DVD is <u>not included</u> with this book. To receive the free DVD, please follow the instructions above.

Praxis II Elementary Education Multiple Subjects 5001 Study Guide 2019 – 2020

TEST PREP WITH PRACTICE TEST QUESTIONS

Table of Contents

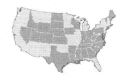

Introduction

Congratulations on choosing to take the Praxis Elementary Education: Multiple Subjects (5001) exam! By purchasing this book, you've taken the first step toward becoming an elementary educator.

This guide will provide you with a detailed overview of the Praxis Elementary Education exam, so you know exactly what to expect on test day. We'll take you through all the concepts covered on the test and give you the opportunity to test your knowledge with practice questions. Even if it's been a while since you last took a major test, don't worry; we'll make sure you're more than ready!

What is the Praxis?

Praxis Series tests are a part of teaching licensure in approximately forty states. Each state uses the tests and scores in different ways, so be sure to check the certification requirements in your state by going to www.ets.org/praxis/states. There, you will find information detailing the role of the Praxis tests in determining teaching certification in your state, what scores are required, and how to transfer Praxis scores from one state to another.

What's on the Praxis?

The content in this guide will prepare you for the Praxis Elementary Education: Multiple Subjects (5001) exam. This test uses multiple-choice and numeric-entry questions to assess whether you possess the knowledge and skills necessary to become an elementary educator. The exam consists of four subtests that each assess your subject knowledge in a different area. Each subtest has a different time limit and number of questions; the approximate number of questions for each subtopic is given below. Altogether, the exam is four hours and fifteen minutes long.

Praxis 5001 Elementary Education				
Section	**Questions per Section**	**Concepts**	**Percentage**	**Number of Questions**
Reading/ Language Arts	80	Reading	47%	38
		Writing, Speaking, and Listening	52%	42
Mathematics	50	Number and Operations	40%	20
		Algebraic Thinking	30%	15
		Geometry and Measurement, Data, Statistics, and Probability	30%	15
Social Studies	55	United States History, Government, and Citizenship	45%	25
		Geography, Anthropology, and Sociology	30%	16
		World History and Economics	25%	14
Science	50	Earth Science	32%	16
		Life Science	34%	17
		Physical Science	34%	17
Total			4.25 hours	235

You will answer approximately eighty multiple-choice questions on reading and language arts. Questions in this section will assess your own reading comprehension and vocabulary usage as well as your understanding of teaching strategies that reinforce vocabulary and language development. The foundations of reading and the use of language in writing will be assessed. You'll need to know the purposes and characteristics of effective listening and communication; likewise, you should understand the barriers that hinder interpersonal exchange.

You will answer approximately fifty multiple-choice questions on mathematics. The test will cover mathematical processes, number sense and numeration, algebraic concepts, informal geometry and measurement, and data organization and interpretation. A scientific calculator will be provided for you on this portion of the test.

You will answer approximately fifty-five multiple-choice questions on social studies. The social studies section is interdisciplinary; it will test your ability to understand relationships among fields in social studies. These fields include geography, anthropology, sociology, world and US history, government/civics/ democracy, economics, and social studies as inquiry. You'll need knowledge of all of these subjects in order to answer the questions correctly.

You will answer approximately fifty multiple-choice questions on science. This section assesses your knowledge of scientific fundamentals in a wide spectrum of the sciences, including earth, life, and physical sciences, science in personal and social perspectives, and science as inquiry. Questions will explore the structure of systems, such as matter, living systems, and earth systems. Be sure to familiarize yourself with the unifying processes of science and science as a process and human endeavor.

How is the Praxis Scored?

The questions are equally weighted. Keep in mind that some multiple-choice questions are experimental questions for the purpose of the Praxis test writers and will not count toward your overall score. However, since those questions are not indicated on the test, you must respond to every question. There is no penalty for guessing on Praxis tests, so be sure to eliminate answer choices and answer every question. If you still do not know the answer, guess; you may get it right!

Your score report will be available on your Praxis account for one year, but you can also opt for a paper report. The score report includes your score and the passing score for the states you identified as score recipients. Your score will be available immediately after the test.

How is the Praxis Administered?

The Praxis Series tests are available at testing centers across the nation. To find a testing center near you, go to http://www.ets.org/praxis/register. At this site, you can create a Praxis account, check testing dates, register for a test, or find instructions for registering via mail or phone. The Praxis Elementary Education: Multiple Subjects (5001) exam is administered as a computerized test. The Praxis website allows you to take a practice test to acclimate yourself to the computerized format.

On the day of your test, be sure to bring your admission ticket (which is provided when you register) and photo ID. The testing facility will provide pencils and erasers and an area outside of the testing room to store your personal belongings. You are allowed no personal effects in the testing area. Cell phones and other electronic, photographic, recording, or listening devices are not permitted in the testing center at all, and bringing those items may be cause for dismissal, forfeiture of your testing fees, and cancellation of your scores. For details on what is and is not permitted at your testing center, refer to http://www.ets.org/praxis/test_day/bring.

About Cirrus Test Prep

Cirrus Test Prep study guides are designed by current and former educators and are tailored to meet your needs as an incoming educator. Our guides offer all of the resources necessary to help you pass teacher certification tests across the nation.

Cirrus clouds are graceful, wispy clouds characterized by their high altitude. Just like cirrus clouds, Cirrus Test Prep's goal is to help educators "aim high" when it comes to obtaining their teacher certification and entering the classroom.

About This Guide

This guide will help you master the most important test topics and also develop critical test-taking skills. We have built features into our books to prepare you for your tests and increase your score. Along with a detailed summary of the test's format, content, and scoring, we offer an in-depth overview of the content knowledge required to pass the test. Our sidebars provide interesting information, highlight key concepts, and review content so that you can solidify your understanding of the exam's concepts. Test your knowledge with sample questions and detailed answer explanations in the text that help you think through the problems on the exam as well as practice tests that reflect the content and format of the Praxis. We're pleased you've chosen Cirrus to be a part of your professional journey!

Part I: Review

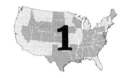

Reading and Language Arts

Reading, writing, speaking, and listening are the four cornerstones of a language arts curriculum in elementary education. Teacher content knowledge is demonstrated in the following areas: reading foundational skills, student comprehension of literature and informational texts, the stages and characteristics of the writing process and effective writing, and techniques for oral communication and collaboration.

Reading: Foundational Skills

Phonological Awareness

Phonological Awareness is an understanding of how sounds, syllables, words, and word parts can be orally manipulated to break apart words, make new words, and create rhymes. It is an important foundational skill for learning to read and literacy development. **Phonemic awareness** is a type of phonological awareness that focuses on the sounds in a language. It is an understanding of how each small unit of sound, or **phoneme**, forms the language by creating differences in the meanings of words. For example, the phonemes /m/ and /s/ determine the difference in meaning between the words *mat* and *sat*.

There are forty-four different phonemes in the English language. These includes letter combinations such as consonant diagraphs like /sh/ and vowel dipthongs like /oi/ where the letters work together to produce one sound. Teachers build phonemic awareness in their students using a variety of techniques such as phoneme blending, phoneme segmentation, phoneme substitution, and phoneme deletion.

Table 1.1. Phoneme Chart

s	t	p	n	m	a	e	i	o
sun	tan	paint	now	mark	apple	edge	innertube	obvious
g	d	c k	r	h	u	ai	ee	igh
girl	dark	cat, kite	ring	heat	under	pain	flee	night
b	f	l	j	v	oa	oo	oo	ar
buy	find	lamb	joy	vehicle	float	foot	scoot	far
w	x	y	z	qu	or	ur	ow	oi
wipe	exit	yellow	zip	quiet	port	turn	brow	foil
ch	sh	th	th	ng	ear	air	ure	er
sandwich	sharp	thick	them	ring	fear	flair	lure	driver

Phoneme blending is combining phonemes to make a word; for example, /m/ /a/ /t/ combines to form *mat*. In contrast, **phoneme substitution** is the replacement of phonemes in words to make new words; removing the /m/ from the beginning of the word *mat* and replacing it with /s/ creates the word *sat*. **Phoneme segmentation** is separating phonemes in words; separating the sounds in the word *mat* isolates the phonemes /m/ /a/ /t/. Finally, in **phoneme deletion**, phonemes are removed from words to make new words. Removing /m/ from *mat* leaves the word *at*.

Building phonemic awareness in students is the latter part of a developmental sequence that contributes to a strong foundation in phonological awareness. Prior to focusing on phonemic awareness, teachers build phonological awareness with exercises that task students with orally manipulating the phonological units of spoken **syllables**. These phonological units are defined as onsets and rimes and can be blended, substituted, segmented, and deleted just like phonemes. The **onset** of a syllable is the beginning consonant or consonant blend. The **rime** includes the syllable's vowel and its remaining consonants. For example, in the word *block*, the consonant blend /bl/ is the onset, and the remainder of the word –*ock* is the rime.

Once students have a solid foundation in phonological awareness, they are ready to begin phonics instruction. **Phonics** is the study of the relationship between the spoken sounds in words and the printed letters that correspond to those sounds, or **letter-sound correspondence**. In explicit phonics instruction, letters and their corresponding sounds are first taught in isolation, then blended into words, and finally applied to decodable text.

Initially, the most common sounds for each letter and **high frequency** letter-sound correspondences, or those that occur most often in the English language, are introduced. In order to assist students beginning to read simple VC (vowel-consonant), VCC (vowel-consonant-consonant), CVCC (consonant-vowel-consonant-consonant), and CVC (consonant-vowel-consonant) words early on, a few short vowel sounds are introduced as well. Letters with names that bear a strong relationship to their sounds are introduced before letters that do not. For example, the sound of the letter *s* can be heard at the end of its name.

Phonics instruction progresses from simple to more complex letter-sound correspondences and sound/spellings (or the spelling of words based on letter-sound correspondences). Short-vowel sound spellings are introduced before long-vowel sound/spellings, and letters that are similar in appearance (e.g., *b* and *d*) or sound (e.g., /m/ and /n/) are taught separately along the instructional continuum. As students move through kindergarten and the primary grades, they progress from decoding two- or three-phoneme words with letters representing their most common sounds to longer words and more complex sound/spelling patterns.

Sight words, words that are repeated most often in text, are taught in conjunction with phonics. These are words that students need to learn to recognize by sight, such as *a*, *in*, *the*, *at*, and *I*, in order to read sentences with optimal fluency. As with letter-sound correspondences and sound/spellings, sight word instruction begins with the most common words, or highest frequency words. Teachers develop sight word lists for students using either the *Dolch List of Basic Sight Words* or *Fry's Numerical List of Instant Words*. These lists change and evolve across grade levels so that students build a large repertoire of instantly recognizable words as they move through the primary grades.

SAMPLE QUESTION

1) A teacher says *hat* and instructs students to produce the sounds they hear in the word. Which strategy is the teacher using to build phoneme awareness?

   A. phoneme blending

   B. phoneme deletion

   C. phoneme segmentation

   D. phoneme substitution

Answers:

   A. Incorrect. The strategy of phoneme blending requires students to combine phonemes to make a word.

   B. Incorrect. The strategy of phoneme deletion requires students to remove phonemes in words to make new words.

   C. Correct. The strategy of phoneme segmentation requires students to separate the phonemes in a word.

   D. Incorrect. The strategy of phoneme substitution requires students to replace phonemes in words to make new words.

ROOTS AND AFFIXES

Beginning in second grade, language arts students also receive instruction in identifying and understanding roots and affixes in order to determine the meanings of unfamiliar words. **Roots** are typically derived from Latin or Greek and establish the basis of new words. *Cent* is a Latin root meaning "one hundred." **Affixes** are added to words or roots to change their meanings. They consist of prefixes, added to the beginning of a word or root, and suffixes, added to the end of a word or root. For example, the prefix *per-* can be added to *cent* to make the word *percent*, effectively changing the meaning to"one part in a hundred." Likewise, the suffix *–ury* can be added to *cent* to make the word *century*, effectively changing the meaning to "a period of one hundred years."

By understanding how roots and affixes work together to form words and change the meanings of words, students can steadily add new words to their automatic memory banks of known words and decode unfamiliar words with greater ease and precision. As with instruction in phonics and sight words, elementary language arts teachers begin with the most common prefixes and suffixes and progress from simple to complex combinations of roots and affixes.

Table 1.2. Common Roots and Affixes

Root	Definition	Example
ast(er)	star	asteroid, astronomy
audi	hear	audience, audible
auto	self	automatic, autograph
bene	good	beneficent, benign
bio	life	biology, biorhythm
cap	take	capture
ced	yield	secede
chrono	time	chronometer, chronic
corp	body	corporeal
crac or crat	rule	autocrat
demo	people	democracy
dict	say	dictionary, dictation
duc	lead or make	ductile, produce
gen	give birth	generation, genetics
geo	earth	geography, geometry
grad	step	graduate
graph	write	graphical, autograph
ject	throw	eject

Root	Definition	Example
jur or jus	law	justice, jurisdiction
log or logue	thought	logic, logarithm
luc	light	lucidity
man	hand	manual
mand	order	remand
mis	send	transmission
mono	one	monotone
omni	all	omnivore
path	feel	pathology
phil	love	philanthropy
phon	sound	phonograph
port	carry	export
qui	rest	quiet
scrib or script	write	scribe, transcript
sense or sent	feel	sentiment
tele	far away	telephone
terr	earth	terrace
uni	single	unicode
vac	empty	vacant
vid	see	video
vis	see	vision

Table 1.3. Common Prefixes

Prefix	Definition	Example
a- (also an-)	not, without; to, toward; of, completely	atheist, anemic, aside, aback, anew, abashed
ante-	before, preceding	antecedent, anteroom
anti-	opposing, against	antibiotic, anticlimax
com- (also co-, col-, con-, cor-)	with, jointly, completely	combat, codriver, collude, confide
dis- (also di-)	negation, removal	disadvantage, disbar
en- (also em-)	put into or on; bring into the condition of; intensify	engulf, entomb
hypo-	under	hypoglycemic, hypothermia
in- (also il-, im-, ir-)	not, without; in, into, toward, inside	infertile, impossible, influence, include

Table 1.3. Common Prefixes (continued)

Prefix	Definition	Example
intra-	inside, within	intravenous, intrapersonal
out-	surpassing, exceeding; external, away from	outperform, outdoor
over-	excessively, completely; upper, outer, over, above	overconfident, overcast
pre-	before	precondition, preadolescent, prelude
re-	again	reapply, remake
semi-	half, partly	semicircle, semiconscious
syn- (also sym-)	in union, acting together	synthesis, symbiotic
trans-	across, beyond	transatlantic
trans-	into a different state	translate
under-	beneath, below	underarm, undersecretary
under-	not enough	underdeveloped

SAMPLE QUESTIONS

2)   Use roots and affixes to determine the meaning of the underlined word:

Monograph most nearly means

A.   a mathematical concept

B.   a written study of a single subject

C.   an illness caused by a virus

D.   a boring piece of art

Answers:

B.   The prefix *mono—* means one, and the word root *graph* means written, so a monograph is a written document about one subject.

3)   Use roots and affixes to determine the meaning of the underlined word:

My sister is a polyglot, and comfortably travels all over the world.

A.   a person who speaks many language

B.   a person who loves to travel

C.   a person who is extremely intelligent

D.   a person who is unafraid of new places

Answers:

A.   The prefix *poly—* means many, and the suffix *–glot* means in a language or tongue. Therefore, the sister speaks many languages.

READING FLUENCY

Language arts teachers apply strategic phonics, sight word, and word analysis strategies to help students become fluent readers who can use their reading skills as a means of accessing literature and deriving information from printed text. In other words, reading to learn is the end-all goal of learning to read and **fluency**, or the ability to read with ease and automaticity, is the key. Reading fluency is composed of three factors: rate, accuracy, and prosody.

Reading **rate** is the speed and fluidity with which a student can read. It is determined by the number of words read correctly per minute or the length of time it takes for a student to read a selected passage. A steady, fluid reading rate is important because it allows the reader to focus on constructing meaning from text without being distracted by the effort it takes to slowly plod through word pronunciations.

Reading **accuracy** refers to a student's ability to recognize or decode words correctly. Meaningful comprehension of reading material is dependent on reading accuracy, which in turn depends upon the reader having a significant inventory of known sight words and an ability to decode words effortlessly. Without accuracy, a student is unlikely to understand what an author or text is communicating. By examining patterns in word-identification errors, the elementary language arts teacher can identify decoding strategies that a student is not using and provide appropriate instruction.

Prosody encompasses the range of vocal expressions a reader uses when reading aloud. It includes rhythm, intonation, and stress patterns. Being able to read text orally while conveying the meaning of what is being read with appropriate vocal cues is evidence of reading prosody. In other words, when a student reads out loud, the spoken words should reflect natural speech patterns. Typically, when prosody is lacking, a student will read in a stilted, monotone voice, which often means the student does not understand the words.

SAMPLE QUESTION

4) Which of the following is an example of prosody?

    A. using appropriate vocal cues when reading aloud

    B. decoding words correctly when reading aloud

    C. reading at an appropriate speed when reading aloud

    D. reading smoothly and steadily when reading aloud

Answers:

    A. **Correct.** Prosody is a reader's ability to use appropriate vocal expressions when reading aloud.

    B. Incorrect. Decoding words correctly while reading aloud is an example of reading accuracy.

C.   Incorrect. Reading aloud at an appropriate speed is an example of reading rate.

D.   Incorrect. Reading smoothly and steadily when reading aloud is an example of reading rate.

Teaching English to Speakers of Other Languages

Many elementary language arts classrooms include both students whose first language is English and students who are learning English as a second language. Five **stages of language acquisition** have been identified for students learning a second language. These stages are defined as preproduction, early production, speech emergence, intermediate fluency, and advanced fluency. These stages correlate to five **levels of language proficiency**, L1 through L5, which are L1) Entering, L2) Beginning, L3) Developing, L4) Expanding, and L5) Bridging.

Table 1.4. Stages of Second-Language Acquisition

Stage	Characteristics
Preproduction	Preproduction is also known as the silent period. Though these learners may have close to 500 words in their receptive vocabulary, they refrain from speaking but will listen and may copy words down. They can respond to visual cues such as pictures and gestures, and they will communicate their comprehension. However, sometimes students will repeat back what they have heard in a process referred to as parroting. This can aid them in adding to their receptive vocabulary, but it should not be mistaken for producing language.
Early Production	In this stage learners have achieved a 1000-word receptive and active vocabulary. They now produce single-word and two- to three-word phrases and can respond to questions and statements. Many learners in this stage enjoy engaging in musical games or word plays that help them to memorize language chunks that they can use later.
Speech Emergence	English language learners have a vocabulary of about 3000 words by the time they reach this stage of second-language acquisition. They are able to chunk simple words and phrases into sentences that may or may not be grammatically correct. They respond to modeling of correct responses better than direct correction. At this stage, learners also are more likely to participate in conversations with native English speakers, as they are gaining confidence in their language skills. These learners can understand simple readings when reinforced by graphics or pictures and can complete some content work with support.

Stage	Characteristics
Intermediate Fluency	By the intermediate fluency stage, English language learners have acquired a vocabulary of about 6000 words. They are able to speak in more complex sentences and catch and correct many of their own errors. They are also willing to ask questions to clarify what they do not understand. Learners at this stage may sound fluent, but they have large gaps in their vocabulary as well as in their grammatical and syntactical understanding of the language. They are often comfortable speaking in group conversation that avoids heavy academic language.
Advanced Fluency	Second-language learners who reach advanced fluency have achieved cognitive language proficiency in their learned language. They demonstrate near-native ability and use complex, multi phrase and clause sentences to convey their ideas. Though accents are still detectable and idiomatic expressions are sometimes used incorrectly, the language learner has become essentially fluent.

The **preproduction stage** of language acquisition is defined as the silent stage during which a student is primarily absorbing new input. At this proficiency level—L1 Entering—a student rarely uses English to communicate and responds nonverbally to instruction, constructing meaning primarily from illustrations, graphs, and charts. This is followed by the early production stage in which a student begins to speak a few words and simple phrases. At this proficiency level—L2 Beginning—a student can communicate basic information in a limited manner but exhibits a number of predictable errors.

During the **emergence of speech stage**, the student begins to speak more clearly and accurately and increases his or her spoken vocabulary. It is during this stage that the student takes steps toward reading and writing in the second language. At this proficiency level—L3 Developing—a student understands more complex speech and can communicate spontaneously in simple sentences. However, the student's vocabulary and comprehension of language structure remain limited.

During the **intermediate fluency stage**, the student gains competency speaking in more complex sentences and demonstrates a larger vocabulary. This is the stage at which a student can begin to think in the second language as well as speak it. At this proficiency level—L4 Expanding—a student can read in the second language with demonstrated fluency, but may still struggle with comprehending text that describes complex or abstract concepts.

Finally, the student enters the **advanced fluency stage** in which he or she can converse fluently and think clearly in the second language. At this proficiency level—L5 Bridging—a student requires only minimal language support and can function at the same level as peers with a first language of English. Progression through these five stages of language acquisition typically takes around two years. It is important for language arts teachers to recognize these stages and proficiency levels in order to best facilitate and recognize student understanding and internalization of both the new language and new content.

5)   Marlin enjoys participating in class discussions with his peers and even initiates them occasionally. Though he sometimes makes errors in his speech, he is able to self-correct and often repeats the correct phrasing back to himself. What stage of second-language acquisition might Marlin be in?

A.   preproduction

B.   early production

C.   speech emergence

D.   intermediate fluency

Answers:

A.   Incorrect. Preproduction is characterized by little speech and much listening. Students may copy words down and respond to visual cues such as pictures and gestures to communicate their comprehension.

B.   Incorrect. Early production is characterized by the building of vocabulary and the production of single word and two- to three-word phrases and responses.

C.   Incorrect. Speech emergence is characterized by the ability to create multi-word responses; however, in this stage students do not yet have a working grasp of grammar concepts and thus must model their sentence structures after others' speech.

D.   Correct. Marlin's interest in conversation and his ability to self-correct indicate that he is moving towards advanced fluency and has reached the intermediate stage.

Reading Literature and Informational Text

In order to effectively teach students to comprehend the literature and informational text they are tasked with reading, the elementary language arts teacher needs to demonstrate an understanding of comprehension strategies, point of view, comparing information from a variety of texts and multimedia sources, and the role of text complexity in reading development.

COMPREHENSION STRATEGIES

Expertise in language arts requires an ability to use key ideas and details from literary or informational text to determine the moral, theme, or central idea; make inferences; and summarize information. Readers must also be able to analyze characters, setting, plot, and relationships among ideas, events, and concepts. The **theme** of a literary text is the basic idea that the author wants to convey. It weaves in and out of the text as the story, play, or poem unfolds. It expresses an underlying opinion related to the text's subject. On the other hand, the **moral** of a literary text is the lesson the author wants to teach the reader. It is more direct than a theme. The basic underlying idea of informational text is referred to as the **central idea**. This is the major focus of the information provided in the text.

The key purpose of reading text is to obtain information or experience a story. In order to do this, readers must have the ability to comprehend what is being read. Without comprehension, reading is simply an exercise in making sounds that have no meaning. Being able to comprehend what is being read is what connects the words an author writes to the reader's experience of the world; it is what gives text meaning and makes it relatable. Elementary language arts teachers help students to comprehend what is being read by teaching students a variety of comprehension strategies. One of these strategies is the ability to make **inferences**, or determine what an author is suggesting by using clues in text. It is the ability to understand what is not directly stated by an author.

Summarization is the distillation and condensation of a text into its main idea and key details. It is a short encapsulation of what the text is about to clarify the general message. However, to properly summarize, it is important to **identify story elements**. More specifically, this is identifying the characters (e.g., main, minor, protagonist, antagonist, dynamic, static), **setting** (where the story takes place), and **plot** development (e.g., exposition, rising action, problem/climax, falling action, resolution) in a text. Understanding the role of a character in a story via the character's actions, traits, relationship, and personality is **character analysis**. Analyzing how a character thinks and behaves allows a reader to understand his or her motivations and beliefs.

Recognizing genre is the ability to name the genre of a text (e.g., poetry, drama, picture book, graphic novel, folktale, myth, fairy tale, tall tale, historical fiction, science fiction) and the features of that genre. Readers who understand and recognize the characteristics of a variety of genres can gain additional insights into an author's purpose or message. For example, a reader is able to comprehend a text with a greater depth and breadth if he or she knows how the **rhyme scheme** (e.g., abab, aabb, aabba) and **meter** (basic rhythmic structure of the lines or verses in poetry) of a poem affect its tone or how **stage directions** develop the rising action in a play.

An author uses a specific point of view to tell a story. When **identifying point of view**, readers use genre and pronoun clues to identify who is telling a story to best form accurate conclusions about the events of the story. Typically, authors use one of five points of view: first-person, second-person, third-person objective, third-person limited omniscient, and third-person omniscient. In **first-person** point of view, one character tells the story from his or her direct experience using pronouns such as *I*, *my*, *mine*, and *we*. In **second-person** point of view, the perspective of the text is from an external "you," whether that be the reader or unknown other. In **third-person**

objective point of view, a detached narrator relates the actions and dialogue of the story, but not the thoughts or feelings of any characters. In **third-person limited omniscient** point of view, a detached narrator tells the story from one character's point of view including that character's internal thoughts and feelings. In **third-person omniscient** point of view, a detached and all-knowing narrator tells the story from the point of view of all of the characters, including all of their thoughts and feelings. Any text told from a third-person point of view includes pronouns such as *he, she, it*, and *they*.

Some texts offer supplemental information outside of the main text. These **text features** include imagery like photographs, drawings, maps, charts, graphs. They also include organizational features like chapter **headings**, titles, **sidebars** (boxes of explanatory or additional information set aside from main text), and **hyperlinks** (highlighted sections or words in digital text that take a reader to another digital location or document for additional information). Readers should be able to **analyze text features** to better comprehend an author's message.

Finally, **analyzing text organization** is the ability to analyze the way a text is organized in order to better comprehend an author's purpose for writing. Different forms of textual organization facilitate an author's message. Some of the more common organizational structures are cause and effect, problem and solution, sequence of events or steps-in-a-process, compare and contrast, and description. Each **text structure** can be identified by the use of particular signal words (words that provide clues to how the author has organized information) and features.

SAMPLE QUESTIONS

6)   **What is an inference based on?**

 A.   facts and specific examples in the text
 B.   details of the text and the reader's knowledge of the topic of the text
 C.   understanding the author's purpose
 D.   recognizing the author's tone

Answers:

 A.   Incorrect. It is true that readers use details of the text to infer meaning. However, an inference is made when certain information is not explicitly stated and readers have to fill in the blank.

 B.   Correct. In order to read between the lines, readers must use their own knowledge as well as draw on the information provided.

 C.   Incorrect. Understanding the author's purpose may help a reader to draw an inference, but it is not necessarily essential to the process.

 D.   Incorrect. Readers can infer an author's tone, but tone itself does not necessarily provide enough information for one to make an inference.

7)   **What is one way students could determine the central idea of a text?**

   A.   by summarizing the passage

   B.   by crossing out all irrelevant detail

   C.   by highlighting all sentences that mention the main topic

   D.   by identifying the main points and deciding which one is supported by all of the points and details

   Answers:

   A.   Incorrect. While a summary would include the main points of the text, it would not necessarily identify the central idea or point.

   B.   Incorrect. Rather than cross out details, students should determine how those details relate to ideas in the passage.

   C.   Incorrect. Most of the sentences relate to the main topic, so this would not be helpful.

   D.   Correct. In a sense, this process could be considered the reverse of the process a writer might use as he or she plans to write, starting with the central idea that he or she wants to communicate and determining the points and details that will make his or her idea clear to the reader.

8)   **Read the excerpt from *Treasure Island* by Robert Louis Stevenson.**

   I remember him as if it were yesterday, as he came plodding to the inn door, his sea-chest following behind him in a hand-barrow—a tall, strong, heavy, nut-brown man, his tarry pigtail falling over the shoulder of his soiled blue coat, his hands ragged and scarred, with black, broken nails, and the sabre cut across one cheek, a dirty, livid white.

   This text is written from which point of view?

   A.   second-person

   B.   first-person

   C.   third-person objective

   D.   third-person omniscient

   Answers:

   A.   Incorrect. Second-person point of view is written from the perspective of an external "you."

   B.   Correct. First-person point of view is written directly from the perspective of one character.

   C.   Incorrect. Third-person objective point of view is written from the perspective of a detached narrator.

   D.   Incorrect. Third-person omniscient point of view is written from the perspective of an all-knowing, detached narrator.

TEXT COMPLEXITY

The teaching of reading comprehension strategies is best facilitated when students are reading text that is at developmentally appropriate reading levels. Students improve their reading skills best when the text provided is neither too easy nor too difficult. **Text leveling**, or complexity, is determined by three factors: quantitative measures, qualitative measures, and reader and task considerations. **Quantitative measures** include readability scores determined by computer algorithms that evaluate text elements such as word frequency and sentence length. **Qualitative measures** include analysis of text elements such as structure (i.e., low or high complexity), language clarity (i.e., literal vs. figurative or familiar vs. unfamiliar), and knowledge demands (i.e., assumptions about what a reader already knows). **Reader and task considerations** are determined by the professional judgment of educators who match texts to particular students, classes, and/or tasks based on their inherent needs.

SAMPLE QUESTION

9) Which of the following is true of quantitative measures of text complexity?

   A. They are task considerations determined by professional judgment.

   B. They are analytical measurements determined by knowledge demands.

   C. They are statistical measurements determined by computer algorithms.

   D. They are leveling measurements determined by text structure.

Answers:

   A. Incorrect. Quantitative measures of text complexity are free of human judgment.

   B. Incorrect. The analysis of knowledge demands is a qualitative measure of text complexity.

   C. Correct. Quantitative measures are objective and based on statistics.

   D. Incorrect. Leveling measurements based on text structure are qualitative measures.

Writing

Elementary school is where students establish a solid foundation of writing skills that lead to a lifelong ability to communicate ideas, opinions, experiences, and beliefs. Language arts teachers across the grades are tasked with building student understanding of writing styles, purposes, and practices.

Table 1.5. Developmental Stages of Writing

Stage	Age	Students in this stage...
Preconventional	3 – 5	▶ are aware that print conveys meaning, but rely on pictures to communicate visually. ▶ include recognizable shapes and letters on drawings. ▶ can describe the significance of the objects in their drawings.
Emerging	4 – 6	▶ use pictures when drawing, but may also label objects. ▶ can match some letters to sounds. ▶ copy print they see in their environment.
Developing	5 – 7	▶ write sentences and no longer rely mainly on pictures. ▶ attempt to use punctuation and capitalization. ▶ spell words based on sound.
Beginning	6 – 8	▶ write several related sentences on a topic. ▶ use word spacing, punctuation, and capitalization correctly. ▶ create writing that others can read.
Expanding	7 – 9	▶ organize sentences logically and use more complex sentence structures. ▶ spell high frequency words correctly. ▶ respond to guidance and criticism from others.
Bridging	8 – 10	▶ write about a particular topic with a clear beginning, middle, and end. ▶ begin to use paragraphs. ▶ consult outside resources (e.g., dictionaries).
Fluent	9 – 11	▶ write both fiction and nonfiction with guidance. ▶ experiment with sentence length and complexity. ▶ edit for punctuation, spelling, and grammar.

Go on →

Table 1.5. Developmental Stages of Writing (continued)		
Stage	**Age**	**Students in this stage...**
Proficient	10 – 13	▶ write well-developed fiction and nonfiction. ▶ use transitional sentences and descriptive language. ▶ edit for organization and style.
Connecting	11 – 14	▶ write in a number of different genres. ▶ develop a personal voice when writing. ▶ use complex punctuation.
Independent	13 and older	▶ explore topics in depth in fiction and nonfiction. ▶ incorporate literary devices in their writing. ▶ revise writing through multiple drafts.

TYPES OF WRITING

There are four main writing **styles** that students learn in elementary school. Each style is selected based on an author's **purpose** for writing—to explain, to entertain, to describe, or to persuade—and the needs of the **audience**, the people reading the material. Different audiences have different needs. For example, people reading a humor blog will most likely prefer an informal style, while the audience for a magazine article explaining environmental problems caused by deforestation will appreciate writing with a well-organized structure and paragraphs that expand on key issues. The four main styles of writing are as follows:

▶ **Expository Writing**: This style of writing is primarily used to explain an idea or concept or inform the reader about a topic. It is most often used in formal essays that include a main idea and supporting details based on fact.

▶ **Narrative Writing**: This style of writing is primarily used to tell a personal or fictional story that entertains the reader. The author includes descriptive details and figurative language in order to maintain the reader's attention with dynamic characters, interesting settings, and captivating plots. Poems that tell stories, or **narrative poems**, also use this writing style.

▶ **Descriptive Writing**: This style of writing emphasizes the production of imagery using words and figurative language that appeal to the reader's five senses. It is a writing style that produces vivid pictures in the reader's imagination and is often used to write poetry or detailed descriptions of experiences or events.

▶ **Persuasive Writing**: This style of writing is used to convince, or persuade, a reader to subscribe to the author's opinion or point of view. It follows a formal progression that aims to sway the reader into accepting the author's stance and often plays on the reader's emotions to achieve its goal. Persuasive writing is often used for **speeches** and **advertisements**.

SAMPLE QUESTION

10) **Which of the following can be classified as persuasive writing?**

    A.   an advertisement for a new product

    B.   a research paper on the effects of climate on ecosystems

    C.   a poem about the ocean on a foggy day

    D.   a short story with a suspenseful plot

Answers:

    A.   **Correct.** Persuasive writing aims to influence the reader to agree with what is stated and to act accordingly.

    B.   Incorrect. A research paper is an example of expository writing and is often neutral in tone.

    C.   Incorrect. A poem using sensory imagery is an example of descriptive writing.

    D.   Incorrect. A short story with a plot arc is an example of narrative writing.

THE WRITING PROCESS

Elementary students also need to learn that writing is a process that begins with an idea and ends with a final draft. The writing process is made up of five key stages: prewriting, drafting, **revising**/editing, rewriting, and publishing. This process allows students to experience writing as it takes place in the profession. It is a process that enables students to capture the inspiration of the initial idea and then carefully shape and polish that idea until it can best capture a reader's interest.

During the prewriting phase of the writing process, authors brainstorm ideas for writing by organizing them in charts, lists, or by other means. This **organization** of ideas is used to write the first draft of a writing piece. During the next stage of the process, a writer reviews the first draft for **coherence** by identifying sections that need elaboration, correction, and/or reorganization. The original draft is revised based on these observations and those of peer editors. Once the **revisions** have been determined, the first draft is rewritten with corrections and changes made. It is only after the first draft has been carefully examined and rewritten that it is ready for an audience during the publishing phase of the writing process.

SAMPLE QUESTION

11) **Which of the following elements shapes each paragraph in a writing task?**

    A.   the thesis

    B.   the topic sentence

    C.   the drafting stage

    D.   the outline

Answers:

    A.   Incorrect. The thesis drives the entire essay.

    B.   **Correct.** The topic sentence for each paragraph introduces the idea that the paragraph will discuss.

    C.   Incorrect. The drafting stage addresses writing the entire document; it does not unify the content within each paragraph.

    D.   Incorrect. The outline drives the overall direction of the essay.

USING SOURCES

As students grow as writers, they begin to learn how to cite sources to support their ideas in research papers. The research paper is an expository essay that contains references to outside materials that legitimize claims made in the essay. Students learn to **paraphrase** supporting information, or briefly restate it in their own words, in order to avoid **plagiarism**, the intentional copying and credit-taking of another person's work. They also learn to include **citations** that name original sources of new information and are taught how to differentiate between primary sources, secondary sources, reliable sources, and unreliable sources.

Primary sources are original materials representative of an event, experience, place, or time period. They are direct or firsthand accounts in the form of text, image, record, sound, or item. **Secondary sources** inform about events, experiences, places, or time periods, but the information is provided by someone who was not directly involved and who used primary sources to discuss the material.

Reliable sources are trustworthy materials that come from experts in the field of study. These sources have **credibility** because they include extensive bibliographies listing the sources used to support the information provided. Some examples of reliable sources are published books, articles in credible magazines, and research studies provided by educational institutions. **Unreliable sources** are untrustworthy materials from a person or institution that does not have the educational background, expertise, or evidence of legitimate sources to support a claim. Some examples of unreliable sources are self-published materials, studies done to sell products, and opinion pieces.

SAMPLE QUESTION

12) **Which of the following is considered a reliable source for research about California?**

    A.   a personal blog about living in California

    B.   a research paper published by the State of California

    C.   an advertisement for California real estate

    D.   a letter to the editor about California roadways

Answers:

    A.   Incorrect. A personal blog is an unreliable source for research on a broad topic.

    B.   **Correct.** A published study by a government institution is a reliable research source.

    C.   Incorrect. Advertisements present biased information and are therefore unreliable sources of information.

    D.   Incorrect. Letters to the editors of newspapers typically include opinions, which are unreliable sources of information.

Language

Throughout elementary school, students are introduced to the conventions of Standard English grammar, usage, mechanics, and spelling as tools to facilitate communication and comprehension when writing, speaking, reading, and listening. They learn how to utilize the English language in both formal and informal contexts through exposure to conversational, academic, and content area language. In addition, they build vocabulary by learning how to use context and word structure to determine the meanings of unknown words and phrases. Elementary language arts teachers are responsible for implementing a curriculum and providing feedback that best help students develop and strengthen these language skills.

> **QUICK REVIEW**
>
> Grammar refers to the structures and systems that make up a language.

PARTS OF SPEECH

The parts of speech are the building blocks of sentences, paragraphs, and entire texts. Grammarians have typically defined eight parts of speech—nouns, pronouns, verbs, adverbs, adjectives, conjunctions, prepositions, and interjections—all of which play unique roles in the context of a sentence. Thus, a fundamental understanding of the parts of speech is necessary in order to form an understanding of basic sentence construction.

Though some words fall easily into one category or another, many words can function as different parts of speech based on their usage within a sentence.

Nouns are the words that describe people, places, things, and ideas. Most often, nouns fill the position of subject or object within a sentence. The category of nouns has several subcategories: common nouns (*chair, car, house*), proper nouns (*Julie, David*), abstract nouns (*love, intelligence, sadness*), concrete nouns (*paper clip, bread, person*), compound nouns (*brother-in-law, rollercoaster*), non-countable nouns (*money, water*), countable nouns (*dollars, cubes*), and verbal nouns (*writing, diving*). There is much crossover between these subcategories (for example, *chair* is common, concrete, and countable), and other subcategories do exist.

> **DID YOU KNOW?**
>
> Sometimes, a word that is typically used as a noun will be used to modify another noun. The word then would be labelled as an adjective because of its usage within the sentence. Here is an example using the word *cabin*: *The family visited the <u>cabin (noun)</u> by the lake. Our <u>cabin (adjective)</u> stove overheated during vacation.*

Pronouns replace nouns in a sentence or paragraph, allowing a writer to achieve a smooth flow throughout a text by avoiding unnecessary repetition. The unique aspect of the pronoun as a part of speech is that the list of pronouns is finite: while there are innumerable nouns in the English language, the list of pronouns is rather limited in contrast.

Pronoun categories are the following: personal, possessive, reflexive/intensive, relative, interrogative, demonstrative, and indefinite.

Personal pronouns act as subjects or objects in a sentence. (<u>*She*</u> *received a letter; I gave the letter to <u>her</u>.*)

Possessive pronouns indicate possession. (<u>*My*</u> *coat is red; <u>our</u> car is blue.*)

Reflexive or **intensive pronouns** intensify a noun or reflect back upon a noun. (*I <u>myself</u> made the dessert. I made the dessert <u>myself</u>.*)

Table 1.6. Personal, Possessive, and Reflexive/Intensive Pronouns

Case	First Person		Second Person		Third Person	
	singular	plural	singular	plural	singular	plural
subject	I	we	you	you (all)	he, she, it	they
object	me	us	you	you (all)	him, her, it	them
possessive	my	our	your	your	his, her, its	their
reflexive/ intensive	myself	ourselves	yourself	yourselves	himself, herself, itself	themselves

Relative pronouns begin dependent clauses. Like other pronouns, they may appear in subject or object case, depending on the clause.

Take, for example, the sentence *Charlie, who made the clocks, works in the basement.* Here, the relative pronoun *who* is substituting for Charlie; that word indicates that Charlie makes the clocks, and so *who* is in the subject case because it is performing the action (*makes the clocks*).

In cases where a person is the object of a relative clause, the writer would use the relative pronoun *whom*. For example, read the sentence *My father, whom I care for, is sick.* Even though *my father* is the subject of the sentence, in the relative clause the relative pronoun *whom* is the object of the preposition *for*. Therefore that pronoun appears in the object case.

When a relative clause refers to a non-human, *that* or *which* is used. (*I live in Texas, which is a large state.*) The relative pronoun *whose* indicates possession. (*I don't know whose car that is.*)

Table 1.7. Relative Pronouns

Pronoun Type	Subject	Object
person	who	whom
thing	which, that	which, that
possessive	whose	whose

Interrogative pronouns begin questions. (*Who worked last evening?*) They request information about people, places, things, ideas, location, time, means, and purposes.

Table 1.8. Interrogative Pronouns

Interrogative Pronoun	Example
who	Who lives there?
whom	To whom shall I send the letter?
what	What is your favorite color?
where	Where do you go to school?
when	When will we meet for dinner?
which	Which movie would you like to see?
why	Why are you going to be late?
how	How did the ancient Egyptians build the pyramids?

Demonstrative pronouns point out or draw attention to something or someone. They can also indicate proximity or distance.

Table 1.9. Demonstrative Pronouns

Number	Subject/ Proximity	Example	Object/ Distance	Example
singular	this (subject)	This is my apartment—please come in!	that (object)	I gave that to him yesterday.
	this (proximity)	This is the computer you will use right here, not the one in the other office.	that (distance)	That is the Statue of Liberty across the harbor.
plural	these (subject)	These are flawless diamonds.	those (object)	Give those to me later.
	these (proximity)	These right here are the books we want, not the ones over there.	those (distance)	Those mountains across the plains are called the Rockies.

Indefinite pronouns simply replace nouns to avoid unnecessary repetition. (_Several_ came to the party to see _both._)

Table 1.10. Common Indefinite Pronouns

Singular		Plural	Singular or Plural
each either neither one everyone no one someone anyone	everybody nobody somebody anybody everything nothing something anything another	both few several many	some any none all most more _These pronouns take their singularity or plurality from the object of the prepositions that follow: Some of the pies were eaten._

Remember that a pronoun takes the place of the noun. For example, instead of writing *Mary, Sue, Ralph, Peter, Michael, and Stephen visited the museum*, within the context of the story, the author could write the following: <u>*All*</u> *visited the museum.* An indefinite pronoun works well to replace a list of names or objects.

Verbs express action (*run, jump, play*) or state of being (*is, seems*).

Verbs also convey mood.

- Indicative verbs state facts: *My brother plays tennis.*
- Subjunctive verbs make a statement of speculation or wish. The subjunctive mood is formed with other words like *that*. However, the verb itself does not usually change. Example:

    The doctor recommends that you take the medication twice a day.

    I wish that I had a dog.
- Conditional sentences, which use the auxiliaries *would, could,* and *should,* use the subjunctive. Example:

    If I took a road trip, I could visit the Grand Canyon.
- Imperative verbs state a command: *Play tennis!*

Finally, verbs are conjugated in active or passive voice.

- Active voice expresses a dynamic action: *They played tennis.*
- Passive voice is used to indicate that the subject is acted upon: *Tennis was played at the club.* It is rarely used and is most frequently seen (when used properly) in math and science where the subject has limited agency in the matter at hand. (*The math problem is easily solved.*) However, overuse of the passive voice is common.

Verbs are conjugated to indicate *person* (first, second, and third person) and *number* (whether they are singular or plural).

Table 1.11. Verb Conjugation (Present Tense)

Person	Singular	Plural
first person	I give	we give
second person	you give	you (all) give
third person	he/she/it/ gives	they give

Verb tense indicates the time of the action.

Table 1.12. Verb Tenses

Tense	Past	Present	Future
simple	I <u>gave</u> her a gift yesterday.	I <u>give</u> her a gift every day.	I <u>will give</u> her a gift on her birthday.
continuous	I <u>was giving</u> her a gift when you got here.	I <u>am giving</u> her a gift; come in!	I <u>will be giving</u> her a gift at dinner.
perfect	I <u>had given</u> her a gift before you got there.	I <u>have given</u> her a gift already.	I <u>will have given</u> her a gift by midnight.
perfect continuous	Her friends <u>had been giving</u> her gifts all night when I arrived.	I <u>have been giving</u> her gifts every year for nine years.	I <u>will have been giving</u> her gifts on holidays for ten years next year.

Linking verbs join the subject to the subject complement: for example, *The dog is cute.* The following chart helps to distinguish among linking, helping, and action verbs.

Table 1.13. Linking, Helping, and Action Verbs

Linking or Helping	Action or Helping	Helping	Linking or Action
am, is, are, was, were, be, being, been	have, has, had, do, does, did	shall, will, should, would, may, might, must, can, could	taste, feel, smell, sound, look, appear, become, seem, grow, remain, stay

Transitive verbs take an object; intransitive verbs do not. Such troublesome verbs include combinations such as *lie* or *lay*, *rise* or *raise*, and *sit* or *set*. The following chart may help to clarify the differences in some pairs of troublesome verbs.

Table 1.14. Intransitive and Transitive Verbs

Intransitive Verbs	Transitive Verbs	
lie – to recline	lay – to put	lay <u>something</u>
rise – to go or get up	raise – to lift	raise <u>something</u>
sit – to be seated	set – to put	set <u>something</u>
Hint: These intransitive verbs have *i* as the second letter. *Intransitive* begins with *I*.	Hint: The word *transitive* begins with a *T*, and it *TAKES* an object.	

Verbs may be regular, following the conventions of regular verbs and their four parts (simple present, present participle, simple past, and past participle) and endings (*walk, walked, walking, have walked*). Some examples follow.

Table 1.15. Regular Verbs and Their Endings			
Simple Present	**Present Participle**	**Simple Past**	**Past Participle**
sit	sitting	sat	(have) sat
set	setting	set	(have) set
lie	lying	lay	(have) lain
lay	laying	laid	(have) laid
rise	rising	rose	(have) risen
raise	raising	raised	(have) raised

Also, verbs may be irregular, not following the convention of the four parts and endings (*swim, swam, swimming, have swum*).

Adverbs take on a modifying or describing role. These parts of speech describe the verb (He *quickly* ran to the house next door.), adjectives (Her *very* effective speech earned her a new job.), other adverbs (Several puppies arrived *rather* happily after they had eaten dog treats.), and entire sentences. (*Instead*, the owner kept his shop.)

Adverbs typically answer the questions *Where? When? Why? How? How often? To what extent? Under what conditions?*

Like adverbs, **adjectives** modify or describe, but they add to the meaning of nouns (*Five thoughtful* students came to work at the farm.) and pronouns only. (*The idea from the committee proved a *smart* one.*) One very important note regarding the adjective is that any word used to describe a noun or pronoun will be classified as an adjective. *Her* could be used as a pronoun or an adjective depending on usage. (*Her [used as an adjective] dog barks until midnight. We gave several books to her [used as a pronoun and object of the preposition to].*) Also, *a, and,* and *the* are always limiting adjectives.

Adjectives typically answer the questions *What kind? Which one? How many? How much? Whose?*

Conjunctions join words into phrases, clauses, and sentences by use of three mechanisms: coordinating conjunctions (*and, but, or, for, nor, yet, so*), correlative conjunctions (*whether/or, either/or, neither/nor, both/and, not only/but also*), and subordinating conjunctions, which join dependent clauses (typically adverbial clauses) to the independent clauses to which they are related. (*Because* we love pizza, we treat ourselves during football season to several orders.)

The following is a list of common subordinating conjunctions:

Table 1.16. Subordinating Conjunctions

Time	after, as, as long as, as soon as, before, since, until, when, whenever, while
Manner	as, as if, as though
Cause	because
Condition	although, as long as, even if, even though, if, provided that, though, unless, while
Purpose	in order that, so that, that
Comparison	as, than

When using correlative conjunctions, be sure that the structure of the word, phrase, or clause that follows the first part of the conjunction mirrors the structure of the word, phrase, or clause that follows the second part. Here is a **correct** example: *I will neither <u>mow the grass</u> nor <u>pull the weeds</u> today.* Here is an **incorrect** example: *I will neither <u>mow the grass</u> nor <u>undertake the pulling of the weeds</u> today.*

Prepositions set up relationships in time (<u>*after*</u> *the party*) or space (<u>*under*</u> *the cushions*) within a sentence. A preposition will always function as part of a prepositional phrase—the preposition along with the object of the preposition. If a word that usually acts as a preposition is standing alone in a sentence, the word is likely functioning as an adverb. (*She hid <u>underneath</u>.*)

A preposition acts as an adverb when it provides more information about a verb: *Several days ago, we took the turkey bones <u>outside</u> because of the smelly garbage.* Here, the preposition explains where the bones were taken.

DID YOU KNOW?

Interjections should generally be avoided in academic writing. However, they are great for adding emotion and excitement to creative writing, journals, and diaries.

Interjections have no grammatical attachment to the sentence itself other than to add expressions of emotion. These parts of speech may be punctuated with commas or exclamation points and may fall anywhere within the sentence itself. Here are a few examples of the usage of the interjection: *Ouch! He stepped on my toe. She shopped at the stores after Christmas and, hooray, found many items on sale. I have seen his love for his father in many expressions of concern—Wow!*

SAMPLE QUESTIONS

Choose the correct verb.

13) Yesterday, I (laid/lay) on the couch for hours.

14) We (sat/set) the ladder upright.

15) The egg was (rising/raising) in the water as it boiled.

Answers:

13) The correct response is **lay**, the intransitive (here, in the past tense), which does not take an object.

14) The correct response is **set**, the transitive, which takes an object (*the ladder*).

15) The correct response is **rising**, the intransitive, which does not take an object.

16) List all of the adjectives used in the following sentence:

Her camera fell into the turbulent water, so her frantic friend quickly grabbed the damp item.

A. turbulent, frantic, damp

B. turbulent, frantic, quickly, damp

C. her, turbulent, her, frantic, damp

D. her, the, turbulent, her, frantic, the, damp

Answer:

D. *Turbulent, frantic,* and *damp* are adjectives; *her* is modifying first *camera* and then *friend*; and *the* is always a limiting adjective—the definite article.

17) List all of the pronouns used in the following sentence:

Several of the administrators who had spoken clearly on the budget increase gave both of the opposing committee members a list of their ideas.

A. several, of, their

B. several, who, both

C. several, who, both, their

D. several, both

Answer:

B. *Several* is an indefinite plural pronoun; *who* is a relative pronoun introducing the adjectival clause *who had spoken clearly on the budget increase; both* is an indefinite plural pronoun.

PHRASES AND CLAUSES

A **phrase** is a group of words that communicates a partial idea and lacks either a subject or a predicate. Several phrases may be strung together, one after another, to add detail and interest to a sentence.

> The animals crossed <u>the large bridge</u> <u>to eat the fish</u> <u>on the wharf</u>.

Phrases are categorized based on the main word in the phrase. A **prepositional phrase** begins with a preposition and ends with an object of the preposition; a **verb phrase** is composed of the main verb along with its helping verbs; and a **noun phrase** consists of a noun and its modifiers.

> prepositional phrase: The dog is hiding <u>under the porch</u>.

> verb phrase: The chef <u>would have created</u> another soufflé, but the staff protested.

> noun phrase: <u>The big, red barn</u> rests beside <u>the vacant chicken house</u>.

An **appositive phrase** is a particular type of noun phrase that renames the word or group of words that precedes it. Appositive phrases usually follow the noun they describe and are set apart by commas.

> My dad, <u>a clock maker</u>, loved antiques.

Verbal phrases begin with a word that would normally act as a verb but is instead filling another role within the sentence. These phrases can act as nouns, adjectives, or adverbs.

> gerund phrase: <u>Writing numerous Christmas cards</u> occupies her aunt's time each year.

> participial phrase: <u>Enjoying the stars that filled the sky</u>, Dave lingered outside for quite a while.

> infinitive phrase: <u>To visit Europe</u> had always been her dream.

QUICK REVIEW

The word *gerund* has an *n* in it, a helpful reminder that the gerund acts as a noun. Therefore, the gerund phrase might act as the subject, the direct object, or the object of the preposition just as another noun would.

SAMPLE QUESTION

18) Identify the underlined phrases in the following sentence:

   <u>**Wrapping packages for the soldiers,**</u> *the kind woman tightly rolled the tee-shirts* <u>to see how much space</u> *remained* <u>for the homemade cookies</u>.

   A.   participial, infinitive, prepositional

   B.   gerund, infinitive, prepositional

   C.   gerund, prepositional, prepositional

   D.   participial, prepositional, adverbial

Answer

A. The underlined phrases are participial, infinitive, and prepositional, respectively.

CLAUSES AND SENTENCE STRUCTURE

Clauses contain both a subject and a predicate. They can be either independent or dependent. An **independent** (or main) **clause** can stand alone as its own sentence:

The dog ate her homework.

Dependent (or subordinate) clauses cannot stand alone as their own sentences. They start with a subordinating conjunction, relative pronoun, or relative adjective, which will make them sound incomplete:

<u>Because</u> the dog ate her homework

Table 1.17. Words That Begin Dependent Clauses	
Subordinating Conjunctions	**Relative Pronouns and Adjectives**
after, before, once, since, until, when, whenever, while, as, because, in order that, so, so that, that, if, even if, provided that, unless, although, even though, though, whereas, where, wherever, than, whether	who, whoever, whom, whomever, whose, which, that, when, where, why, how

Sentences can be classified based on the number and type of clauses they contain. A **simple sentence** will have only one independent clause and no dependent clauses. The sentence may contain phrases, complements, and modifiers, but it will comprise only one independent clause, one complete idea.

The cat ran under the porch.

A **compound sentence** has two or more independent clauses and no dependent clauses:

The cat ran under the porch, and the dog ran after him.

A **complex sentence** has only one independent clause and one or more dependent clauses:

The cat, who is scared of the dog, ran under the porch.

A **compound-complex sentence** has two or more independent clauses and one or more dependent clause:

The cat, who is scared of the dog, ran under the porch, and the dog ran after him.

Table 1.18. Sentence Structure and Clauses

Sentence Structure	Independent Clauses	Dependent Clauses
Simple	1	0
Compound	2 +	0
Complex	1	1 +
Compound-complex	2 +	1 +

Writers can diversify their use of phrases and clauses in order to introduce variety into their writing. Variety in **sentence structure** not only makes writing more interesting but also allows writers to emphasize that which deserves emphasis. In a paragraph of complex sentences, a short, simple sentence can be a powerful way to draw attention to a major point.

SAMPLE QUESTION

19) **Which sentence is correct in its sentence structure label?**

   A. The grandchildren and their cousins enjoyed their day at the beach. *Compound*

   B. Most of the grass has lost its deep color despite the fall lasting into December. *Complex*

   C. The members who had served selflessly were cheering as the sequestration ended. *Simple*

   D. Do as you please. *Complex*

   Answer

   D. This sentence is complex because it has one independent clause (*Do*) and one dependent (*as you please*).

PUNCTUATION

Many of the mechanical choices writers must make relate to **punctuation.** While creative writers have liberty to play with punctuation to achieve their desired ends, academic and technical writers must adhere to stricter conventions.

The **period** is the most common **terminal punctuation** mark, used to end declarative (statement) and imperative (command) sentences. Examples:

   ▶ *Sarah and I are attending a concert.*

   ▶ *Meet me outside the concert hall one hour before the show.*

The **question mark**, another common terminal punctuation mark, is used to end interrogative sentences (questions). Example: *How many people are attending the concert?*

While the difference between the period and the question mark is usually obvious, confusion sometimes occurs when questions are stated indirectly. In that case, the period is usually preferable. Example: *I wonder how many people are attending the concert.*

Exclamation points end exclamatory sentences, in which the writer or speaker is exhibiting intense emotion or energy; thus, writers should carefully consider their use of exclamations. In fact, the exclamation point should be used reservedly or not at all in academic writing unless the exclamation point is within a quotation that a writer incorporates into the text. The emphatic usage of *what* or *how* without asking a question, however, demands the usage of the exclamation point. Example: *What a great show that was!*

> **HELPFUL TIP**
>
> The exclamation point has impact only in contrast to its frequency of usage. That is, if the exclamation point is used frequently, each exclamation will be less impactful. On the other hand, if the exclamation point is used sparingly, its use will draw the reader's attention and emphasize the information contained in the sentence.

The **colon** and the **semicolon**, though often confused, each have a unique set of rules surrounding their use. While both punctuation marks are used to join clauses, the construction of the clauses and the relationship between them varies.

The **semicolon** is used to show a general relationship between two independent clauses (IC; IC). Example: *The disgruntled customer tapped angrily on the counter; she had to wait nearly ten minutes to speak to the manager.*

When using the semicolon with a conjunctive adverb to join two independent clauses, the pattern is as follows: independent clause, semicolon, conjunctive adverb, comma, independent clause. Example: *She may not have to take the course this year; however, she eventually will have to sign up for that specific course.*

The **colon**, somewhat less limited than the semicolon in its usage, is used to show a relationship between two clauses and, moreover, to highlight the information contained in the second clause—usually a list, definition, or clarification. While the clause preceding the colon must be an independent clause, the clause that follows doesn't have to be. Examples:

- ▶ Incorrect. *The buffet offers three choices that include: ham, turkey, or roast beef.*
- ▶ Correct. *The buffet offers three choices: ham, turkey, or roast beef.*
- ▶ Correct. *The buffet offers three choices that include the following: ham, turkey, or roast beef.*

A writer should also use the colon to separate a title from a subtitle (Title: Subtitle), to separate the hour and the minutes (9:30 a.m.), to follow certain parts of a letter or memo (To:, From:, Date:, RE:), and to follow a formal salutation (To whom it may concern:).

Neither the semicolon nor the colon should be used to set off an introductory phrase from the rest of the sentence.

▸ Incorrect. *After the trip to the raceway; we realized that we should have brought ear plugs.*

▸ Incorrect. *After the trip to the raceway: we realized that we should have brought ear plugs.*

▸ Correct. *After the trip to the raceway, we realized that we should have brought ear plugs.*

> **HELPFUL HINT**
>
> *Let's eat Grandma,* OR *Let's eat, Grandma.* While this well-known example is humorous, it also demonstrates the need for comma accuracy.

Many people are taught that, when reading, a comma represents a pause for breath. While this trick may be useful as a way of helping young readers build fluency, it is not a helpful guide for comma usage when writing. Rather, proper comma usage is guided by a set of specific rules.

The following list summarizes the most important comma usage rules:

1. Commas are used to separate two independent clauses along with a coordinating conjunction.

   George ordered the steak, but Bruce preferred the ham.

2. Commas are used to separate coordinate adjectives.

   The shiny, regal horse ran majestically through the wide, open field.

3. Commas are used to separate items in a series.

   The list of groceries included cream, coffee, donuts, and tea.

4. Commas are used to separate introductory words and phrases from the rest of the sentence.

   Slowly, Nathan became aware of his surroundings after the concussion.

   For example, we have thirty students who demand a change.

5. Commas are used to set off non-essential information and appositives.

   Estelle, our newly elected chairperson, will be in attendance.

6. Commas are used to set off introductory words from quoted words if the introductory words are not an independent clause.

   Elizabeth said sadly, "I want to go home right now for spring break."

7. Commas are used to set off the day and month of a date within a text.

   My birthday makes me feel quite old because I was born on February 16, 1958, in Minnesota.

8. Commas are used to set up numbers in a text of more than four digits.

   We expect 25,000 visitors to the new museum.

Quotation marks are used for many purposes, the most common of which are related to academic writing and citation. First, quotation marks enclose titles of short, or relatively short, literary works such as short stories, chapters, and poems. (The titles of longer works, like novels and anthologies, are italicized.) Additionally, quotation marks are used to enclose direct quotations within the text of a document where the quotation is integrated into the text. If a quotation is within another quotation, then the inner quotation uses single quotation marks.

Writers also use quotation marks to set off dialogue. Occasionally, quotation marks are used to enclose words used in special sense or for a non-literary purpose. (*The shady dealings of his Ponzi scheme earned him his ironic name "Honest Abe."*)

When considering quotation marks versus italics in notating a title, the question of short versus long is a useful guide. A chapter title is written in quotation marks, while the book title itself is italicized. Short poetry titles are written in quotation marks; long epic poem titles are italicized. An article title is written in quotation marks, while the name of the newspaper is italicized.

Apostrophes, sometimes referred to as single quotation marks, have several different purposes.

1. show possession: *boy's watch, John and Mary's house*
2. replace missing letters, numerals, and signs: *do not = don't, 1989 = '89*
3. form plurals of letters, numerals, and signs: *A's*

Other marks of punctuation include the **en dash** (to indicate a range of dates, for example), the **em dash** (to indicate an abrupt break in a sentence and emphasize the words within the em dashes), the **parentheses** (to enclose insignificant information), the **brackets** (to enclose added words to a quotation and to add insignificant information within parentheses), the **slash** (to separate lines of poetry within a text or to indicate interchangeable terminology), and the **ellipses** (to indicate information removed from a quotation, to indicate a missing line of poetry, or to create a reflective pause).

SAMPLE QUESTION

20) **Identify the marks of punctuation needed in the following sentence:**

Freds brother wanted the following items for Christmas a red car a condo and a puppy.

A.   Fred's / Christmas; / car, /condo,

B.   Fred's / Christmas: / car, / condo,

C.   Fred's / Christmas: / car,

D.   Fred's / items' / Christmas: / car, / condo,

Answer

B.   To be possessive, *Fred's* requires an apostrophe before the *s. Christmas* needs a colon to indicate the upcoming list, and *car* and *condo* should be followed by commas since they are items in a series.

Listening and Speaking

Listening and speaking are a child's first pathway to literacy. Children typically enter elementary school with an ability to orally communicate ideas, experiences, and concepts. The role of the elementary language arts teacher is to help students hone this skill set for academic and social growth. Students learn how to use strategies for listening and speaking that contribute to their abilities to listen carefully, think critically, differentiate relevant from irrelevant information, articulate clearly, and use appropriate vocal cues and word choice. Students are tasked with communicating for a variety of purposes, audiences, and contexts and have opportunities to engage in active listening during discussions of text, topics, and community.

Active listening is listening that is focused and empathetic. It is listening to authentically "hear" a perspective, feeling, or point of view. The following characteristics make up active listening:

- ▶ **Focusing**: Students practice keeping their attention on the person who is speaking.

- ▶ **Using positive nonverbal cues**: Students demonstrate interest by looking at the speaker and by using appropriate facial expressions and body language.

- ▶ **Allowing speaker to finish uninterrupted**: Students wait for a speaker to finish and concentrate on the message before formulating a response.

- ▶ **Not judging**: Students listen and respond with respect for the speaker's views and feelings. They agree or disagree using methods that maintain respect within the whole group.

- ▶ **Paraphrasing**: Students verify understanding by restating the speaker's main points concisely and in different words.

Students in elementary school also learn how to prepare and engage in small group and individual oral presentations. They learn the steps necessary to organize the information they want to present and techniques for presenting the information in ways that capture and maintain the attention of the audience. The following oral presentation skills provide an overview of what elementary school students need to know in order to effectively communicate with their audience:

- ▶ **Logical structure**: Ideas follow a logical line of reasoning.

- ▶ **Supporting evidence**: Information is supported by relevant evidence.

- ▶ **Word choice**: Only necessary and relevant words and sentences are included.

- ▶ **Collaboration**: Group presentations are creative, cohesive, and logical.

- ▶ **Eye contact**: Eyes are directed at the audience to the extent possible.

- ▶ **Articulation**: Enunciation is clear.

- ▶ **Volume**: Intonation is natural and neither too soft nor too loud.

▶ **Audience**: The style of presentation matches the needs of the audience.
▶ **Displays**: Visuals, props, and/or sounds that enhance presentation are used.

SAMPLE QUESTIONS

21) **Which of the following quotes is a demonstration of active listening?**

   A.   "If I understand correctly, you think the classroom needs a pet."
   B.   "I think you meant to say that you wish you had a pet at home."
   C.   "You didn't talk about the kind of pet our classroom should have."
   D.   "There's no way the principal will let us have a classroom pet."

   Answers:

   A.   **Correct.** This quote demonstrates active listening because the listener is paraphrasing the message to clarify understanding.
   B.   Incorrect. This quote does not demonstrate active listening because the message is changed to what the listener thinks instead of remaining as the speaker intended.
   C.   Incorrect. This quote does not demonstrate active listening because the listener changes the topic; furthermore, the listener speaks in a critical manner.
   D.   Incorrect. This quote does not demonstrate active listening because the listener dismisses the message.

22) **Students have been placed in small groups to prepare reader's theater presentations that they will perform for each other. How might each group best meet the needs of its audience?**

   A.   by reciting their lines in quiet voices during the performance
   B.   by passing around a script to read from during the performance
   C.   by using classroom materials as props during the performance
   D.   by skipping some parts of the story during the performance

   Answers:

   A.   Incorrect. Reciting lines in quiet voices makes it difficult for an audience to hear important details.
   B.   Incorrect. Reading from a shared script interrupts the flow of a performance and causes the audience to become restless.
   C.   **Correct.** Props add interesting visuals to a performance and reinforce comprehension.
   D.   Incorrect. Skipping some parts of a story is confusing to an audience.

Terms

academic language: language used in formal settings and academic writing

active listening: listening that is focused and empathetic

adjective: a word that modifies a noun or pronoun

advanced fluency stage of language acquisition: learners demonstrate near-native ability and use complex, multiphrase and multiclause sentences to convey their ideas

adverb: a word that modifies an adjective, adverb, verb, phrase, or clause

affixes: added to words or roots to change their meanings; include prefixes (added to the beginning of a word or root) and suffixes (added to the end of a word or root)

analyzing text organization: analyzing how a text is organized in order to better comprehend an author's purpose for writing

audience: the reader/readers

central idea: the basic underlying idea of informational text

character analysis: understanding the role of a character in a story via the character's actions, traits, relationships, and personality

citations: identification of original sources of outside information

clause: a group of words with both a subject and a predicate

complex sentence: a sentence made up of an independent clause and one or more dependent clauses

compound sentence: a sentence made up of two independent clauses (or simple sentences)

compound-complex sentence: a sentence that has two or more independent clauses and one or more dependent clauses

conjunction: joins words into phrases, clauses, and sentences

connotation: the intended meaning of a word beyond its literal meaning

conversational language: familiar and informal language

credibility: proof of the reliability of a source

denotation: the literal meaning of a word

descriptive writing: a writing style that emphasizes the production of imagery using words and figurative language that appeal to the reader's five senses

dialect: language that is particular to a geographical location or consolidated social group

early production stage of language acquisition: learners produce single-word and two- to three-word phrases and can respond to questions and statements

expository writing: a writing style that explains an idea or concept or informs the reader about a topic

figurative language: language that conveys images and ideas separate from the actual meanings of the words used

first-person point of view: one character tells the story from his or her direct experience using pronouns such as *I*, *my*, *mine*, and *we*

fluency: the ability to read with ease and automaticity

genre: type of a text (e.g., poetry, drama, picture book, graphic novel, folktale, myth, fairy tale, tall tale, historical fiction, science fiction)

grammar: the way parts of speech work together in sentences and how words are grouped to make meaning such as in phrases or clauses

high frequency letter-sound correspondences: letter-sound correspondences that occur most often in the English language

identifying point of view: using genre and pronoun clues to identify who is telling a story to best form accurate conclusions about the events of the story

inferences: conclusions about what an author suggests in a text based on context clues

interjection: a word that expresses emotion

intermediate fluency stage of language acquisition: learners are able to speak in more complex sentences and catch and correct many of their errors

letter-sound correspondence: the relationship between the spoken sounds in words and the printed letters that correspond to those sounds

levels of language proficiency: L1) entering, L2) beginning, L3)

developing, L4) expanding, and L5) bridging

literal: the most basic or exact meaning of a word

mechanics: the conventions of print that are not necessary in spoken language, such as punctuation, capitalization, and indentation (spelling is a component of mechanics but is treated as a separate category in elementary school)

meter: the basic rhythmic structure of the lines or verses in poetry

misplaced modifier: a modifier that causes confusion because it does not modify its intended word or phrase

modifiers: words or phrases that change the meanings of or add details to other words or phrases in a sentence

moral: the lesson the author intends to teach the reader in a literary text

morphemes: the smallest units of language that contain meaning

narrative poems: poems that tell stories

narrative writing: a writing style that tells a personal or fictional story that entertains the reader

noun: a person, place, thing, or idea

onset: the beginning consonant or consonant blend of a syllable

paraphrasing: briefly restating information in one's own words

persuasive writing: a writing style that convinces, or persuades, a reader to subscribe to the author's opinion or point of view (often used for speeches and advertisements)

phoneme: each small unit of sound in a language

phoneme blending: combining phonemes to make a word

phoneme deletion: removing phonemes from words to make new words

phoneme segmentation: separating phonemes in words

phoneme substitution: replacing phonemes in words to make new words

phonemic awareness: a type of phonological awareness; an understanding of how phonemes form a language by creating differences in the meanings of words

phonics: the study of the relationship between the spoken sounds in words and the printed letters that correspond to those sounds

phonological awareness: an understanding of how sounds, syllables, words, and word parts can be orally manipulated to break apart words, make new words, and create rhymes

phrase: a group of words with either a subject or a predicate

plagiarism: intentionally copying and taking credit for another person's work

plot development: the exposition, rising action, problem/climax, falling action, and resolution

preposition: describes relationships in time and space

preproduction stage of language acquisition: the silent period; learners refrain from speaking but will listen, may copy words down, and can respond to visual cues

primary sources: original materials representative of an event, experience, place, or time period

pronoun: a word that replaces a noun

prosody: the range of vocal expressions a reader uses when reading aloud, including rhythm, intonation, and stress patterns

punctuation: periods, commas, question marks, exclamation marks, and other markings that divide text or help a reader know when to change pace or read with inflection

qualitative measures: contributors to text leveling that include analysis of text elements such as structure, language clarity, and knowledge demands

quantitative measures: contributors to text leveling that include readability scores determined by computer algorithms that evaluate text elements such as word frequency and sentence length

reader and task considerations: matching texts to particular students, classes, and/or tasks based on their inherent needs as determined by the professional judgment of educators

reading accuracy: the ability to recognize or decode words correctly

reading rate: the speed and fluidity with which a reader can read

register: particular styles of language determined by purpose, audience, and social context

reliable sources: trustworthy materials that come from experts in the field of study

rhyme scheme: rhyme pattern in a poem; may be represented as letters (e.g., *abab, aabb, aabba*)

rime: a syllable's vowel and its remaining consonants (not including the onset)

roots: the basis of many words in the English language, typically derived from Latin or Greek

secondary sources: sources that inform about events, experiences, places, or time periods using primary sources but that were not directly involved in the event in any way

second-person point of view: a narrative perspective from an external "you," whether that be the reader or unknown other

setting: where a story takes place

sight words: words that are repeated most often in text

silent period: the preproduction stage of language acquisition

simple sentence: a sentence that contains a subject, a verb, and a completed thought

speech emergence stage of language acquisition: learners can chunk simple words and phrases into sentences that may or may not be grammatically correct and can understand simple readings when reinforced by graphics or pictures

stages of language acquisition: preproduction, early production, speech emergence, intermediate fluency, and advanced fluency

structural analysis: an analysis of the roots and affixes of words

summarization: distilling and condensing a text into its main idea and key details by identifying story elements

syllables: phonological units composed of onsets and rimes that can be blended, substituted, segmented, and deleted like phonemes

syntax: the grammatical formations and patterns of sentences

text features: supplemental information outside of the main text such as chapter headings, titles, sidebars (boxes of explanatory or additional information set aside from main text) and hyperlinks

text leveling: complexity of text as determined by quantitative measures, qualitative measures, and reader and task considerations

text structure: organizational structures like cause and effect, problem and solution, sequence of events or steps-in-a-process, compare and contrast, and description

theme: the basic idea that the author wants to convey in a literary text

third-person limited omniscient point of view: a narrative perspective in which a detached narrator tells the story from one character's point of view, including that character's internal thoughts and feelings

third-person objective point of view: a narrative perspective in which a detached narrator relates the actions and dialogue of the story, but not the thoughts or feelings of any characters

third-person omniscient point of view: a narrative perspective in which a detached and all-knowing narrator tells the story from the point of view of all of the characters, including all of their thoughts and feelings

tone: the attitude of a text

unreliable sources: untrustworthy materials from a person or institution that does not have the educational background, expertise, or evidence of legitimate sources to support a claim

usage: common rules for how language is used under certain conditions or within particular styles

verb: a word that expresses action or being

writing styles: specific types of writing that convey the author's purpose for writing—to explain, to entertain, to describe, or to persuade

Mathematics

Numbers and Operations

PLACE VALUE

While historically some civilizations have used other numbering systems, today most of the world uses the base-10 system. In the **base-10** system, each **digit** (the numeric symbols 0 – 9) in a number is worth ten times as much as the number to the right of it.

Table 2.1. Place Value Chart

1,000,000	100,000	10,000	1,000	100	10	1		1/10	1/100
10^6	10^5	10^4	10^3	10^2	10^1	10^0	.	10^{-1}	10^{-2}
millions	hundred thousands	ten thousands	thousands	hundreds	tens	ones	decimal	tenths	hundredths

For example, in the number 321 each digit has a different value based on its location. This is called **place value.** Knowing the place value of each digit allows students to write a number in expanded form. **Expanded form** is breaking up a number by the value of each digit. For example, the expanded form of 321 is written as 300 + 20 + 1.

CHECK YOUR UNDERSTANDING

How does learning expanded notation deepen a student's understanding of the concept of a number?

3	2	1
Hundreds	Tens	Ones

Figure 2.1. Expanded Form

SAMPLE QUESTION

1) **Which digit is in the hundredths place when 1.3208 is divided by 5.2?**

   A. 0

   B. 4

   C. 5

   D. 8

Answer:

C. Divide 1.3208 by 5.2.

```
        .254
52 ) 13.208
       104
       280
       260
        208
        208
          0
```

There is a **5** in the hundredths place.

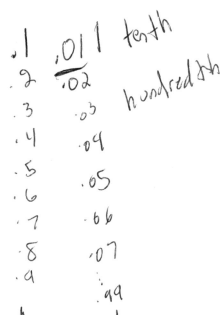

NUMBER THEORY

A basic foundation in numeracy is vital for establishing the groundwork for understanding advanced mathematical concepts. Students begin working with **natural numbers**, which are used when counting (e.g., 1, 2, 3, etc.). Once a basic understanding of natural numbers is achieved, more advanced concepts, such as whole numbers and integers, can be introduced. **Whole numbers** are similar to natural numbers, except that whole numbers include zero. **Integers** are positive or negative whole numbers (not fractions or decimals).

CHECK YOUR UNDERSTANDING

What are some examples of concrete objects that could be used to teach numeracy in the classroom?

Rational numbers are numbers that can be made by dividing two integers. Rational numbers must be expressed as a terminating or a repeating decimal, such as 0.125 or $0.\overline{66}$. Pi (π) would not be a rational number because it does not terminate or repeat (π = 3.14159265...); instead, pi goes on forever with no repeating pattern. Integers are rational numbers because they can be written as a fraction with a denominator of 1.

Figure 2.2. Number Line

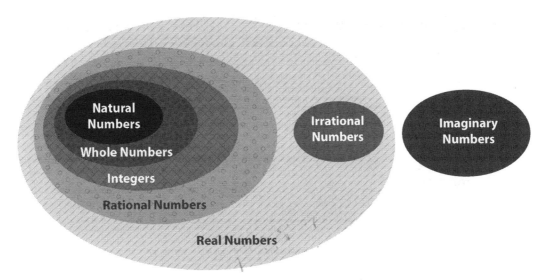

Figure 2.3. Types of Numbers

The set of rational and irrational numbers make up the set of **real numbers**. Real numbers can be represented on a **number line**, where 0 is in the middle, positive numbers are to the right, and negative numbers are to the left. Figure 2.2 is an example of a number line; remember that fractions and decimals are between the integers shown.

The **opposite** of a number is the negative version of that number (or positive version if the number is negative). Remember that the distance between a number and 0 on the number line is the same as the distance between the opposite of that number and 0.

Negative numbers with larger opposites are actually smaller than negative numbers with smaller opposites. For example,

$$-40 < -2.4 < 0 < .1 < 20$$

The **absolute value** (| |) of a number is the positive value of a number or its opposite; for example, $|-3| = 3$ and $|3| = 3$.

Every whole number (except 1) is either a prime number or a composite number. A **prime number** is a natural number greater than 1 that can be divided evenly only by 1 and itself. For example, 7 is a prime number because it can only be divided by the numbers 1 and 7.

On the other hand, a **composite number** is a natural number greater than 1 that can be evenly divided by at least one other number besides 1 and itself. For example, 6 is a composite number because it can be divided by 1, 2, 3, and 6.

Go on

SAMPLE QUESTIONS

2) **To which of the following number sets does 3 NOT belong?**

A. irrational

B. rational

C. whole

D. integer

Answer:

A. The number 3 is not irrational because it can be written as the fraction $\frac{3}{1}$.

3) **Classify the number $\frac{13}{14}$.**

A. irrational

B. imaginary

C. rational

D. integer

C. $\frac{13}{14}$ is a rational number because it can be written as a fraction but not as a whole number (without the fraction). It is not imaginary because it does not have an *i* component.

OPERATIONS WITH WHOLE NUMBERS

Rational numbers can be used to perform mathematical operations. **Addition** is combining numbers, while **subtraction** requires finding the difference between numbers.

Multiplication is the repeated addition of the same number to itself; in contrast, **division** is splitting a number into equal parts. Addition and subtraction are considered **inverse operations** because each operation cancels out the other operation. For example, 2 + 3 = 5 is true, and so is the inverse, 5 – 3 = 2. Multiplication and division are also inverse operations because 2 × 3 = 6 and the inverse, 6 ÷ 3 = 2, are both true. Knowing inverse operations allows students to check their answers.

In multiplication, the two numbers multiplied together are called **factors**. The answer is called the **product**. For example, in the operation 3 × 2 = 6 (3 added to itself 2 times), the numbers 3 and 2 are factors, and the number 6 is the product.

Multiplication may be presented in several ways. One way to visually present a multiplication problem is with an **array**, such as the one shown next. In an array, each of the two factors is represented by the appropriate number of rows or columns, and the product will be the total number of boxes in the array.

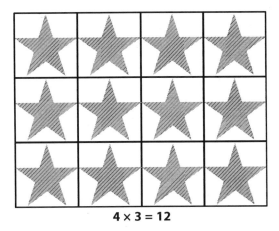

4 × 3 = 12

Figure 2.4. Array

Another way to represent multiplication is by using **area models** (also called the box method). Although this is a non-traditional approach to multiplication, it promotes the understanding of place value.

In division, the number that is being divided into groups is called the **dividend**. The number by which the number is divided is the **divisor**. The answer is called the **quotient**. For example, in the operation 12 ÷ 3 = 4, 12 is the dividend, 3 is the divisor, and 4 is the quotient.

$$5 \times 14$$

	10	4
5	50	20

$$5 \times 14 =$$
$$(5 \times 10) + (5 \times 4) =$$
$$50 + 20 = 70$$

Figure 2.5. Area Models

Sometimes in a division problem, the dividend cannot be divided equally. The number that is left over when a number does not divide evenly into another number is called the **remainder**. For example, when 12 items are divided into 5 groups, each group will have 2 items in it, and there will be 2 items left over, meaning the remainder is 2.

In the figure below, 12 squares are divided into 5 different groups, each represented by a different color. There are 2 squares in each group (the quotient). Two squares are left, meaning there are not enough squares to put 3 squares in each group. Thus, the remainder is 2.

1	2	3	4
5	1	2	3
4	5		

Figure 2.6. Remainder

SAMPLE QUESTIONS

4)   **What is the remainder when 397 is divided by 4?**

    A.   0

    B.   1

    C.   2

    D.   4

Answer:

    B.   Find the highest possible multiple of 4 that is less than or equal to 397, and then subtract to find the remainder.

$$99 \times 4 = 396$$

$$397 - 396 = \mathbf{1}$$

5)   **A teacher has 50 notebooks to hand out to students. If she has 16 students in her class, and each student receives 2 notebooks, how many notebooks will she have left over?**

    A.   2

    B.   16

    C.   18

    D.   32

Answer:

    C.   If each student receives 2 notebooks, the teacher will need $16 \times 2 = 32$ notebooks. After handing out the notebooks, she will have $50 - 32 = \mathbf{18}$ notebooks left.

FACTORS AND MULTIPLES

Composite numbers can be broken down into prime numbers using factor trees. For example, the number 54 is 2×27, and 27 is 3×9, and 9 is 3×3, as shown in Figure 2.7.

The **greatest common factor (GCF)** of a set of numbers is the greatest number (other than 1) that each number in the set is divisible by without any remainders. The GCF may be one of the numbers; for example, for the numbers 4 and 8, the GCF is 4, since 4 goes into both 4 and 8. The greatest common factor can also be called the **greatest common divisor**.

To get the GCF of a set numbers, list all the prime factors of the numbers, and multiply the factors that appear on both sides. (If the factor appears twice on both sides, include both factors.)

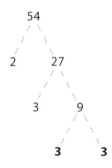

Figure 2.7. Factor Tree

As an example, the GCF of 12 and 18 is 2 × 3 = 6, since the factors 2 and 3 are factors of both 12 and 18. Note also that 6 is the largest number that goes into both 12 and 18.

The **least common multiple (LCM)** is more often known as the **least common denominator (LCD)**, especially when it is used to add and subtract fractions.

To find the LCM of numbers, find the smallest common multiple of those numbers, which is the smallest number that can be divided by both numbers without a remainder. For example, the LCM of 6 and 8 is 24, since 24 is the smallest number that is divisible by both 6 and 8. Write out all the multiples and look for the smallest number that is in both lists:

6: 6, 12, 18, **24**, 30

8: 8, 16, **24**, 32

Once the number has been broken down into its simplest form, the composite number can be expressed using exponents. An **exponent** shows how many times a number (the base) should be multiplied by itself. In the factor tree, Figure 2.7, the number 54 can be written as 2 × 3 × 3 x 3 or $2 × 3^3$. With **negative exponents**, take the reciprocal of the base, and then make the exponent positive. For example:

$$3^{-2} = \left(\frac{1}{3}\right)^2 = \frac{1}{9}$$

A **radical** is the opposite of an exponent and is an expression that has a square root, cube root, or a higher root. For example, $\sqrt{16} = 4$ since $4^2 = 16$ and $\sqrt[3]{8} = 2$ since $2^3 = 8$.

SAMPLE QUESTIONS

6)   What is the least common multiple of the numbers 10 and 12?

A.   2

B.   24

C.   60

D.   120

Answer:

C.   Write out the multiples for each number until reaching a number in both lists.

10: 10, 20, 30, 40, 50, **60**

12: 12, 24, 36, 48, **60**

7)   What is the square root of 169?

A.   9

B.   13

C.   16

D.   19

Answer:

B.   The square root of 169 is **13**.

OPERATIONS WITH POSITIVE AND NEGATIVE NUMBERS

When adding or subtracting negative numbers, look at a number line. When adding two numbers, whether they are positive or negative, count to the right; when subtracting, count to the left. Note that adding a negative value is the same as subtracting. Subtracting a negative value is the same as adding.

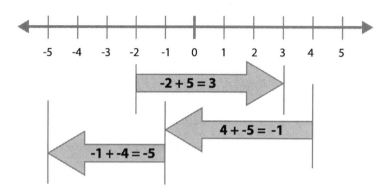

Figure 2.8. Adding Positive and Negative Numbers

> **HELPFUL HINT**
>
> Subtracting a negative number is the same as adding a positive
>
> $5 - (-10) = 5 + (+10) = 5 + 10 = 15$

Multiplying and dividing with negative and positive numbers is somewhat easier. Multiplying two numbers with the same sign gives a positive result, and multiplying two numbers with different signs gives a negative result. The same rules apply to division.

Table 2.2. Operations with Positive and Negative Numbers

Addition and Subtraction	Multiplication and Division
Positive + Positive = Positive $4 + 5 = 9$	Positive × Positive = Positive $5 × 3 = 15$
Negative + Negative = Negative $-4 + -5 = -9$ $-4 - 5 = -9$	Negative × Negative = Positive $-6 × -5 = 30$
Negative + Positive = Depends When adding a positive number and negative number, subtract the absolute values of the two numbers (larger – smaller absolute values) and make the sign the same sign of the largest absolute value of the numbers. $-15 + 9 = -6$	Negative × Positive = Negative $-5 × 4 = -20$ $3 × -6 = -18$

SAMPLE QUESTION

8) Which of the following has the greatest value?

    A.   −4(3)(−2)

    B.   −16 − 17 + 31

    C.   18 − 15 + 27

    D.   −20 + 10 + 10

Answer:

    C.   Evaluate to find the expression with the greatest value.

$$-4(3)(-2) = 24$$

$$-16 - 17 + 31 = -2$$

$$18 - 15 + 27 = \mathbf{30}$$

$$-20 + 10 + 10 = 0$$

Properties of Numbers and the Order of Operations

An **algorithm** is a set of steps to follow when performing mathematical operations. Even the simplest of computations has an algorithm. As problems become more complicated, there are rules, or properties, that guide the problem-solver.

Table 2.3. Mathematical Properties

Name	Description	Applies to	Example
Commutative Property	The order of the operation doesn't matter.	addition	$a + b = b + a$
		multiplication	$ab = ba$
Associative Property	Grouping of numbers doesn't matter.	addition	$(a + b) + c = a + (b + c)$
		multiplication	$(a \times b) \times c = a \times (b \times c)$
Distributive Property	Multiply a value by all the values inside brackets, then add.	multiplication	$a(b + c) = ab + ac$
Identity Property	Adding zero or multiplying by one will not change the original value.	addition	$a + 0 = a$
		multiplication	$a \times 1 = a$
Zero Property	Multiplying any value by zero yields a result of zero.	multiplication	$a \times 0 = 0$

When solving a multi-step equation, the **order of operations** must be used to get the correct answer. Generally speaking, the problem should be worked in the following order: (1) parentheses and brackets, (2) exponents and square roots, (3) multiplication and division, and (4) addition and subtraction. The acronym PEMDAS can be used to remember the order of operations.

Please Excuse My Dear Aunt Sally

P – Parentheses

E – Exponents

M – Multiplication

D – Division

A – Addition

S – Subtraction

The steps "Multiplication–Division" and "Addition–Subtraction" go in order from left to right. In other words, divide before multiplying if the division problem is on the left. For example, the expression $(3^2 - 2)^2 + (4)5^3$ is simplified using the following steps:

1. Parentheses: Because the parentheses in this problem contain two operations (exponents and subtraction) use the order of operations within the parentheses. Exponents come before subtraction.

   $(3^2 - 2)^2 + (4)5^3 = (9 - 2)^2 + (4)5^3 = (7)^2 + (4)5^3$

2. Exponents:

   $(7)^2 + (4)5^3 = 49 + (4)125$

3. Multiplication and division:

   $49 + (4)125 = 49 + 500$

4. Addition and subtraction:

   $49 + 500 = 549$

SAMPLE QUESTIONS

9) **Which expression is equivalent to dividing 400 by 16?**

   A. $2(200 - 8)$ $400 - 16$ 2^3

   B. $(400 \div 4) \div 12$

   C. $(216 \div 8) + (184 \div 8)$

   D. $(216 \div 16) + (184 \div 16)$

   Answers:

   A.   Incorrect. Solve inside the parentheses first: $200 - 8 = 192$. Then, multiply by 2: $192 \times 2 = 384$.

   B.   Incorrect. Solve inside the parentheses first: $(400 \div 4) = 100$. Then, divide: $100 \div 12 = 8.333....$

   C.   Incorrect. Solve inside the parentheses first, then add: $(216 \div 8) + (184 \div 8) = 27 + 23 = 50$.

   D.   **Correct.** Solve inside the parentheses first, then add: $(216 \div 16) + (184 \div 16) = 13.5 + 11.5 = 25$.

10) What number is equal to $(5^2 + 1)^2 + 3^3$?

A. 703
B. 694
C. 30
D. 53

Answer:

A.   Use the order of operations.

$(5^2 + 1)^2 + 3^3 = (25 + 1)^2 + 3^3 = (26)^2 + 3^3 = 676 + 27 = 703$.

OPERATIONS WITH FRACTIONS AND DECIMALS

Fractions use two numbers separated by a horizontal bar to show parts of a whole. Fractions include a **numerator**, the number on top of a fraction, and a **denominator**, the number on the bottom of a fraction. The denominator is the "whole," and the numerator is the "part." For example, if there are 12 students on the chess team, and 5 of the students are selected to represent the school in a tournament, the fraction of the chess team going to the tournament is $\frac{5}{12}$.

If the numerator of a fraction is 1, it is called a **unit fraction**. In the chess team example, $\frac{1}{12}$ is the unit fraction. Five $\frac{1}{12}$ units represent the part of the team that is going to the tournament. As the "whole" gets larger, one "part" becomes smaller and smaller. Think of cutting a cake: cutting 8 slices creates smaller slices than cutting the same cake into 4 slices. So, as the denominator of unit fractions increases, the value of the fraction itself decreases.

The same basic operations that can be performed with whole numbers can also be performed on fractions, with a few modifications. When adding and subtracting fractions, each fraction must have a **common denominator**. The operation is performed in the numerator, and the denominator remains the same. For example, if 3/12 of the chess team described above is eliminated in the second round of the tournament, the total fraction of the team remaining will be $\frac{5}{12} - \frac{3}{12} = \frac{5-3}{12} = \frac{2}{12}$.

In $\frac{2}{12}$, both the numerator and the denominator are divisible by 2, meaning the fraction is not in its simplest form. To simplify the fraction, reduce the numerator and denominator by dividing both by the same value: $\frac{2}{12} = \frac{2 \div 2}{12 \div 2} = \frac{1}{6}$.

If the fractions to be added or subtracted do not have a common denominator, the **least common multiple** of the denominators (also known as the **least common denominator**) must be found. In the operation $\frac{2}{3} - \frac{1}{2}$, the common denominator will be a **multiple** of both 3 and 2. Multiples are found by multiplying the denominator by whole numbers until a common multiple is found:

▸   multiples of 3 are **3** (3 × 1), **6** (3 × 2), **9** (3 × 3), ...

▸   multiples of 2 are **2** (2 × 1), **4** (2 × 2), **6** (2 × 3), ...

Since 6 is the smallest multiple of both 3 and 2, it is the least common multiple and can be used as the common denominator. Both the numerator and denominator of each fraction should be multiplied by the appropriate whole number:

$$\frac{2}{3}\left(\frac{2}{2}\right) - \frac{1}{2}\left(\frac{3}{3}\right) = \frac{4}{6} - \frac{3}{6} = \frac{1}{6}.$$

When multiplying fractions, simply multiply each numerator together and each denominator together. To divide two fractions, invert the second fraction (swap the numerator and denominator) then multiply normally. Note that multiplying fractions creates a value smaller than either original value.

▶ $\frac{5}{6} \times \frac{2}{3} = \frac{10}{18} = \frac{5}{9}$

▶ $\frac{5}{6} \div \frac{2}{3} = \frac{5}{6} \times \frac{3}{2} = \frac{15}{12} = \frac{5}{4}$

Another way to represent parts of a whole is by using decimals. A **decimal** is any real number in the base-10 system, but it often refers to numbers with digits to the right of the decimal point.

5	4	×	3	2
$5 \times 10^1 =$ $5 \times 10 =$ 50	$4 \times 10^0 =$ $4 \times 1 =$ 4		$3 \times 10^{-1} =$ $3 \times \frac{1}{10} =$ 0.3	$2 \times 10^{-2} =$ $2 \times \frac{1}{100} =$ 0.02
Tens	Ones	Decimal Point	Tenths	Hundredths
		$50 + 4 + 0.3 + 0.02 = 54.32$		

Figure 2.9. Decimals and Place Value

Fractions can be converted to decimals by simply dividing the numerator by the denominator. To convert a decimal to a fraction, place the numbers to the right of the decimal over the appropriate base-10 power and simplify the fraction. To convert a decimal to a percentage, multiply the decimal by 100, or move the decimal point two digits to the right. To convert a percentage to a decimal, divide by 100, or move the decimal point two digits to the left.

▶ $\frac{1}{2} = 1 \div 2 = 0.5$

▶ $0.375 = \frac{375}{1,000} = \frac{3}{8}$

$2\frac{2}{3}$

- 0.375 = 37.5%
- 50% = 0.50 = 0.5 1.5×2

$1\frac{1}{4} = \frac{5}{4}$

SAMPLE QUESTIONS

11) Simplify: $\left(1\frac{1}{2}\right)\left(2\frac{2}{3}\right) \div 1\frac{1}{4}$

A. $3\frac{1}{12}$ 3.06

B. $3\frac{1}{5}$ 3.2

C. 4

D. 5

$1\frac{1}{2} = \frac{3}{2}$

$2\frac{2}{3} = \frac{8}{3}$

$\frac{3}{2} \times \frac{8}{3} = \frac{24}{6} = 4$

$4 \div 1\frac{1}{4}$

Answer: $(1.5) \; 2(.67)$

B. Convert each term to an improper fraction and multiple/divide left to right.

$1\frac{1}{2} = \frac{3}{2}$

$2\frac{2}{3} = \frac{8}{3}$

$1\frac{1}{4} = \frac{5}{4}$

$\left(1\frac{1}{2}\right)\left(2\frac{2}{3}\right) \div 1\frac{1}{4}$

$= \left(\frac{3}{2}\right)\left(\frac{8}{3}\right) \div \frac{5}{4}$

$= \frac{24}{6} \div \frac{5}{4}$

$= \frac{4}{1} \times \frac{4}{5} = \frac{16}{5} = 3\frac{1}{5}$

$(1.5)(2.67)$

$4.005 \div 1.25$

3.204

$\frac{1}{5}$

$4 - 75 = .5$

$2.5 = 3.25$

12) Allison used $2\frac{1}{2}$ cups of flour to make a cake, and $\frac{3}{4}$ of a cup of flour to make a pie. If she started with 4 cups of flour, how many cups of flour does she have left?

A. $\frac{3}{4}$

B. 1

C. $\frac{5}{2}$

D. $\frac{13}{4}$

$1.5 - .75$

$.75$

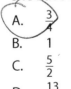 $2\frac{1}{2} = 1\frac{1}{2}$

$2.5 \quad .75$

4

$\frac{6}{4} \cdot \frac{3}{4} = \frac{3}{4}$

$-\frac{3}{4}$

$.5 - .75$

Answer:

A. Add the fractions and subtract the result from the amount of flour Allison started with.

$2\frac{1}{2} + \frac{3}{4} = \frac{5}{2} + \frac{3}{4} = \frac{10}{4} + \frac{3}{4} = \frac{13}{4}$

$4 - \frac{13}{4} = \frac{16}{4} - \frac{13}{4} = \frac{3}{4}$

PROPORTIONAL RELATIONSHIPS

Ratios compare two things. For example, if Jamie has 6 pairs of jeans and 8 T-shirts, then the ratio of jeans to T-shirts is 6:8. Like fractions, ratios can be reduced when both values are multiples of the same number. For example, the ratio 6:8 can be reduced by dividing both parts by 2: 6:8 = 3:4. The value of the ratio doesn't change because a ratio only describes a relationship. Whether Jamie has 3 jeans and 4 shirts; 6 jeans and 8 shirts; or 12 jeans and 16 shirts, the ratio remains the same. In other words, for every 3 pairs of jeans Jamie has, she has 4 T-shirts.

Problems involving ratios can often be solved by setting up a **proportion**, which is an equation stating that two ratios are equal. For example, if Jamie wants to buy 9 pairs of jeans and maintain the ratio described above, a proportion can be used to find the number of shirts she'll need to purchase: $\frac{jeans}{T\text{-}shirts} = \frac{3}{4} = \frac{9}{x}$.

The two fractions can then be **cross-multiplied** to give the equation $3x = 36$, and the variable isolated: $x = 12$ shirts.

HELPFUL HINT	When working with ratios, pay attention to

cross-multiplication:
$\frac{a}{b} = \frac{c}{d} \rightarrow ad = bc$

When working with ratios, pay attention to whether part-to-part or part-to-whole comparisons are being used. For example, if there are 6 boys and 4 girls in a class, the ratio of boys to girls is 6:4, but the ratio of boys to the total is 6:10.

Unit rates are the ratio of two measurements in which the second term is 1. For example, if Patrick earns $240 in 12 hours, he earns $20 in one hour: $\frac{dollars}{hours} = \frac{240}{12} = \frac{x}{1}$, so $x = \$20$.

Percentages are another way to represent parts of a whole. In a percentage, the whole is always 100.

$$\frac{part}{whole} = \frac{percent}{100}$$

In the example above, Jamie bought 9 jeans and 12 shirts, for a total of 21 items of clothing. To find the percentage of her purchase representing shirts, a proportion can be set up where the shirts are the part and the total number of items are the whole: $\frac{12}{21} = \frac{x}{100}$. By cross-multiplying, the equation can be solved to give a percentage: 0.57. Note that when using this equation, the percent is given as a decimal value. To find the percent, simply multiply by 100: $0.57 \times 100 = 57\%$.

SAMPLE QUESTIONS

13) In a theater, there are 4,500 lower-level seats and 2,000 upper-level seats. What is the ratio of lower-level seats to total seats?

A. $\frac{4}{9}$

B. $\frac{4}{13}$

C. $\frac{9}{13}$

D. $\frac{9}{4}$

Answer:

C. Find the total number of seats and set up a proportion.

total seats = 4,500 + 2,000

$$\frac{\text{lower seats}}{\text{total seats}} = \frac{4,500}{6,500} = \frac{9}{13}$$

14) If a car uses 8 gallons of gas to travel 650 miles, how many miles can it travel using 12 gallons of gas?

    A.   870 miles

    B.   895 miles

    C.   915 miles

    D.   975 miles

Answer:

    D.   Set up a proportion and solve.

$$\frac{8}{650} = \frac{12}{x}$$

$$12(650) = 8x$$

$$x = \textbf{975 miles}$$

PERCENTAGES AND PERCENT CHANGES

When working with percentages, it helps to remember that *of* equals *times*. For example, "20% off *of* something" can be translated to "20 divided by 100 *times* the original price" to find the discount.

Percentages cannot be used in math computations; they must be turned into decimals. Again, to turn a percentage into a decimal, move the decimal 2 places to the *left* (divide by 100). To turn a decimal back into a percentage, move the decimal 2 places to the *right* (multiply by 100).

Percent problems can either be set up using equations or ratios; it's helpful to remember "is/of" or "part/whole" in the fractions for the ratios. Also, don't forget to cross-multiply to solve ratios.

Table 2.4. Solving Percent Problems

Percent Problem	Solve Using Equations	Solve Using Ratios
What is 20% of 50?	20% of 50 = 0.2 × 50 = 10	$\left(\frac{\text{is}}{\text{of}}\right) \frac{20}{100} = \frac{x}{50}$ $100x = 1,000$ $x = 10$
120 is what percentage of 80?	$120 = ?\% \times 80$ $?\% = \frac{120}{80} = 1.5 = 150\%$	$\left(\frac{\text{is}}{\text{of}}\right) \frac{120}{80} = \frac{p}{100}$ $80p = 12,000$ $p = 150\%$
200 is 40% of what number?	$200 = 40\% \times ?$ $200 = 0.4 \times ?$ $\frac{200}{0.4} = 500$ $? = 500$	$\left(\frac{\text{part}}{\text{whole}}\right) \frac{40}{100} = \frac{200}{x}$ $40x = 20,000$ $x = 500$

Percent Change can either be percent decrease (going down) or percent increase (going up). To find the percent of increase or decrease, use the following formulas:

$$\text{percent increase} = \frac{\text{new amount} - \text{original amount}}{\text{original amount}} \times 100$$

$$\text{percent decrease} = \frac{\text{original amount} - \text{new amount}}{\text{original amount}} \times 100$$

So, for example, to know the percent increase of a house that has gone up in value from $100,000 to $150,000, use the formula:

$$\text{percent increase} = \frac{150,000 - 100,000}{100,000} \times 100 = 50\%$$

Percent decrease can be demonstrated with an example of an item that is discounted. The new price is found using the equation

$$\text{new lower price} = \text{original price} - \left(\text{original price} \times \frac{\text{percentage off}}{100}\right)$$

For example, if the regular price of a TV is $200 and it's on sale for 30% off, the new price is

$$200 - \left(200 \times \frac{30}{100}\right) = \$140$$

A good example of a **percent increase** problem is adding sales tax to an amount. The new price is found using the equation

$$\text{price with tax} = \text{original price} + \left(\text{original price} \times \frac{\text{percent increase}}{100}\right)$$

As an example, if the price of the TV is $140 with an 8.25% sales tax, the total price is

$$\text{price with tax} = 140 + (140 \times 0.0825) = \$151.55$$

SAMPLE QUESTIONS

15) 40% of what number is equal to 17?

A.   2.35

B.   6.8

C.   42.5

D.   680

Answer:

C.   Solve using ratios.

$$\frac{\text{part}}{\text{whole}} = \frac{40}{100} = \frac{17}{x}$$

$$40x = 100(17)$$

$$x = 42.5$$

(handwritten: 3,000)

(handwritten margin notes: 6000 – 5700 / 5700 – 57,000 / 60,000 – 57,000)

16) What is the percent increase in an employee's salary if it is raised from $57,000 to $60,000?

(handwritten: 57,000 to 60,000)

A. 0.3%

B. 3%

C. 4%

D. 5%

Answer:

D. Use the formula for percent increase.

$$\text{percent increase} = \frac{\text{new amount} - \text{original amount}}{\text{original amount}} \times 100$$

$$= \frac{60{,}000 - 57{,}000}{57{,}000} \times 100 = \mathbf{5\%}$$

SCIENTIFIC NOTATION

65000000.
7 6 5 4 3 2 1
↓
6.5×10^7

.0000987
-1-2-3-4-5
↓
9.87×10^{-5}

Figure 2.10. Scientific Notation

Scientific notation is a notation that can be used with very small and very large numbers that are difficult to work with. It's relatively easy to go back and forth between standard notation numbers ("regular" numbers) and scientific notation numbers, which are numbers that are multiplied by powers of 10.

For scientific notation, use a number between 1 and 10 (not including 10; for example, 9.99 would work) and multiply it by 10 raised to a number. To turn a number greater than 10 into scientific notation, move the decimal point to the left and use a positive exponent. To turn a number less than 1 into scientific notation, move the decimal point to the right and use a negative exponent. Count left or right either from the decimal point if there is one, or from the end of the number (at the right), if there isn't one.

Scientific notation is used by simplifying numbers with numbers between 1 and 10. These numbers are then multiplied by **10** raised to

HELPFUL HINT

When converting a decimal to scientific notation, if the number between 1 and 10 is larger than the number you started with, the power of 10 will be negative. If the number between 1 and 10 is smaller than the number you started with, the power of 10 will be positive.

an exponent. For example, for the number 870,000,000, abbreviate it to 8.7×10^8. Also, $0.000045 = 4.5 \times 10^{-5}$.

Table 2.5. Scientific Notation

Math	Explanation
$8,500 = 8.5 \times 10^3$	8.5 is between 1 and 10; to go from a *larger number to smaller number,* move the decimal to the left 3 places, and use a *positive exponent* (3).
$0.0012 = 1.2 \times 10^{-3}$	1.2 is between 1 and 10; to go from a *smaller number to larger number,* move the decimal to the right 3 places, and use a *negative exponent* (–3).
$3.4 \times 10^5 = 340,000$	Because of the *positive exponent,* move the decimal 5 places *to the right* (adding zeros) to end up with a larger number.
$6.6 \times 10^{-4} = 0.00066$	Because of the *negative exponent,* move the decimal 4 places *to the left* (adding zeros from the decimal point) to end up with a *smaller number.*

SAMPLE QUESTION

17) **Which of the following is the correct scientific notation for the number 34,500,000?**

A. 3.45×10^{-7}

B. 3.45×10^6

C. 34.5×10^6

D. 3.45×10^7

Answer:

D. Move the decimal until it is between the 3 and the 4, making a number between 1 and 10. Count the number of spots the decimal moved and make this value the exponent on the 10.

$34,500,000 = 3.45 \times 10^7$

REASONABLENESS

Since minor mistakes can lead to major errors, mathematicians need quick and easy ways to assess the **reasonableness**, or common sense, of their answers. **Rounding**, or simplifying a number to any predetermined place value, enables a student to make an estimation. An **estimation** is a close prediction that involves minor calculations.

When rounding to a specific place value, the number in that place is rounded up if the digit immediately to the right is 5 or higher, and it remains the same if the number is less than 5. For example, the operation 22 × 8 is difficult to do quickly. However, rounding 22 to 20 and 8 to 10 allows for a quick and easy calculation: 20 × 10. This estimate will provide a product close enough to check for reasonableness of exact calculations. Math that can be done in the student's head without the use of tools is called **mental math**.

SAMPLE QUESTION

18) What is 498,235 rounded to the nearest thousands?

- A. 498,000
- B. 498,200
- C. 499,000
- D. 500,000

Answer:

A. The 8 is in the thousands place. Because the value to the right of the 8 is less than 5, the 8 remains the same and all values to its right become zero. The result is **498,000**.

Algebraic Thinking

ALGEBRAIC EXPRESSIONS

Algebraic expressions contain numbers, variables, and at least one mathematical operation. Each group of numbers and variables in an expression is called a **term** (e.g., $3x$ or $16y$). A **binomial** is an algebraic expression with two terms (e.g., $3x + 16y$), a **trinomial** has three terms, and a **polynomial** has more than three terms. Algebraic expressions can be evaluated for a specific value by plugging that value into the expression and simplifying.

> **HELPFUL HINT**
>
> To multiply binomials, use FOIL:
> First – Outer – Inner – Last. For example,
> $(a + b)(c + d) = ac + ad + bc + bd$.

To add or subtract linear algebraic expressions, add the variables and numbers (constants) separately. For example, $(5x − 3) + (3x − 2) = (5x + 3x) + (−3 − 2) = 8x − 5$. Now subtract, making sure that the minus sign is distributed through the parentheses:

$$(13x − 5y + 2) − (8x − y − 3) = (13x − 8x) + (−5y − −y) + (2 − −3) =$$
$$(13x − 8x) + (−5y + y) + (2 + 3) = 5x − 4y + 5.$$

Remember that two negatives in a row is the same as a positive.

To **evaluate** an algebraic expression for a certain value, simply "plug in" that value into the variable wherever it appears. For example, evaluate $3x + 5y − z^2 + x^2$ when $x = 2$, $y = −4$, and $z = −1$: $3(2) + 5(−4) − (−1)^2 + 2^2 = 6 − 20 − 1 + 4 = −11$.

SAMPLE QUESTIONS

19) If $x = 5$, what is the value of the algebraic expression $2x - x$?

A. 5

B. 10

C. 15

D. 20

Answer:

A. Substitute 5 for x.

$2(5) - 5 = 10 - 5 = 5$

20) $(3x + 2)^2 =$

A. $9x^2 + 4$

B. $9x^2 + 6x + 4$

C. $9x^2 + 10x + 4$

D. $9x^2 + 12x + 4$

Answer:

D. Use FOIL to solve.

$(3x + 2)(3x + 2) =$

$9x^2 + 6x + 6x + 4 = \mathbf{9x^2 + 12x + 4}$

ALGEBRAIC EQUATIONS

In an **equation**, two expressions are joined by an equal sign, which indicates that the two expressions are equal to each other. The two sides of an equation act like a balanced scale: operations can be performed on equations as long as the same operation is performed on both sides to maintain the balance.

> ### HELPFUL HINT
>
> Remember that usually when a problem is talking about a rate (sometimes expressed as "per" something else), this is typically the slope.

This property can be used to solve the equation by performing operations that isolate the variable on one side. For example, the equation $4x + 12 = 2x + 48$ can be solved for x using the following steps:

1. Subtract 12 from both sides of the equation:

   $(4x + 12) - 12 = (2x + 48) - 12 \rightarrow 4x = 2x + 36$

2. Subtract $2x$ from both sides of the equation:

Figure 2.11. Equations

$(4x) - 2x = (2x + 36) - 2x \rightarrow 2x = 36$

3. Divide both sides by 2:

$$\frac{2x}{2} = \frac{36}{2} \rightarrow x = 18$$

Linear equations follow a specific pattern that results in a straight line when graphed. The most common way to write a linear equation is **slope-intercept form**, y = $mx + b$. In this equation, b is the y-intercept, which is the point where the line crosses the y-axis, or where x equals zero. Slope is represented by the letter m and describes how steep the line is. Slope is often described as "rise over run" because it is calculated as the difference in y-values (rise) over the difference in x-values (run):

$$m = \frac{y_2 - y_1}{x_2 - x_1}$$

HELPFUL HINT

Linear equations with the same slope are parallel. When two slopes are reciprocal negatives (such as 2 and $-\frac{1}{2}$), the lines are perpendicular.

SAMPLE QUESTIONS

21) Solve for x: $5x - 4 = 3(8 + 3x)$

   A. −7
   B. $-\frac{3}{4}$
   C. $\frac{3}{4}$
   D. 7

   Answer:

   A. Isolate the variable x on one side of the equation.

   $5x - 4 = 3(8 + 3x)$

   $5x - 4 = 24 + 9x$

   $-4 - 24 = 9x - 5x$

   $-28 = 4x$

   $\frac{-28}{4} = \frac{4x}{4}$

   $x = -7$

22) Which of the following is an equation of the line that passes through the points (4, −3) and (−2, 9) in the xy-plane?

   A. $y = -2x + 5$
   B. $y = -\frac{1}{2}x - 1$
   C. $y = \frac{1}{2}x - 5$
   D. $y = 2x - 11$

Answer:

A.   Use the points to find the slope.

$$m = \frac{y_2 - y_1}{x_2 - x_1} = \frac{-3 - 9}{4 - (-2)} = -2$$

Use the point-slope equation to find the equation of the line.

$$(y - y_1) = m(x - x_1)$$

$$y - (-3) = -2(x - 4)$$

$$\boldsymbol{y = -2x + 5}$$

FUNCTIONS

Functions demonstrate a relationship between sets of values, called the inputs and outputs. The input is the **independent variable**, and the output is called the **dependent variable** because it depends on the input. Usually (but not always) x is the independent variable, and y is the dependent variable. The coordinates found in the function table can then be plotted on a set of axes to find the corresponding graph.

Tables may be used to connect the y-value (dependent variable) to the x-value (independent variable) in an equation. The values may be plotted to see whether the relationship is linear, and if it is, to identify a slope and y-intercept. Here is table of values to be evaluated:

Table 2.6. Function Table

$3x + y = 12$

x	y	
1	9	$3(1) + y = 12$ $3 + y = 12$ $y = 9$
2	6	$3(2) + y = 12$ $6 + y = 12$ $y = 6$
3	3	$3(3) + y = 12$ $9 + y = 12$ $y = 3$

x	2	3	4	5
y	8	11	14	17

HELPFUL HINT

If the difference between x values and the difference between y values are constant, then the function is linear.

Plotting the points shows that the relationship is linear with a slope of 3. Another way to determine the relationship is to notice a pattern where the difference between each x-value is 1, and the difference between each y-value is 3. Since these differences are the same for all x- and y-values, the data can be modeled as a linear equation. The slope is: $\frac{\text{change in } y}{\text{change in } x} = \frac{3}{1} = 3$. To get the y-intercept, when $x = 2$, add 2 more to $3x$ to get 8, the y-value. Thus, the equation is $y = 3x + 2$.

Here's an example of a table with **non-linear** values:

x	1	2	3	4
$f(x)$	2	5	10	17

Note that each value for $f(x)$ (equivalent of the y-value above) is the x-value squared, plus 1. This quadratic pattern can be modeled by $f(x) = x^2 + 1$.

SAMPLE QUESTION

23) Which equation describes the relationship between x and y shown in the table?

x	y
3	11
5	15
7	19

A. $y = -2x - 5$
B. $y = 2x + 5$
C. $y = 4x + 2$
D. $y = x^2 + 2$

Answer:

B. The difference between the x values (2) and the difference between the y values (4) are both constant, so the function is linear. Find the slope to identify the right equation:

$$m = \frac{y_2 - y_1}{x_2 - x_1} = \frac{15 - 11}{5 - 3} = 2$$

$y = 2x + 5$ is a linear relationship because $11 = 2(3) + 5$. The slope is 2, since there is a constant difference of 2 for the x-values and a difference of 4 for the y-values. Substitute the x- and y-values into the equation.

INEQUALITIES

Inequalities are similar to equations, but both sides of the problem are not equal ($\neq$). Inequalities may be represented as follows: greater than ($>$), greater than or equal to ($\geq$), less than ($<$), or less than or equal to ($\leq$).

Figure 2.12. Inequality

Inequalities may be represented on a number line, as shown below. A circle is placed on the end point with a filled circle representing ≤ and ≥, and an empty circle representing < and >. An arrow is then drawn to show either all the values greater than or less than 3.

Inequalities can be solved by manipulating them much like equations. However, the solution to an inequality is a set of numbers, not a single value. For example, simplifying $4x + 2 \leq 14$ gives the inequality $x \leq 3$, meaning every number less than 3 or equal to 3 would be included in the set of correct answers.

$x \leq 3$

Figure 2.13. Inequality Line Graph

SAMPLE QUESTION

24) Which of the following is a solution to the inequality $2x + y \leq -10$?

A. (0, 0)

B. (10, 2)

C. (10, 10)

D. (−10, −10)

Answer:

D. Plug in each set of values and determine if the inequality is true.

$2(0) + 0 \leq -10$ FALSE

$2(10) + 2 \leq -10$ FALSE

$2(10) + 10 \leq -10$ FALSE

$2(-10) + (-10) \leq -10$ **TRUE**

ALGEBRA WORD PROBLEMS

Math word problems involve translations (almost word-for-word, like a language) from English to math; they also take a lot of practice.

Table 2.7. Translating Word Problems

English Word(s)	Math Translation
is, will be, yields	=
what number, how much	"*n*" (or any variable)
in addition to, increased by, added to	+
sum of *x* and *y*	$x + y$
difference of *x* and *y*	$x - y$

English Word(s)	Math Translation
product of x and y	$x \times y$
quotient of x and y	$x \div y$ or $\frac{x}{y}$
opposite of x	$-x$
ratio of x to y	$x \div y$ or $\frac{x}{y}$
a number n less 2	$n - 2$
a number n less than 2	$2 - n$
a number n reduced by 2	$n - 2$
of	times
p percent	$\frac{p}{100}$, or move decimal left 2 places
half, twice	$\frac{x}{2}$, $2x$
average of x, y, and z (and so on)	$\dfrac{x + y + z + \ldots}{\text{how many numbers are on top}}$
y increased by x%	$y + (y \times x/100)$
y decreased by x%	$y - \left(y \times \frac{x}{100}\right)$
y is at least (or no less than) x	$y \geq x$
y is at most (or no more than) x	$y \leq x$

- ▶ Usually the question in the problem is a key for what the variable(s) should be.
- ▶ For consecutive integers, use n, $n + 1$, $n + 2$, and so on.
- ▶ For even or odd consecutive integers, use n, $n + 2$, $n + 4$, and so on.
- ▶ Use easier numbers to figure the problem out (such as the number 100 in percent problems) before using the actual numbers.
- ▶ If the problem asks for a **unit rate**, determine the ratio of the y-value (sometimes a dollar amount) to the x-value, when the x-value is 1. This is basically the slope of the linear functions. Some examples of unit rates are feet per second, miles per hour, and costs per unit.

AGE PROBLEM

Twice a man's age is no more than 5 years less than his father's age. If m represents the man's age, and f his father's age, what is the inequality that would represent this situation?

Solution: Translate almost word-for-word from English to math: $2m \leq f - 5$.

UNIT RATE PROBLEM

A shopper buys 6 pounds of apples for $4.80. What is the unit rate of a pound of apples?

Solution: To get the unit rate, find the amount for one pound of apples; this is when x apples equals 1. Set up a ratio: $\frac{4.8}{6} = \frac{x}{1}$; $x = \$0.80$.

MULTI-VARIABLE PROBLEM

If b books cost d dollars each and each student must buy 2 books, how much will each student pay for his or her books?

Solution: Make it into an easier problem. If 100 books cost $2,000, each student would have to pay $\frac{2,000}{100} \times 2$, or $40. This is the same as, $\frac{d}{b} \times 2$, or $\frac{2d}{b}$.

DISTANCE PROBLEM

If a car is going 57 miles per hour, how many hours does it take the car to go 228 miles?

Solution: Since Distance = Rate × Time, solve for Time: Time = $\frac{\text{Distance}}{\text{Rate}} = \frac{228}{57}$ = 4 hours.

PERCENTAGE PROBLEM

In a clothing store, the manager earns $\frac{1}{4}$ more than her salesperson. What percentage of the manager's salary is the salesperson's salary?

Solution: Translate: $m = s + 0.25s$; $m = 1.25s$; $s = \frac{m}{1.25} = \frac{1}{1.25} \times m = 0.8m = 80\%$. The salesperson's salary is 80% of the manager's salary.

SAMPLE QUESTION

25) Valerie receives a base salary of $740 a week for working 40 hours. For every extra hour she works, she is paid at a rate of $27.75 per hour. If Valerie works t hours in a week, which of the following equations represents the amount of money, A, she will receive?

    A. $A = 740 + 27.75(t - 40)$
    B. $A = 740 + 27.75(40 - t)$
    C. $A = 27.75t - 740$
    D. $A = 27.75t + 740$

Answer:

A.   Valerie will receive her base pay plus 27.75 for every hour she worked in addition to her 40 hours.

    A = base pay + 27.75 × extra hours

    $A = 740 + 27.75(t - 40)$

Geometry and Measurement

UNITS AND MEASUREMENT

The standard units for the metric and American systems are shown below, along with the prefixes used to express metric units.

Table 2.8. Units and Conversion Factors

Dimension	American	SI
length	inch/foot/yard/mile	meter
mass	ounce/pound/ton	kilogram
volume	cup/pint/quart/gallon	liter
force	pound-force	newton
pressure	pound-force per square inch	pascal
work and energy	cal/British thermal unit	joule
temperature	Fahrenheit	kelvin
charge	faraday	coulomb

Table 2.9. Metric Prefixes

Prefix	Symbol	Multiplication Factor
tera	T	1,000,000,000,000
giga	G	1,000,000,000
mega	M	1,000,000
kilo	k	1,000
hecto	h	100
deca	da	10
base unit	--	--
deci	d	0.1
centi	c	0.01
milli	m	0.001
micro	μ	0.0000001
nano	n	0.0000000001
pico	p	0.0000000000001

Units can be converted within a single system or between systems. When converting from one unit to another unit, a **conversion factor** (a numeric multiplier used to convert a value with a unit to another unit) is used. The process of converting between units using a conversion factor is sometimes known as **dimensional analysis**.

Table 2.10. Conversion Factors	
1 in. = 2.54 cm	1 lb. = 0.454 kg
1 yd. = 0.914 m	1 cal = 4.19 J
1 mi. = 1.61 km	$1°F = \frac{5}{9}(°F - 32°C)$
1 gal. = 3.785 L	$1 cm^3 = 1 mL$
1 oz. = 28.35 g	1 hr = 3600 s

SAMPLE QUESTION

26) **Convert the following measurements:**

   A.   4.25 kilometers to meters

   B. $8 m^2$ to mm^2

   C.   12 feet to inches

   D.   23 meters to feet

Answers:

   A. $4.25 \text{ km}\left(\frac{1000 \text{ m}}{1 \text{ km}}\right) = \textbf{4250 m}$

   B. $\frac{8 m^2}{\square} \times \frac{1000 \text{ mm}}{1 \text{ m}} \times \frac{1000 \text{ mm}}{1 \text{ m}} = \textbf{8,000,000 mm}^2$
         Since the units are *square* units (m^2), multiply by the conversion factor *twice*, so that both meters cancel (and $mm \times mm = mm^2$).

   C. $12 \text{ ft}\left(\frac{12 \text{ in}}{1 \text{ ft}}\right) = \textbf{144 in}$

   D. $23 \text{ m}\left(\frac{3.28 \text{ ft}}{1 \text{ m}}\right) = \textbf{75.44 ft}$

CLASSIFYING GEOMETRIC FIGURES

Geometric figures are shapes comprised of points, lines, or planes. A **point** is simply a location in space; it does not have any dimensional properties such as length, area, or volume. A collection of points that extends infinitely in both directions is a **line**, and one that extends infinitely in only one direction is a **ray**. A section of a line with a beginning and end is a **line segment**. Lines, rays, and line segments are examples of **one-dimensional** objects because they can only be measured in one dimension (length).

Figure 2.14. One-Dimensional Object

Lines, rays, and line segments can intersect to create **angles**, which are measured in degrees or radians. Angles between 0 and 90 degrees are **acute**, and angles between 90 and 180 degrees are **obtuse**. An angle of exactly 90 degrees is a

right angle, and two lines that form right angles are **perpendicular**. Lines that do not intersect are described as **parallel**.

Two angles with measurements that add up to 90 degrees are **complementary**, and two angles with measurements that add up to 180 degrees are **supplementary**. Two adjacent (touching) angles are called a **linear pair**, and they are supplementary. The **sum of angles in a triangle** is 180 degrees.

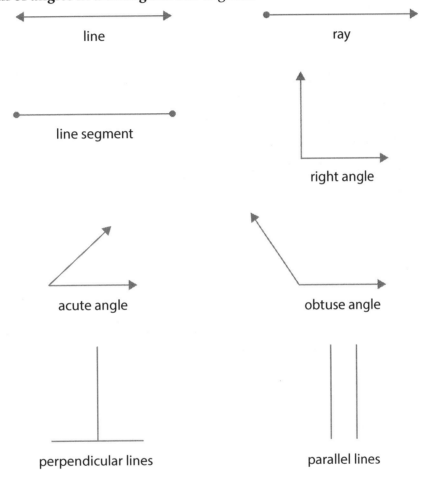

Figure 2.15. Lines and Angles

Two-dimensional objects can be measured in two dimensions (length and width). A **plane** is a two-dimensional object that extends infinitely in both dimensions. **Polygons** are two-dimensional shapes, such as triangles and squares, that have three or more straight sides. **Regular polygons** are polygons with sides that are all the same length. The sum of all the interior angle measurements in a polygon with n sides is $(n - 2) \times 180$ degrees, and the sum of all the exterior angles is 360 degrees for any polygon.

Figure 2.16. Two-Dimensional Object

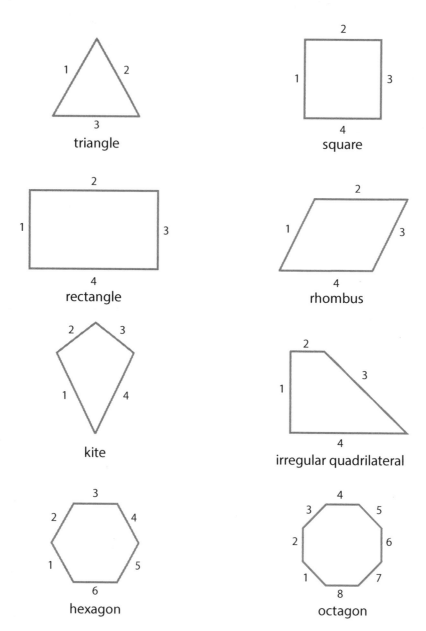

Figure 2.17. Polygons

Three-dimensional objects, such as cubes, can be measured in three dimensions (length, width, and height). Three-dimensional objects are also called **solids**, and the shape of a flattened solid is called a **net**.

Figure 2.18. Three-Dimensional Object

Figure 2.19. Net

SAMPLE QUESTION

27) **What is the measure of each exterior angle of a regular 300-gon?**

A. 1.2°

B. 2.4°

C. 178.8°

D. 360°

360

√ᵢ Don't be fooled- must equal 360 regardless

Answer:

A. The sum of all the exterior angles of a regular *n*-gon is always 360°. Because there are 300 vertices in a 300-gon, the exterior angle at each vertex is $\frac{360}{300}$ = **1.2°**.

PROPERTIES OF SHAPES

The **length**, or distance from one point to another on an object, can be determined using a tape measure or a ruler. The size of the surface of a two-dimensional object is its **area**. The area of an object is its length times its width and is measured in square units. For example, if a wall is 3 feet long and 2 feet wide, its area would be 6 square feet. The distance around a two-dimensional figure is its **perimeter**, which can be found by adding the lengths of all the sides.

Table 2.11. Area and Perimeter of Basic Shapes

Shape	Areas	Perimeter
Triangle	$A = \frac{1}{2}bh$	$P = s_1 + s_2 + s_3$
Square	$A = s^2$	$P = 4s$
Rectangle	$A = l \times w$	$P = 2l + 2w$
Circle	$A = \pi r^2$	$C = 2\pi r$ (circumference)

For the rectangle below, the area would be 8 m² because 2 m × 4 m = 8 m². The perimeter of the rectangle would be 12 meters because the sum of the length of all sides is 2 m + 4 m + 2 m + 4 m = 12 m.

4m

2m

Figure 2.20. Fencing

The **surface area** of a three-dimensional object can be figured by adding the areas of all the sides. For example, the box below is 4 feet long, 3 feet wide, and 1 foot deep. The surface area is found by adding the areas of each face:

- ▶ top: 4 ft. × 3 ft. = 12 ft²
- ▶ bottom: 4 ft. × 3 ft. = 12 ft²
- ▶ front: 4 ft. × 1 ft. = 4 ft²
- ▶ back: 4 ft. × 1 ft. = 4 ft²
- ▶ right: 3 ft. × 1 ft. = 3 ft²
- ▶ left: 3 ft. × 1 ft. = 3 ft²

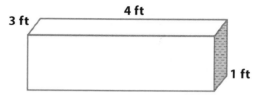

Figure 2.21. Surface Area

A **net** (flattened out three-dimensional solid) can also be used to find the surface area of solids. For example, for a square pyramid with a base with side 6 m and slant height (height in the middle of the triangular faces) of 8 m, the surface area can be calculated with a square and four triangles:

Surface Area = Area of Square Base + Area of 4 Triangles = $6^2 + 4\left[\frac{1}{2}(6 \times 8)\right]$ = 36 + 96 = 132 m².

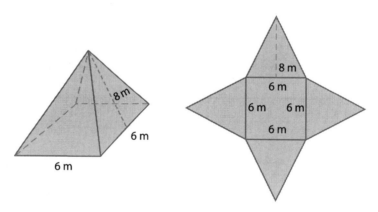

Figure 2.22. Surface Area of a Pyramid

Volume is the amount of space that a three-dimensional object takes up. Volume is measured in cubic units (e.g., ft³ or mm³). The volume of a solid can be determined by multiplying length times width times height. In the rectangular prism below, the volume is 3 in. × 1 in. × 1 in. = 3 in³.

Figure 2.23. Volume

Here are formulas for the surface area and volume of basic solids. Note that lateral area (LA) is the surface area of the solids without the bases, which are the two parallel faces between the height.

Table 2.12. Area and Volume of Basic Solids

Solid	Volume	Surface Area
Sphere (r is radius)	$V = \frac{4}{3}\pi r^3$	$SA = 4\pi r^2$
Cube (s is side)	$V = s^3$	$SA = 6s^2$
Cylinder (r is radius of base; B is area of base)	$V = \pi r^2 h$	$SA = LA + 2B = 2\pi rh + 2\pi r^2$
Right Rectangular Prism (LA, or lateral area, is the perimeter of base times height; B is area of base)	$V = Bh$	$SA = LA + 2B$

Here's an example of finding the volume and surface area of a **right rectangular prism** with a height of 8 cm and square bases with sides of 2 cm. Remember that the bases are the two squares that are on either side of the height.

$SA = LA + 2B = [(2 + 2 + 2 + 2) \times 8] + [2 \times (2 \times 2)] = 64 + 8 = 72$ cm^2

Note that the SA can also be found by adding the areas of all the sides:

$SA = (2 \times 8) + (2 \times 8) + (2 \times 8) + (2 \times 8) + (2 \times 2) + (2 \times 2) = 64 + 8 = 72$ cm^2

Figure 2.24. Surface Area of a Right Rectangular Prism

SAMPLE QUESTION

28) What is the perimeter of the regular polygon?

regular equals perfect.

$2 \times 5 = 10$

A.   4 in.

B.   8 in.

C.   10 in.

D.   32 in.

Answer:

C.   Add the length of each side to find the perimeter:
2 in. + 2 in. + 2 in. + 2 in. + 2 in. = 10 in.

CIRCLES

Circles are a fundamental shape in geometry. A **circle** is the set of all the points in a plane that are the same distance from a fixed point (called the center). The distance from the center to any point on the circle is the **radius** of the circle. The distance around the circle (the perimeter) is called the **circumference**.

The ratio of a circle's circumference to its diameter is a constant value called pi (π), an irrational number which is commonly rounded to 3.14. The formula to find a circle's circumference is $C = 2\pi r$. The formula to find the enclosed area of a circle is $A = \pi r^2$.

Circles have a number of unique parts:

▸ The **diameter** is the largest measurement across a circle. It passes through the circle's center, extending from one side of the circle to the other. The measure of the diameter is twice the measure of the radius.

▸ A line that cuts across a circle and touches it twice is called a **secant** line.

▸ The part of a secant line that lies within a circle is called a **chord**.

▸ A line that touches a circle or any curve at one point is **tangent** to the circle or the curve. A line tangent to a circle and a radius drawn to the point of tangency meet at a right angle (90°).

▸ An **arc** is any portion of a circle between two points on the circle. The measure of an arc is in degrees, whereas the length of the arc will be in linear measurement (such as centimeters or inches).

▸ An angle with its vertex at the center of a circle is called a **central angle**.

▸ A **sector** is the part of a circle that is inside the rays of a central angle (its shape is like a slice of pie).

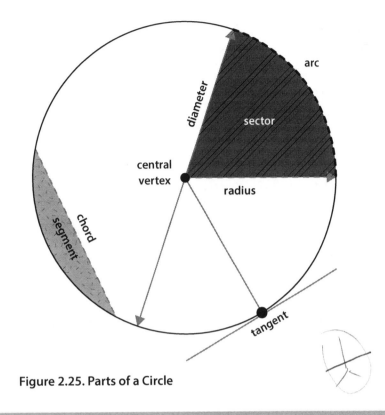

Figure 2.25. Parts of a Circle

29) *W, X, Y,* and *Z* lie on a circle with center *A*. If the diameter of the circle is 75, what is the sum of $\overline{AW}, \overline{AX}, \overline{AY}$, and $\overline{AZ}$?

    A.   75

    B.   300

    C.   150

    D.   106.5

Answer:

    C.   All the points lie on the circle, so each line segment is a radius. The sum of the 4 lines will be 4 times the radius.

$$r = \frac{75}{2} = 37.5$$

$$4r = \mathbf{150}$$

TRIANGLES

Triangles have three sides, and the three interior angles always sum to 180°. The formula for the area of a triangle is $A = \frac{1}{2}bh$ or one-half the product of the base and height (or altitude) of the triangle.

Triangles can be classified in two ways: by sides and by angles.

A **scalene triangle** has no equal sides or angles. An **isosceles triangle** has two equal sides and two equal angles (often called base angles). In an **equilateral triangle**, all three sides are equal as are all three angles. Moreover, because the sum of the angles of a triangle is always 180°, each angle of an equilateral triangle must be 60°.

A **right triangle** has one right angle (90°) and two acute angles. An **acute triangle** has three acute angles (all angles are less than 90°). An **obtuse triangle** has one obtuse angle (more than 90°) and two acute angles.

For any triangle, the side opposite the largest angle will have the longest length, while the side opposite the smallest angle will have the shortest length. The **triangle inequality theorem** states that the sum of any two sides of a triangle must be greater than the third side. This leads to the **third-side rule**: if b and c are two sides of a triangle, then the measure of the third side a must be between the sum of the other two sides and the difference of the other two sides: $c - b < a < c + b$.

Solving for missing angles or sides of a triangle is a common type of triangle problem. Often a right triangle will come up on its own or within another triangle. The relationship among a right triangle's sides is known as the **Pythagorean theorem**: $a^2 + b^2 = c^2$, where c is the hypotenuse and is across from the 90° angle.

Triangles Based on Sides

Triangles Based on Angles

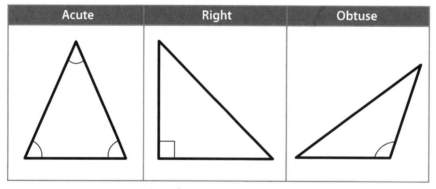

Figure 2.26. Types of Triangles

30) Which of the following could be the perimeter of a triangle with two sides that measure 13 and 5?

    A.   24.5

    B.   26.5

    C.   36

    D.   37

    Answer:

    B.   Use the third-side rule to find the possible values for the third side, then calculate the possible perimeters.

$$13 - 5 < s < 13 + 5$$

$$8 < s < 18$$

$$13 + 5 + 8 < P < 13 + 5 + 18$$

$$26 < P < 36$$

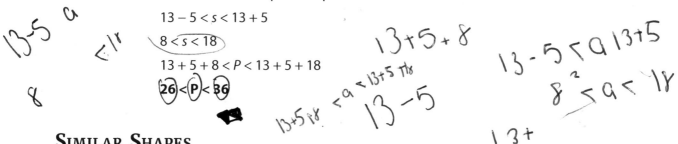

SIMILAR SHAPES

Similar shapes have the same angle measurements and sides that are proportional. The **scale factor** is the ratio of corresponding sides of the figures. If the dimensions of a figure are **dilated** (made smaller or larger with proportional dimensions) by a scale factor of $\frac{a}{b}$, then the surface area of the new dilated solid is multiplied by $\frac{a^2}{b^2}$, and the volume of the new dilated solid is multiplied by $\frac{a^3}{b^3}$.

For example, in the solids below, the scale factor is $\frac{16}{8} = 2$. Therefore, the surface area of the second solid is equal to the surface area of the first solid multiplied by $2^2 = 4$, and the volume of the second solid is equal to the volume of the first solid's volume multiplied by $2^3 = 8$.

$SA = 72$ cm² $SA = 72 \times 2^2 = 288$ cm²

$V = 32 \times 2^3 = 256$ cm³

Figure 2.27. Dilated Solids

31) Cone *A* is similar to cone *B* with a scale factor of 3:4. If the volume of cone *A* is 54π, what is the volume of cone *B*?

    A. 72π

    B. 128π

    C. 162π

    D. 216π

Answer:

B. Set up a proportion. Cube the scale factor when calculating volume.

$$\frac{54\pi}{x} = \frac{3^3}{4^3}$$

$$x = 128\pi$$

GRAPHING ON A COORDINATE PLANE

A **coordinate plane** is a plane containing the x- and y-axes. The **x-axis** is the horizontal line on a graph where $y = 0$. The **y-axis** is the vertical line on a graph where $x = 0$. The x-axis and y-axis intersect to create four **quadrants**. The first quadrant is in the upper right, and other quadrants are labeled counter-clockwise using the roman numerals I, II, III, and IV. **Points**, or locations, on the graph are written as **ordered pairs**, (x,y), with the point $(0,0)$ called the **origin**. Points are plotted by counting over x places from the origin horizontally and y places from the origin vertically.

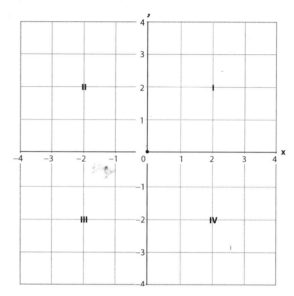

Figure 2.28. Four Quadrants

SAMPLE QUESTION

32) Using Figure 2.28, in which quadrant is the point $(-5, 2)$ located?

A. I

B. II

C. III

D. IV

Answer:

B. Starting at the origin, move 5 units to the left, and then up 2 units.

Data, Statistics, and Probability

STATISTICS

Statistics is the study of data. Analyzing data requires using **measures of center** (mean, median, and mode) to identify trends or patterns.

The **mean** is the average; it is determined by adding all outcomes and then dividing by the total number of outcomes. For example, the average of the data set $\{16, 19, 19, 25, 27, 29, 75\}$ is equal to $\frac{16 + 19 + 19 + 25 + 27 + 29 + 75}{7} = \frac{210}{7} = 30$.

The **median** is the number in the middle when the data set is arranged in order from least to greatest. For example, in the data set $\{16, 19, 19, \mathbf{25}, 27, 29, 75\}$, the median is 25. When a data set contains an even number of values, finding the median requires averaging the two middle values. In the data set $\{75, 80, 82, 100\}$, the two numbers in the middle are 80 and 82. Consequently, the median will be the average of these two values: $\frac{80 + 82}{2} = 81$.

HELPFUL HINT

Mode is <u>most</u> common. Median is in the middle (like a median in the road). Mean is average.

Finally, the **mode** is the most frequent outcome in a data set. In the set $\{16, 19, 19, 25, 27, 29, 75\}$, the mode is 19 because it occurs twice, which is more than any of the other numbers. If several values appear an equal and most frequent number of times, both values are considered the mode.

Other useful indicators include range and outliers. The **range** is the difference between the highest and the lowest number in a data set. For example, the range of the set $\{16, 19, 19, 25, 27, 29, 75\}$ is $75 - 16 = 59$. **Outliers**, or data points that are much different from other data points, should be noted as they can skew the central tendency. In the data set $\{16, 19, 19, 25, 27, 29, 75\}$, the value 75 is far outside the other values and raises the value of the mean. Without the outlier, the mean is much closer to the other data points.

CHECK YOUR UNDERSTANDING

Why should teachers recognize the importance of outliers when looking at student data?

▸ $\frac{16 + 19 + 19 + 25 + 27 + 29 + 75}{7} = \frac{210}{7} = 30$

▸ $\frac{16 + 19 + 19 + 25 + 27 + 29}{6} = 22.5$

When a data distribution is symmetrical, the mean, median, and mode tend to be in the center of the data. Generally, the median is a better indicator of a central tendency if outliers are present to skew the mean. If a distribution is **skewed left** (outliers tend to be smaller numbers), typically the mean is less than the median, and the median is the best indicator. If the distribution is **skewed right** (outliers tend to be larger numbers), typically the mean is greater than the median, and again, the median is the best indicator. So, the mean tends to be pulled toward the longer "tails" of the data.

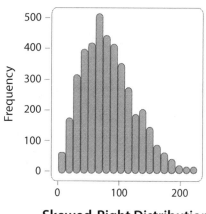

Figure 2.29. Skew

33) Ken has 6 grades in English class. Each grade is worth 100 points. Ken has a 92% average in English. If Ken's first five grades are 90, 100, 95, 83, and 87, what did Ken earn for the sixth grade?

   A.   80

   B.   92

   C.   97

   D.   100

   Answer:

   C.   If Ken has six scores that average 92%, his total number of points earned is found by multiplying the average by the number of scores:

   $92 \times 6 = 552$

   To find how many points he earned on the sixth test, subtract the sum of the other scores from 552:

   $90 + 100 + 95 + 83 + 87 = 455$

   $552 - 455 = 97$

34) What is the relationship between the mean and the median in a data set that is skewed right?

   A.   The mean is greater than the median.

   B.   The mean is less than the median.

   C.   The mean and median are equal.

   D.   The mean may be greater than, less than, or equal to the median.

   Answer:

   A.   If the data is skewed right, the set includes extreme values that are to the right, or high. The median is unaffected by these high values, but the mean includes these high values and would therefore be greater.

DATA PRESENTATION

Data can be presented in a variety of ways. The most appropriate depends on the data being displayed.

Box plots (also called box-and-whisker plots) show data using the median, range, and outliers of a data set. They provide a helpful visual guide, showing how data is distributed around the median. In the example below, 81 is the median and the range is 100 − 0, or 100.

Figure 2.30. Box Plots

Bar graphs use bars of different lengths to compare data. The independent variable on a bar graph is grouped into categories such as months, flavors, or locations, and the dependent variable will be a quantity. Thus, comparing the length of bars provides a visual guide to the relative amounts in each category. **Double bar graphs** show more than one data set on the same set of axes.

Histograms similarly use bars to compare data, but the independent variable is a continuous variable that has been "binned" or divided into categories. For example, the time of day can be broken down into 8:00 a.m. to 12:00 p.m., 12:00 p.m. to 4:00 p.m., and so on. Usually (but not always), a gap is included between the bars of a bar graph but not a histogram.

Figure 2.31. Bar Graph

Dot plots display the frequency of a value or event data graphically using dots, and thus can be used to observe the distribution of a data set. Typically, a value or category is listed on the *x*-axis, and the number of times that value appears in the data set is represented by a line of vertical dots. Dot plots make it easy to see which values occur most often.

Figure 2.32. Double Bar Graph

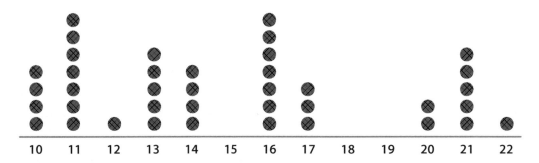

Figure 2.33. Dot Plot

Scatterplots use points to show relationships between two variables which can be plotted as coordinate points. One variable describes a position on the *x*-axis, and the other a point on the *y*-axis. Scatterplots can suggest relationships between variables. For example, both variables might increase, or one may increase when the other decreases.

Figure 2.34. Scatterplot

Line graphs show changes in data by connecting points on a scatterplot using a line. These graphs will often measure time on the *x*-axis and are used to show trends in the data, such as temperature changes over a day or school attendance throughout the year. **Double line graphs** present two sets of data on the same set of axes.

Figure 2.35. Line Graph

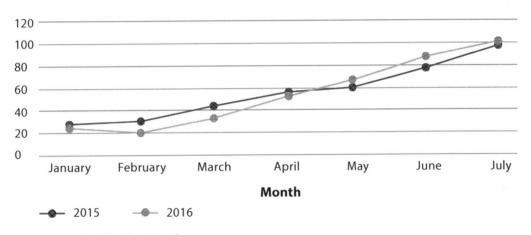

Figure 2.36. Double Line Graph

Circle graphs (also called pie charts) are used to show parts of a whole: the "pie" is the whole, and each "slice" represents a percentage or part of the whole.

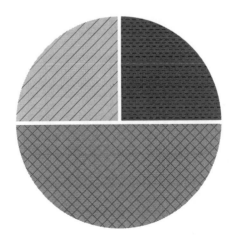

Figure 2.37. Circle Graph

SAMPLE QUESTION

35) The pie graph below shows how a state's government plans to spend its annual budget of $3 billion. How much more money does the state plan to spend on infrastructure than education?

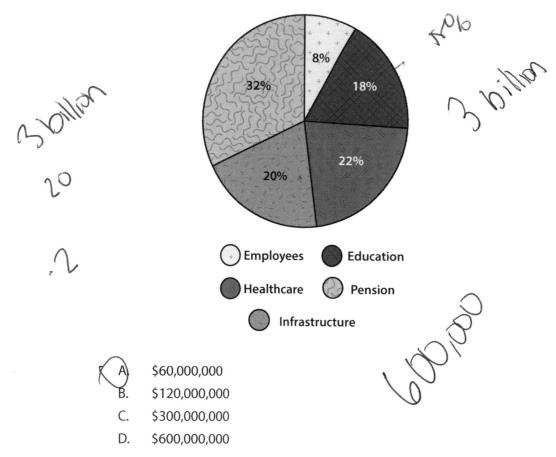

A. $60,000,000
B. $120,000,000
C. $300,000,000
D. $600,000,000

Answer:

A. Find the amount the state will spend on infrastructure and education, and then find the difference.

infrastructure = 0.2(3,000,000,000) = 600,000,000

education = 0.18(3,000,000,000) = 540,000,000

600,000,000 − 540,000,000 = **$60,000,000**

PROBABILITY

Probability is the likelihood, or chance, that something will happen. Probability is expressed as a fraction with the numerator being the number of successful outcomes and the denominator being the total number of outcomes. For example, if there are 25 marbles in a bag and 4 marbles are red, the probability of randomly pulling a red marble out of the bag is $\frac{4}{25}$ (also written as 0.16 or 16%).

Another example involves a spinner with 8 sections, with 3 that are choice A, 2 that are choice B, and 3 that are choice C. The probability of landing on choice A would be $\frac{3}{8}$ (also written as 0.375 or 37.5%).

Probabilities are always numbers between 0 and 1, inclusive. If there is no chance of something occurring, its probability is 0; if there's a 100% chance of something occurring, its probability is 1.

Replacement means putting something back the way it was before an event occurred. For example, the probability of drawing 4 red marbles out of 25 marbles twice, with replacement, would be $\frac{4}{25} \times \frac{4}{25} = \frac{16}{625}$. The same probability without replacement would be $\frac{4}{25} \times \frac{3}{24} = \frac{12}{600} = \frac{1}{50}$ since there would be one less red marble and one less of the total marbles. Note that probabilities are multiplied when the events are independent from each other.

For the probability of something happening at least one time, take the probability of the event not happening at all, and subtract this probability from 1. For example, the probability of rolling a two on at least one of two dice would be *1 minus the probability of not rolling a two on either die*, which would be $1 - \left(\frac{5}{6} \times \frac{5}{6} \right)$ $= 1 - \frac{25}{36} = \frac{11}{36}$.

SAMPLE QUESTION

36) Some of a hotel's 400 rooms have an ocean view and the rest of the rooms do not. If the probability of getting a room with an ocean view is 35%, how many rooms do NOT have an ocean view?

   A. 140
   B. 200
   C. 260
   D. 300

Answer:

   C. The probability of getting a room without an ocean view is equal to 1 minus the probability of getting a room with an ocean view.

   $P_{view} = 1 - P_{no\ ocean\ view}$

   $P_{view} = 1 - 0.35 = 0.65$

   Use the equation for percentages to find the number of rooms without a view.

   part = percentage × whole = (0.65)400 = **260 rooms**

Terms

acute: angle between 0 and 90 degrees

acute triangle: has three acute angles

addition: the process of combining two or more numbers

algebraic expressions: contain numbers, variables, and a mathematical operation

algorithm: a set of steps to follow when solving a problem

angle: a shape formed by two rays that share a common point

arc: any portion of a circle between two points on the circle

area: the size of a surface measured in square units

area model (also called the box method): a non-traditional approach to multiplication that promotes understanding of place value

array: a pictorial representation of a multiplication problem

associative property: in multiplication and addition, the way numbers are grouped in parentheses does not matter, $(a + b) + c = a + (b + c)$

bar graph: a graph that uses lengths of rectangles to show data

base-10: the numbering system where each digit is worth ten times as much as the digit to the right of it

binomial: an algebraic expression with two different variables

box plot (also called box-and-whisker plots): data is shown using the median and range of a data set

central angle: an angle with its vertex at the center of a circle

chord: the part of a secant line that lies within a circle

circle: set of all the points in a plane that are the same distance from a fixed point

circle graph: a pie chart where each "piece" demonstrates a quantity

circumference: the distance around a circle

commutative property: in multiplication and addition, the order of the numbers on each side of the equation does not matter: $ab = ba$

composite number: a natural number greater than 1 that can be divided by at least one other number besides 1 and itself

coordinate plane: the plane containing the x-axis and y-axis

customary units: units of measure used in the United States

decimal: any real number in the base-10 system, but often refers to numbers with digits to the right of the decimal point

denominator: the number on the bottom of a fraction

dependent variables: variables with a value dependent on other variables

diameter: the largest measurement across a circle

digits: any number 0 – 9

distributive property: multiplication distributes over addition, $a(b + c) = ab + ac$

dividend: a number that is being divided by another number

division: splitting a number into equal parts

divisor: the number by which another number is divided

dot plot: a graphical display of data using dots

double bar graphs: bar graphs that present more than one type of data

double line graph: a line graph that presents more than one type of data

equations: algebraic expressions that use an equal sign

equilateral triangle: all three sides are equal as are all three angles

estimation: a close prediction that involves minor calculations

expanded form: breaking up a number by the value of each digit

exponent: the number written to the upper right of another number that indicates how many times that number should be multiplied by itself

factors: numbers that are multiplied with each other

figures: geometric forms made up of points, lines, or planes

formulas: mathematical relationships expressed in symbols

fraction: a part of a whole

function: a relationship between input and output

histogram: bar graph showing continuous data over time

independent variables: values that determine the value of other variables

inequalities: two mathematical quantities that are not equal to each other

integers: positive or negative whole numbers that are not fractions or decimals

inverse operation: an operation that reverses another operation

isosceles triangle: has two equal sides and two equal angles

length: the measurement of something from end to end

line: a one-dimensional geometric shape that is infinitely long

linear equation: an equation that results in a straight line when graphed

line graph: a graph that uses points connected by lines to show data

line segment: a part of a line that connects two points

mean: the average

measures of center: include mean, median, and mode

median: the number in the middle when the data set is arranged from least to greatest

mental math: math that can be done in the student's head without the use of tools

metric units: the universal units of measure

mode: the most frequent

model: a mathematical representation of the real-world

multiples: the product of two whole numbers

multiplication: repeated addition of the same number to itself

natural numbers: numbers used when counting; do not include zero, fractions, or decimals

net: the shape of a flattened three-dimensional object

numerator: the number on top of a fraction

obtuse: angle between 90 and 180 degrees

obtuse triangle: has one obtuse angle and two acute angles

one-dimensional: having only length

order of operations: work the problem in the following order: (1) parentheses and brackets, (2) exponents and square roots, (3) multiplication and division, and (4) addition and subtraction

ordered pair: two numbers written to show the position of a point in a coordinate plane

origin: the point (0, 0) on a graph

outlier: a data point that is vastly different from the other data points

parallel lines: lines that remain the same distance apart over their entire length and never cross

percentage: a part of a whole conveyed per 100

perimeter: distance around a two-dimensional shape

perpendicular lines: lines that cross at a 90-degree angle

place value: the value of the location of a digit within a number

point: location in a coordinate plane

polygons: two-dimensional shapes that have 3 or more straight sides

prime number: a natural number greater than 1 that can be divided only by 1 and itself

probability: the likelihood that something will happen

product: the result of multiplying two or more numbers

quadrants: the four areas created by the intersection of the x-axis and y-axis

quotient: the result of dividing one number into another

radius: the distance from the center to any point on a circle

range: the difference between the highest number and the lowest number in a data set

ratio: a comparison of two things

rational number: a number that can be made by dividing two integers; includes fractions and terminating or repeating decimals

ray: a shape that starts at one point and goes infinitely in one direction

reasonableness: making common sense

remainder: the number that is left over when one number does not divide evenly into another

right triangle: has one right angle and two acute angles

rounding: simplifying a number to any given place value

scalene triangle: has no equal sides or angles

scatterplot: a graph of plotted points that compares two data sets

secant: a line that cuts across a circle and touches it twice

sector: the part of a circle that is inside the rays of a central angle

similar: shapes that have the same angles and whose sides have a constant proportion

slope: in a linear relationship, the change in y divided by the change in x. This is the measurement of the steepness of a line.

solids: three-dimensional objects

statistics: the study of data

subtraction: finding the difference between two numbers

surface area: the sum of the areas of all sides of a three-dimensional object

tangent: a line that touches a circle or any curve at one point

three-dimensional: having length, width, and height

trends: two sets of data that show a pattern

triangle inequality theorem: that the sum of any two sides of a triangle must be greater than the third side

two-dimensional: having length and width

unit fraction: a fraction where the numerator is 1

unit rate: the ratio of two measurements in which the part is 1

volume: the amount of space that an object occupies as measured in cubic units

whole numbers: counting numbers, including zero, that are not fractions or decimals

x-axis: horizontal position on a graph where $y = 0$

y-axis: vertical position on a graph where $x = 0$

Social Studies

The social studies portion of the elementary education test covers content aligned with state and national standards. Questions focus on concepts appropriate to elementary-level anthropology, sociology, economics, geography, world history, United States history, United States government, civics, and social studies skills and processes. Not only do teachers need to understand these subjects individually, but they also need to understand the relationships among these subjects and why they are taught at the elementary level.

Geography, Anthropology, and Sociology

GEOGRAPHY

The study of geography is the study of spatial distribution. It stresses analyzing information based on the distribution, location, and interactions of different human and physical features of the earth. Geography is divided into two main areas. **Physical geography** explores the natural process of the earth, whereas **human geography** explores the impact of people on the physical world, such as how humans alter their environments. It also looks at **social structures** as they relate to geography, such as how social events relate to places. An example of that would be how immigration affected urban populations in the US during the nineteenth century.

Geography uses maps to determine spatial distributions, such as ethnic demographics in various **regions**, languages in a particular country, or even the number of volcanoes in a determined area. The main reason for creating a map or developing a geographic information system is to assess the **spatial relationships** between features. An example of a spatial relationship is the distance between residential areas and transportation stops.

All maps use **cardinal directions**: north, south, east, and west. Some maps also feature **intermediate directions** between each point. All of these are featured on a compass rose, which is used to determine locations and directions.

Absolute location describes a location identifiable by specific geographic coordinates. For example, latitude and longitude delineate specific coordinates, so the absolute location of New York City is 40°70'58" N, 74°11'81" W. Addresses are also absolute locations: for instance, the absolute location of the White House is 1600 Pennsylvania Avenue NW, Washington, DC 20500. **Relative location** describes where a place is situated in relation to another place or places. For example, the state of Illinois is located in the Midwest region of the United States; it borders Wisconsin to the north, Indiana to the east, Iowa and Missouri to the west, and Kentucky to the south.

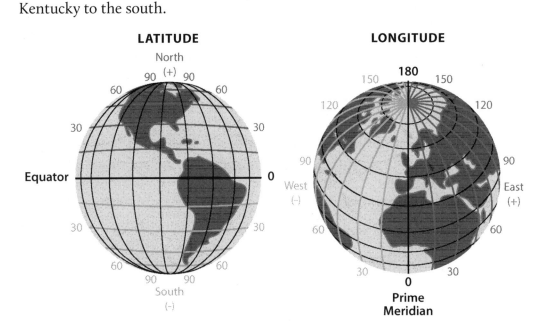

Figure 3.1. Longitude and Latitude

Maps display **geographic features**, physical features like continents, bodies of water, plains, plateaus, mountains, and valleys. Raised elevations and bodies of water are indicated through shading or coloring; they are also labeled. In addition, maps show **political features** like towns and cities, and county, state, or national borders. They may also include significant bodies of water.

Despite their differences, physical and human geography are interconnected. For example, physical features can determine the feasibility of living in certain locations or practicing certain lifestyles. Physical features dictate the availability of **natural resources** such as fresh water, arable land, fuel, livestock, and game; they also affect climate patterns. Manmade resources also intersect with physical and human geography; for example, the Hoover Dam manages the Colorado River, a natural resource, in order to provide water and electricity to certain parts of the southwestern United States.

Physical regions of the world are broken down by distance from the equator. The **low latitudes**, from the equator to latitudes 23.5° north and south, have three distinct climates. **Tropical rainforests** can be found in the equatorial lowlands in

Central Africa, Southeast Asia, and the Amazon basin. North and south of the rainforest is the **savannah**. The savannah is dry in the winter and wet in the summer, experiencing an average of 10 to 30 inches of rain. The **desert** lies beyond the savannah to the north and south. Deserts are the hottest and driest parts of the earth and receive less than 10 inches of rainfall a year. The best known deserts in the world are the Sahara Desert, the Australian Outback, and the Arabian Desert.

The **middle latitudes**, from latitudes 23.5° to 66.5° north and south, have a greater variety of climates, determined more by proximity to water than by the exact latitude. Three climates in the middle latitudes receive the most rain and therefore are the most fertile. The first is the **Mediterranean climate**, found in lands between latitudes 30° and 40° north and south that include land bordering the Mediterranean Sea, a small part of southwestern Africa, southern and southwestern Australia, a small part of the Ukraine near the Black Sea, central Chile, and southern California.

The **humid subtropical climate** is located on coastal areas north and south of the tropics. This climate receives warm ocean currents and warm winds year round, leading to a climate that is warm and moist. This is also the climate that supports the greatest percentage of the world's population. Japan, southeastern China, northeastern India, southeastern South Africa, the southeastern United States, and parts of South America all have subtropical climates.

Finally, several areas that are near or surrounded by water experience the **marine climate**. Marine climates are warm and rainy, resulting in part from the warm ocean winds. Western Europe, the British Isles, the US and Canadian Pacific Northwest, southern Chile, southern New Zealand, and southeastern Australia all have marine climates.

The climate best for farming is the **humid continental climate**, the true four-season climate. This climate can be found in the northern and central United States, south-central and southeastern Canada, northern China, and the western and southeastern parts of the former Soviet bloc. Those areas of continents far from the ocean are called **steppes**, or prairie. Flatlands with minimal rainfall, steppes can even become deserts if rainfall consistently dips below 10 inches per year.

The **high latitudes**, from latitudes 66.5° north and south to the poles, are home to two climates: **tundra** and **taiga**. The tundra features extremely cold and long winters; while the ground is frozen for most of the year, during the short summer the ground becomes mushy. With no arable land, it is home to few people. The taiga can be found south of the tundra in Northern Russia, Sweden, Norway, Finland, Canada, and Alaska. Home to the world's largest forestlands, the taiga also exhibits many swamps and marshes; importantly, it contains extreme mineral wealth. While there is a growing season, it is so short that meaningful agriculture is impossible; thus, the taiga is sparsely populated.

Students should understand that human activity, such as agriculture, ranching, logging, mining, and urban and suburban development impact the earth and the environment by interrupting ecosystems. Furthermore, they should also understand that **industrialization**, the process of manufacturing, creates byproducts that affect and can harm the environment.

Urbanization, or the development of cities, became a feature of human development at the advent of the nineteenth-century Industrial Revolution, when unskilled jobs in factories offered higher wages for workers than an agricultural lifestyle did. Urbanization and **suburbanization** continue today as cities develop and as urban dwellers move to growing suburbs. Development necessarily results in the destruction of surrounding environment; however, new urban ecosystems result, and **urban planning** is itself a geographic specialty.

Another way to illustrate human and social behavior is by mapping **migration** patterns. This is the study of movement from one place to another, with the intention of settling permanently at the new location. As discussed above, urbanization is one type of migration. Some migration is internal—people moving from one place to another within the same region, like urbanization. Other migration involves people moving from one region of the world to another. Many immigrants have migrated to the United States from other countries. Push and pull factors cause people to migrate: economic, cultural, sociopolitical, or environmental reasons. Pull factors like job opportunities or better living standards attract people to new locations. Push factors like famine, drought, war, lack of economic opportunities, and political persecution drive people to leave their homes in search of relief.

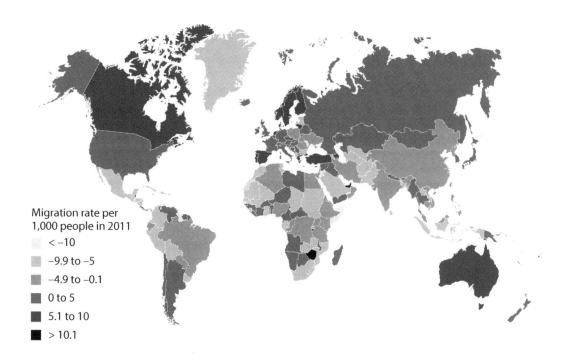

Migration rate per
1,000 people in 2011

  < −10

  −9.9 to −5

  −4.9 to −0.1

  0 to 5

  5.1 to 10

  > 10.1

Figure 3.2. Migration Streams

SAMPLE QUESTIONS

1) Which of the following are major physical regions in the continental United States?

   A.   humid continental, humid subtropical, Mediterranean, marine, desert

   B.   humid continental, humid subtropical, taiga, tundra, Mediterranean

   C.   humid continental, Mediterranean, marine, taiga, tropical rainforest

   D.   the Sun Belt, the Bible Belt, and the Coasts

   Answers:

   A.   **Correct.** These are all major physical regions in North America.

   B.   Incorrect. While Alaska has taiga and tundra, it is not considered part of the continental United States.

   C.   Incorrect. While Hawaii and US territories in the Caribbean and Pacific Ocean have tropical rainforest, they are not considered part of the continental United States.

   D.   Incorrect. These terms may be used in human geography, anthropology, or history but not in physical geography.

2) Which of the following is NOT an example of human geography?

   A.   studying the importance of trade among Central American countries

   B.   examining regional differences in cuisine around the world

   C.   studying the distribution of fauna and flora in North America

   D.   deciding whether to build retail outlets based on local population

   Answers:

   A.   Incorrect. Studying international trade explores how the physical environment (differing countries) affects human behavior (trade agreements).

   B.   Incorrect. Studying dishes from different regions relates to studying human behavior, consumption, and resource use in a geographical area.

   C.   **Correct.** Studying only flora and fauna is physical geography; the geographer is not studying human interactions with or impact on the earth.

   D.   Incorrect. Studying population and developing a commercial zone is an exercise in human geography and urban development.

ANTHROPOLOGY AND SOCIOLOGY

The elementary social studies curriculum also covers elements of **anthropology** and **sociology**. At the elementary level, these fields provide students insight into the behavior of individuals and groups relative to their location. Students should develop a knowledge of major world ethnic groups, organizations, and institutions, including understanding the major regions of the world and the general dominant cultures, religions, and languages therein. Students also begin developing their own personalities and learning the boundaries and limits of personal and social behavior.

Understanding personal identity in relation to peers, family, and institutions provides the tools for analyzing the reasons behind their behavior. Developing personal identity entails exploring and analyzing how individuals relate to others. **Socialization** is a process where individuals learn skills, beliefs, values, and behavior patterns of society and how these can influence their own norms and customs. For example, family roles differ depending on age and gender, and there are norms that dictate how certain family members should act.

Primary socialization occurs when children learn the values, actions, and attitudes that are appropriate for members of their particular culture. For example, if a family eats dinner together every night, that child will likely assume that he or she must regularly communicate with the closest and most important people in his or her life.

Secondary socialization occurs when an individual learns the appropriate values, actions, attitudes, and behaviors as a member of a smaller group within a larger society. Secondary socialization generally occurs in adolescence or young adulthood, and influences will be teachers, employers, and other authority figures.

Examining **conflict, cooperation,** and **exchange** is a feature of social studies; students encounter these in history, economics, and geography. **Conflict** is the process of disagreement and is usually resolved when one of the two parties receives either the entirety or a satisfactory amount of their desired goal. **Cooperation**, on the other hand, is the process of working together to achieve similar goals; it often leads to positive outcomes. **Exchange** is the process of giving one thing and receiving another (usually with similar value) in return.

Students learn that **institutions** are extensions of core social values and are created in response to varying individual and group needs. Institutions are formally structured groups that comprise society. At the macro level they include government, private enterprise, religious institutions, and academic institutions. At the micro level, they include local communities and the family unit. They are composed of a usually formal, often top-down structure with a small governing body in charge (either the executives in a government or private company or the parents in the family unit). For example, labor unions fight for better conditions for workers; governments maintain social stability; businesses provide goods, services, and profit; and religious organizations fulfill social and personal needs.

The study of institutions also includes understanding how they are maintained and changed, as well as how they exert influence among individuals. Studying communities helps clarify how individuals, families, and institutions socialize and come together to form values, beliefs, and behavior patterns, and how they may differ from those of other communities.

More broadly, studying culture relates to understanding human and group behavior. Studying culture helps students understand that individuals develop culture and also adapt to it in changing circumstances (such as migration). Examining different belief systems and practices, such as celebrations, languages, and other norms, exposes students to multiple cultural perspectives on shared human experiences. Studies may also explore the similarities and differences among cultures and how they evolve in various regions.

SAMPLE QUESTION

3) **What are the three major forms of sociological interactions?**

   A.   culture, counterculture, and subculture

   B.   celebrations, languages, and belief systems

   C.   government, schools, and businesses

   D.   cooperation, exchange, and conflict

Answers:

   A.   Incorrect. Culture is not a form of interaction; it describes the beliefs and actions of a particular group. Countercultures and subcultures develop in opposition to a culture or as subsets of that culture.

   B.   Incorrect. Celebrations, languages, and belief systems are all part of culture.

   C.   Incorrect. Government, schools, and businesses are all examples of institutions; they are not interactions.

   D.   **Correct.** Cooperation, exchange, and conflict are the primary forms of social interaction.

World History

ANCIENT (CLASSICAL) CIVILIZATIONS

Classical civilizations have had a lasting influence on human history. Elementary-level students should be aware of the ancient civilizations in the Fertile Crescent (including ancient Egypt), ancient Greece and Rome, and ancient China.

Around 2500 BCE (or possibly earlier) the **Sumerians** emerged in the Near East (eventually expanding into parts of Mesopotamia). Developing irrigation and advanced agriculture, they also developed **cuneiform**, the earliest known example of writing to use characters to form words. Sumer featured city-states, the potter's wheel, early astronomy and mathematics, early education, literary and artistic developments, and religious thought. Cuneiform also allowed advanced governance and administration.

Later, **Assyria** and **Babylonia** developed as important empires in the region. The Assyrians had based much of their culture on Sumer, contributing unique sculpture and jewelry, establishing military dominance, and playing an important role in regional trade. Babylonia also inherited elements of Sumerian civilization and developed them further. In the eighteenth century BCE, King Hammurabi in Babylonia had developed courts and an early codified rule of law—**the Code of Hammurabi**—which meted out justice on an equal basis: "an eye for an eye, a tooth for a tooth."

Meanwhile, development had been under way in the **Nile Valley** in ancient **Egypt**. The fertile land on the banks of the Nile River allowed the early Egyptians to develop settled communities thanks to agriculture and irrigation. Known for their pyramids, art, use of papyrus as paper, and pictorial writing (**hieroglyphs**), the ancient Egyptians emerged as early as 5000 BCE and were united under one monarch, or **pharaoh**.

Around 2500 BCE, Egypt's civilizational institutions, administrative structure, written language, art, and architecture were becoming well developed. In addition, the religious framework of ancient Egypt had become established, with a complex mythology of various gods. The ancient Egyptians also developed astronomy and the twenty-four-hour system of measuring time. It was during this period that the famous **pyramids** were erected at Giza; these structures were actually burial tombs for pharaohs. Major pharaohs included Hatshepsut, Thutmose III, Akhenaten, and Ramesses II.

Egyptian architecture also influenced many civilizations in the Western world. The use of columns in Pharaoh Hatshepsut's temple in Luxor is an example. It influenced Greek architectural design, which was copied by the Romans and many civilizations since.

In **China**, the Shang Dynasty, the first known dynasty, emerged around the second millennium BCE and developed the earliest known Chinese writing, which helped unite Chinese-speaking people throughout the region. Like other early civilizations, the Shang Dynasty featured the use of bronze technology, horses, wheeled technology, walled cities, and other advances. Later, under the Zhou dynasty, China developed the concept of the **Mandate of Heaven**, in which the emperor had a divine mandate to rule, based on an understanding that land was divinely inherited. **Confucius** lived toward the end of this dynasty (c. 551–479 BCE). His teachings would be the basis for Confucianism, the foundational Chinese philosophy emphasizing harmony and respect for hierarchy.

The Qin dynasty (221–206 BCE) was characterized by a centralized administration, expanded infrastructure, standardization in weights and measures, writing, currency, and strict imperial control. The administrative bureaucracy was established by the first emperor, **Qin Shihuangdi**, and it was the foundation of Chinese administration until the twentieth century. In addition, the emperor constructed the **Great Wall of China**; his tomb is guarded by the famous **terracotta figurines**.

Ancient Greece was composed of small **city-states** like **Athens**, the first known **democracy**, and the military state **Sparta**. Around 460 BCE, Athens became a revolutionary democracy controlled by the poor and working classes. In fact, the term *democracy* comes from the Greek word *demokratia*—"people power." It was participatory rather than representative; officials were chosen by groups rather than elected. Athenian ideals have influenced politics and governance throughout history.

Athens was the strongest of the many small political bodies (in fact, the word *political* comes from the Greek word ***polis*** meaning "city-state" or "community") and much of Greece became unified under Athens following the Peloponnesian War between Athens and Sparta. It was during this period, the **Golden Age** of Greek civilization, that much of the Hellenic art, architecture, and philosophy known today emerged, including the **Parthenon** and other masterpieces of ancient Greek sculpture and architecture. **Socrates** began teaching philosophy, influencing later philosophers like **Plato** and **Aristotle**, establishing the basis for modern Western philosophical and political thought. Mathematical advances included the Pythagorean Theorem, Euclidean geometry, and the calculation of the circumference of the earth. Playwrights like **Sophocles** and **Euripides** emerged; their work influenced later Western literature. The Greeks practiced the Olympic Games to honor their gods, a diverse panoply of deities with a detailed mythology.

The Greeks established numerous colonies across the Black Sea, southern Italy, Sicily, and the eastern Mediterranean, spreading Greek culture throughout the Mediterranean world; it was eventually conquered by the rising Mediterranean power, Rome.

Figure 3.3. Pax Romana

Originally a kingdom, Rome became a republic in 509 BCE, and as such, Romans elected lawmakers (senators) to the **Senate**. The Romans developed highly advanced infrastructure, including aqueducts and roads, some still in use today. Economically powerful, Rome began conquering areas around the Mediterranean with its increasingly powerful military, including Greece, expanding westward to North Africa. With conquest of territory and expansion of trade came increased slavery, and working-class Romans were displaced; at the same time, the wealthy ruling class became more powerful and corrupt.

The people, or *Populare*, wanted a more democratic republic. As the Senate weakened due to its own corruption, **Julius Caesar**, a popular military leader widely supported by the *Populare*, emerged. Forcing the corrupt Senate to give him control, Caesar began to transition Rome from a republic to what would become an empire. Caesar was assassinated in 44 BCE; however, in that short time he had been able to consolidate and centralize imperial control. His nephew Octavian eventually gained control of Rome in 27 BCE, taking the name **Augustus Caesar** and becoming the first Roman emperor.

At this time, Rome reached the height of its power, and the Mediterranean region enjoyed a period of stability known as the **Pax Romana**. Rome controlled the entire Mediterranean region, Europe, and much of the Middle East and North Africa. Latin literature flourished, as did art, architecture, philosophy, mathematics, science, and international trade throughout Rome and beyond into Asia and Africa.

SAMPLE QUESTIONS

4) According to Confucianism, an ideal society

   A.   is based on respect for authority and wisdom, making harmonious interaction a priority.

   B.   allows respectful debate and discussion to encourage learning and the development of wisdom.

   C.   encompasses a diverse group of people, to gather wisdom from different cultures.

   D.   values hierarchy and enforces a caste system.

   Answers:

   A.   **Correct.** Confucius taught others to respect authority (filial piety) and encouraged group harmony.

   B.   Incorrect. Confucianism does not encourage the questioning of authority; this would risk harmonious interaction with others.

   C.   Incorrect. Confucianism does not focus on cultural diversity.

   D.   Incorrect. While Confucianism values hierarchy, it does not feature a caste system.

5) During the *Pax Romana*, the Mediterranean region was all of the following EXCEPT

    A. experiencing a period of relative stability under Roman rule.

    B. a center of commercial activity.

    C. ruled by Augustus Caesar.

    D. under the control of a powerful Senate.

Answers:

    A. Incorrect. This is true: the Roman Empire controlled the Mediterranean and much of the land bordering it.

    B. Incorrect. This is true: Rome was enormously commercially powerful during the *Pax Romana*.

    C. Incorrect. This is true: Rome was ruled by Augustus Caesar during this time period.

    D. **Correct**. This is false: After Julius Caesar took power from the Senate, Rome was ruled by a powerful emperor.

BYZANTIUM AND FEUDALISM

Eventually, Rome weakened and split in two. The Eastern Roman Empire later became the Byzantine Empire, a strong civilization and a place of learning based in Constantinople, a strategically-located commercial center connecting Asian trade routes with Europe. The Western Roman Empire eventually collapsed; the Christian church remained important politically and culturally, but different rulers took power throughout Europe.

In Europe, the early **Middle Ages** (or Dark Ages) from the fall of Rome to about the tenth century, was a chaotic, unstable, and unsafe time. What protection and stability existed were represented and maintained by the Catholic Church and the feudal system.

Society and economics were characterized by decentralized, local governance, or **feudalism**, a hierarchy where land and protection were offered in exchange for loyalty. In exchange for protection, **vassals** would pledge fealty, or pay homage to **lords**, landowners who would reward their vassals' loyalty with land, or **fiefs**. Economic and social organization consisted of manors, self-sustaining areas possessed by lords but worked by peasants. The peasants were **serfs**, not slaves but not entirely free. Tied to the land, they worked for the lord in exchange for protection; however they were not obligated to fight. Usually they were also granted some land for their own use. While not true slaves, their lives were effectively controlled by the lord.

Warriors who fought for lords, called **knights**, were rewarded with land and could become minor lords in their own right. Lords themselves could be vassals of other lords; that hierarchy extended upward to kings or the Catholic Church. The Catholic Church itself was a major landowner and political power. In a Europe not yet dominated by sovereign states, the **pope** was not only a religious leader, but also a political one.

Small kingdoms and alliances extended throughout Europe, and stable trade was difficult to maintain. The Celts controlled Britain and Ireland until the invasion of the Saxons; around 600 C.E., the Saxons conquered Britain while the Celts were pushed to Ireland, Scotland, and Brittany in northwest France. While the Church was gaining power, it was insecure in Italy as the Germanic tribes vied for control in Germany and France. Monasteries in Ireland and England retained and protected classical learning in the wake of the fall of Rome and insecurity in Italy. The Germanic tribes themselves were threatened by Asian invaders like the Huns, increasing instability in central and eastern parts of Europe, where Slavs also fought for supremacy north of Byzantium.

> **DID YOU KNOW?**
>
> There were limits on sovereign power, however. In 1215, long before the revolution, English barons forced King John to sign the **Magna Carta**, which protected their property and rights from the king and was the basis for today's parliamentary system in that country.

One exception to the chaos was the Scandinavian **Viking** civilization. From the end of the eighth century until around 1100, the Vikings expanded their influence from Scandinavia, ranging from the Baltic Sea to the East to the North Sea through the North Atlantic, thanks to their extraordinary seafaring skills and technology. The Vikings traded with the Byzantine Empire and European powers. They traveled to and sometimes raided parts of Britain, Ireland, France, and Russia.

Meanwhile, by the eighth century the North African **Moors**, part of the expanding Islamic civilization, had entered Iberia and were a threat to Christian Europe. **Charles Martel**, leader of the Franks in what is today France, defeated the Moors at the **Battle of Tours (or Poitiers)** in 732 CE, effectively stopping any further Islamic incursion into Europe from the south. After Martel's death, **Charlemagne**, the son of a court official, eventually took over the kingdom.

Charlemagne was able to maintain Frankish unity and extend his rule into Central Europe, even defending the Papal States in central Italy. In what is considered the reemergence of centralized power in Europe, parts of Western and Central Europe were organized under Charlemagne, who was crowned emperor of the Roman Empire by the pope in 800 CE. While in retrospect this seems long after the end of Rome, at the time many Europeans still perceived themselves as somehow still part of a Roman Empire.

It was also under Charlemagne that the feudal system became truly organized, bringing more stability to Western Europe. In 962 CE, the **Holy Roman Empire** was formed in Central Europe, a confederation of small states which remained an important European power until its dissolution in 1806.

In 1066, **William the Conqueror** left Normandy in northwest France. The Normans established organization in England, including a more consolidated economy and kingdom supported by feudalism. They also consolidated Christianity as the local religion. English possessions included parts of France. However, conflict between Britain and France would continue for several centuries, while rulers in Scandinavia and Northwest Europe consolidated power.

SAMPLE QUESTION

6)   **In feudal Europe, serfs were**

   A.   enslaved by the lords and knights.

   B.   bonded to the land but under the protection of the lords.

   C.   forced to fight for the lords.

   D.   able to eventually purchase their freedom from the knights in exchange for support fighting.

Answers:

   A.   Incorrect. Serfs, while limited in their freedom, were not truly slaves; they could not be bought or sold.

   B.   Correct. Serfs were bonded to the land—they had to work it for the lord—however, the lord was obligated to protect them.

   C.   Incorrect. Serfs did not fight.

   D.   Incorrect. Serfs could not purchase individual freedom by fighting for their lords.

CONFLICT AND CULTURAL EXCHANGE

Meanwhile, Arab-Islamic empires characterized by brisk commerce, advancements in technology and learning, and urban development arose in the Middle East.

In Arabia itself, the Prophet **Muhammad** was born in Mecca around 570 CE; he began receiving messages from God (Allah), preaching them around 613 as the last affirmations of the monotheistic religions and writing them as the **Qur'an**, the Islamic holy book. Driven from **Mecca** to Medina in 622, Muhammad and his followers were able to recapture the city and other major Arabian towns by the time of his death, establishing Islam and Arab rule in the region.

After Muhammad's death in 632, his followers went on to conquer land beyond Arabia north into the weakening Byzantine Empire. The Arab-Islamic empires, or caliphates, were first based in Damascus. The first caliphate, the Umayyad, was overthrown by the Arab-Muslim Abbasid family, which established a new capital in Baghdad.

Expansion under the Prophet Muhammad, 612 – 632

Expansion under the Rashidun, 632 – 655

Expansion under the Umayyad Caliphate, 661 – 750

Figure 3.4. Islamic Expansion

Building on the Umayyad Caliphate, Abbasid administration was highly organized, allowing efficient taxation. The administration and stability provided by the caliphates fostered an Arabic literary culture. Stability permitted open trade routes, economic development, and cultural interaction throughout Asia, the Middle East, North Africa, and parts of Europe, while other parts of Europe remained relatively unstable following the collapse of Rome.

Thanks to the universality of the Arabic language, scientific and medical texts from varying civilizations—Greek, Persian, Indian—could be translated into Arabic and shared throughout the Islamic world. Arab thinkers studied Greek and Persian astronomy and engaged in further research. Arabs studied mathematics from around the world and developed algebra, enabling engineering, technological, and architectural achievements. Finally, Islamic art is well known for its geometric designs.

Around this time, China experienced tremendous development and economic growth. Characterized by increasing urbanization, Song Dynasty China featured complex administrative rule, including the difficult competitive written examinations required to obtain prestigious bureaucratic positions in government. China engaged not only in overland trade along the Silk Road, exporting silk, tea, ceramics, jade, and other goods, but also sea trade with Korea, Japan, Southeast Asia, India, Arabia and even East Africa.

International commerce was vigorous along the **Silk Road,** trading routes which stretched from the Arab-controlled Eastern Mediterranean to Song Dynasty China.

The Silk Road reflected the transnational nature of Central Asia: the nomadic culture of Central Asia lent itself to trade among the major civilizations of China, Persia, the Near East, and Europe. Buddhism and Islam spread into China. Chinese, Islamic, and European art, pottery, and goods were interchanged—essentially, early globalization. The Islamic tradition of the **hajj**, or the pilgrimage to Mecca, also spurred cultural interaction. Islam had spread from Spain throughout North Africa, the Sahel, the Middle East, Persia, Central Asia, India, and China; peoples from all these regions traveled and met in Arabia as part of their religious pilgrimage.

Figure 3.5. Silk Road

Islam also spread along trans-Saharan trade routes into West Africa and the Sahel. Brisk trade between the gold-rich **Kingdom of Ghana** and Muslim traders based in Morocco brought Islam to the region around the eleventh century. The Islamic **Mali Empire** (1235–1500), based farther south in Timbuktu, eventually extended beyond the original Ghanaian boundaries all the way to the West African coast, and controlled the valuable gold and salt trades. At the empire's peak, the ruler **Mansa Musa** made a pilgrimage to Mecca in 1324. However, by 1500, the **Songhai Empire** had overcome Mali and eventually dominated the Niger River area.

Loss of Byzantine territory to the Islamic empires meant loss of Christian lands in the Levant—including Jerusalem and Bethlehem—to Muslims. In 1095 CE, the Byzantine Emperor asked the pope for help to defend Jerusalem and protect Christians. With a history of Muslim

QUICK REVIEW

How did the Silk Road and Islam both contribute to global cultural exchange?

incursions into Spain and France, anti-Muslim sentiment was strong in Europe and Christians there were easily inspired to fight them in the Levant, or **Holy Land**; the Pope offered lords and knights the chance to keep lands and bounty they won from conquered Muslims (and Jews) in this **Crusade**. He also offered Crusaders

indulgences—forgiveness for sins committed in war and guarantees they would enter heaven.

Despite conflict in Europe, Christians found they had more in common with each other than with Muslims, and were able to unite to follow the Pope's call to arms to fight in the Middle East. The decline of the Abbasids had left the Levant vulnerable, and Christian Crusaders were able to establish settlements and small kingdoms in Syria and on the Eastern Mediterranean coast, conquering major cities and capturing Jerusalem by 1099 in the **First Crusade**.

> **DID YOU KNOW?**
>
> During the Hundred Years' War, **Joan of Arc** led the French in the 1429 Battle of Orléans, reinvigorating French resistance to English incursions.

The Crusades continued over several centuries. While they never resulted in permanent European control over the Holy Land, they did open up trade routes between Europe and the Middle East, stretching all the way along the Silk Road to China. This increasing interdependence helped lead to the European Renaissance.

Ongoing interactions between Europeans and Muslims exposed Europeans, who could now afford them thanks to international trade, to improved education and goods. However, the **Bubonic (Black) Plague** also spread to Europe as a result of global exchange, killing off a third of its population from 1347 – 1351. The plague had a worldwide impact: empires fell in its wake.

Back in Europe, conflict reached its height throughout the thirteenth and fourteenth centuries known as the **Hundred Years' War** (1337 – 1453). France was in political chaos during the mid-fourteenth century, decentralized and at times without a king, suffering the effects of the Black Plague, and periodically under English rule. While conflict would continue, England lost its last territory in France, Bordeaux, in 1453.

In al-Andalus (Spain), despite some coexistence between Christians and Muslims under Muslim rule, raids and conflict were ongoing during the lengthy period of the **Reconquista**, which did not end until 1492 when Christian powers took Grenada. From the zenith of Muslim rule, Christian raids continued. The marriage of Ferdinand of Castilla and Isabella of Aragon in 1479 connected those two kingdoms, and the monarchs were able to complete the Reconquista by taking Grenada and uniting Spain.

SAMPLE QUESTIONS

7) **While the Crusades enriched Europe in many ways, they did NOT**

   A. bring new knowledge to the West.

   B. result in lasting land gains.

   C. provide religious indulgences for crusaders.

   D. offer the opportunity to gain personal wealth.

Answers:

A.   Incorrect. Crusaders returned to Europe having been exposed to new knowledge and technology from the Middle East.

B.   Correct. European powers controlled some areas in the Levant, but only temporarily.

C.   Incorrect. Crusaders were entitled to indulgences—forgiveness for any sins committed in conflict.

D.   Incorrect. One incentive for Europeans to fight in the Crusades was the possibility of amassing personal wealth through plunder.

8)   **The Kingdom of Mali developed due to its**

A.   control of the trans-Saharan trade routes.

B.   ability to repel Islamic influences from the north.

C.   control over gold and salt resources.

D.   control of the trans-Saharan slave trade.

Answers:

A.   Incorrect. Mali did not control the trans-Saharan trade routes.

B.   Incorrect. The Kingdom of Mali embraced Islam.

C.   Correct. Mali became wealthy due to gold and salt, valuable natural resources.

D.   Incorrect. Mali did not control the trans-Saharan slave trade.

EMPIRES IN TRANSITION

The collapse of the Abbasid Caliphate in the thirteenth century led to instability and decentralization of power in Mesopotamia, Persia, and Central Asia; smaller sultanates (territories ruled by sultans, regional leaders) emerged, and production and economic development declined. China closed its borders and trade on the Silk Road declined.

Despite the lack of political cohesion, Islam remained a unifying force throughout the region, and political instability and decentralization paradoxically allowed local culture to develop, particularly Persian art and literature.

The **Mongol Empire** was based in Central Asia; led by **Genghis Khan**, the Mongols expanded throughout Asia thanks to their abilities in horsemanship and archery. Despite the rich history of transnational activity across Asia, the continent was vulnerable. Central Asia lacked one dominant culture or imperial power; Southwest Asia was fragmented following the decline of the Abbasids. These weaknesses allowed the Mongols to take over most of Eurasia.

In China, the Mongols destroyed local infrastructure, including the foundation of Chinese society and administration—the civil service examinations (which were eventually reestablished). However, the Mongol **Yuan Dynasty** maintained most of the administrative policy of the preceding Song Dynasty. The Yuan did, however, upend Chinese social hierarchy; placing Mongols at the top, followed by non-ethnic Han Chinese and then Han Chinese. Yet attempts at imperial expansion, threats from the Black Plague, financial problems, and flooding led to the decline of the Yuan Dynasty and the rise of the ethnic Chinese **Ming Dynasty** in 1368.

The Ming reasserted Chinese control and continued traditional methods of administration; the construction of the **Forbidden City**, the home of the emperor in Beijing, helped consolidate imperial rule. The Ming also recharged international trade; demand for ceramics in particular, in addition to silk and tea, was high abroad, and contact with seafaring traders like the Portuguese and Dutch in the sixteenth century was strong. China itself explored the oceans.

Mongol decline was not only isolated to China. In Russia, **Ivan the Great** brought Moscow from Mongol under Slavic Russian control, achieving Moscow's independence in 1480. He consolidated a Russia that was the foundation for an empire and a sovereign nation that sought diplomatic relations with Europe. A century later, the first tsar, **Ivan the Terrible**, expanded Russian territory farther into Europe. Ivan reformed government, the military, and strengthened Russian Orthodox Christianity; however, his despotic reputation gave him his name.

In India, the **Mughal Empire** developed from the small kingdoms that made up the Subcontinent. The Mughals would rule India from the sixteenth century until the eighteenth century and nominally control parts of the country until British takeover in the nineteenth century.

Despite the instability inland, Indian Ocean trade routes had continued to function since at least the seventh century. The ocean acted as a unifying force throughout the region, and the monsoon winds permitted Arab, Persian, Indian, and Chinese merchants to travel to East Africa in search of goods such as ivory and gold—and slaves.

Despite the achievements of the Islamic empires, China, and the Central Asian and Indian empires that would emerge from the Mongols, the **East African slave trade** remained vigorous until the nineteenth century. Arabs, Asians, and other Africans kidnapped African people and sent them to lives of slavery throughout the Arab world and South Asia. Later, Europeans would take part in the trade, forcing Africans into slavery in colonies throughout South and Southeast Asia, and on plantations in Indian Ocean islands such as Madagascar.

The major East African port was Zanzibar, from which slaves, gold, coconut oil, ivory, and other African exports made their way to Asia and the Middle East. However, enslaved persons from Sub-Saharan Africa were also forced north overland to markets in Cairo, where they were sold and dispersed throughout the Arab-Islamic, Fatimid, and Ottoman empires.

Farther north, the Ottoman Turks represented a threat to Central Europe. Controlling most of Anatolia from the late thirteenth century, the Ottomans spread west into the Balkans. In 1453 they captured Istanbul, from which the **Ottoman Empire** would come to rule much of the Mediterranean world.

Under the leadership of **Mehmed the Conqueror** in the fifteenth century and his successors, the Ottomans would conquer Pannonia (Hungary), North Africa, the Caucasus, the Levant and Mesopotamian regions, western Arabia, and Egypt. Under **Suleiman the Magnificent** (1520 – 1566), the **Ottoman Empire** consolidated control over the Balkans, the Middle East, and North Africa and would hold that land until the nineteenth century.

The capture of Istanbul (Constantinople) had represented the true end of the Byzantine Empire; the remaining Christian Byzantines, mainly isolated to coastal Anatolia, Constantinople, and parts of Greece, fled to Italy, bringing Greek, Middle Eastern, and Asian learning with them and enriching the emerging European Renaissance.

SAMPLE QUESTIONS

9) **Russia built its empire by**

    A.   strengthening its navy to colonize overseas.

    B.   overland expansion, moving eastward into Asia and Siberia, and westward into Europe.

    C.   remaining isolated, avoiding expansion and focusing on industrialization instead.

    D.   converting Asian peoples from Islam to Russian Orthodox Christianity

Answers:

    A.   Incorrect. Russia's strategy was land-based expansion; it did not have a strong navy until the twentieth century.

    B.   **Correct.** Russia expanded to the east, taking control of Siberia. Russia also moved westward, controlling parts of Eastern Europe.

    C.   Incorrect. Russia expanded and employed developmental strategies under a number of tsars.

    D.   Incorrect. Russia was not actively seeking to convert Muslims to Christianity.

10) **Which of the following was a result of the rise of the Ottoman Turks?**

    A.   Christian Byzantines left Constantinople for Western Europe, bringing classical learning with them.

    B.   The Ottomans were able to conquer large areas, establishing a vast Islamic empire.

    C.   The Ottomans represented an Islamic threat to European Christendom.

    D.   All of the above

Answer:

D. **Correct.** All the answers are true. Byzantine scholars did leave Constantinople and bring classical learning to Europe, especially Rome. At its height under Suleiman the Magnificent, the Ottoman Empire stretched from Morocco through Anatolia and the Levant to Persia. The Ottomans represented a serious threat to Europe for centuries, as they controlled the Balkans.

THE EUROPEAN RENAISSANCE

The **Renaissance**, or *rebirth,* included the revival of ancient Greek and Roman learning, art, and architecture in Europe. However, the roots of the Renaissance stretched farther back to earlier interactions between Christendom, the Islamic World, and even China, during the Crusades and through Silk Road trade. Not only did the Renaissance inspire new learning and prosperity in Europe, enabling exploration, colonization, profit, and later imperialism, but it also led to scientific and religious questioning and rebellion against the Catholic Church and, later, monarchical governments.

Reinvigoration of classical knowledge was triggered in part by Byzantine refugees from the Ottoman conquest of Constantinople, including scholars who brought Greek and Roman texts to Italy and Western Europe. The fall of Constantinople precipitated the development of **humanism** in Europe, a mode of thought emphasizing human nature, creativity, and an overarching concept of truth.

Art, considered not just a form of expression but also a science in itself, flourished in fifteenth century Italy, particularly in **Florence**. Major figures who explored anatomy in sculpture, design and perspective, and innovation in architecture included Leonardo da Vinci, Botticelli, and Michelangelo. Leonardo is particularly known for his scientific pursuits in addition to artistic achievement.

Meanwhile, scholars like Galileo, Isaac Newton, and Copernicus made discoveries in what became known as the **Scientific Revolution**, rooted in the scientific knowledge of the Islamic empires, which had been imported through economic and social contact initiated centuries prior in the Crusades. Scientific study and discovery threatened the power of the Church, whose theological teachings were often at odds with scientific findings and logical reasoning.

QUICK REVIEW

The Scientific Revolution changed European thinking. What was the impact of using reason and scientific methodology rather than religion to understand the world?

Also in the mid-fifteenth century, in Northern Europe, Johannes Gutenberg invented the **printing press**. With the advent of printing, texts could be more widely and rapidly distributed, and people had more access to information beyond what their leaders told them. Combined with humanism and increased emphasis on secular thought, the power of the church and of monarchs who ruled by divine right was under threat. Here lay the roots of the **Enlightenment**, the basis for reinvigorated European culture and political thought that would drive its development for the next several centuries—and inspire revolution.

Transnational cultural exchange had also resulted in the transmission of technology to Europe. During the sixteenth century, European seafaring knowledge, navigation, and technology benefitted from Islamic and Asian expertise; European explorers and traders could now venture beyond the Mediterranean. Trade was no longer dependent on the Silk Road. Europeans eventually arrived in the Western Hemisphere, heretofore unknown to the peoples of Eurasia and Africa.

SAMPLE QUESTION

11) **Major influences on the European Renaissance included**

    A. cultural discoveries in North America.

    B. African music and culture.

    C. the ideas of the Greek Orthodox Church.

    D. scientific knowledge from the Islamic empires.

Answers:

A. Incorrect. While the Americas were of interest to many Renaissance figures, the historical movement did not rely on information from civilizations of the Western Hemisphere.

B. Incorrect. African music and culture had no bearing on the Renaissance.

C. Incorrect. While Christians came from Constantinople, their influence on the Renaissance came from the classical texts and learning they brought, not from their Christian faith.

D. **Correct.** Science and technology imported from the Middle East during the Crusades helped inspire the Renaissance.

COLONIZATION OF THE WESTERN HEMISPHERE

Interest in exploration grew in Europe during the Renaissance period. Technological advancements made complex navigation and long-term sea voyages possible, and economic growth resulting from international trade drove interest in market expansion. Global interdependence got a big push from Spain when King Ferdinand and Queen Isabella agreed to sponsor **Christopher Columbus'** exploratory voyage in 1492 to find a sea route to Asia, in order to speed up commercial trade there. Instead, he stumbled upon the Western Hemisphere, which was unknown to Europeans, Asians, and Africans to this point.

Columbus landed in the Caribbean; he and later explorers would claim the Caribbean islands and eventually Central and South America for Spain and Portugal. However, those areas were already populated by the major American civilizations.

The **Maya**, who preceded the Aztecs in Mesoamerica, had dominated the Yucatan peninsula around 300 CE. They developed a complex spiritual belief system accompanied by relief art, a detailed calendar, a written language, and pyramidal temples that still stand today. In addition, they studied astronomy and mathematics. Maya political administration was organized under monarchial city-states from around 300 until around 900, when the civilization began to decline.

As smaller Mesoamerican civilizations had weakened and collapsed, the **Aztecs** had come to dominate Mexico and much of Mesoamerica. Their military power and militaristic culture allowed the Aztecs to dominate the region and regional trade. The main city of the Aztec empire, **Tenochtitlan**, was founded in 1325 and, at its height, was a major world city home to several million people.

Meanwhile in the Andes, the **Incas** had emerged. Based in **Cuzco**, the Incas had consolidated their power and strengthened in the area, likely due to a surplus of their staple crop maize, around 1300. Inca engineers built the citadel of **Machu Picchu** and imperial infrastructure, including roads, throughout the Andes. In order to subdue local peoples, they moved conquered groups elsewhere in the empire and repopulated conquered areas with Incas.

In Mexico, the ruler **Montezuma II** led the Aztecs during their first encounter with Spain; explorer **Hernan Cortés** met with him in Tenochtitlan after invading other areas of Mexico in 1519. Spain was especially interested in subduing the Aztec religion, which included ceremonies with human blood and human sacrifice, and in controlling Mexican and Mesoamerican gold. Cortés arrested Montezuma; Spain then began the process of colonizing Mexico and Central America, and the Aztec Empire collapsed.

In South America, as in Mexico and Central America, the Spanish were interested in economic exploitation and spreading Christianity, accessing the continent in the early sixteenth century. In 1533, the Spanish conquistador **Francisco Pizzaro** defeated the Inca king **Atahuallpa** and installed a puppet ruler, marking the decline of the Inca Empire. While the empire remained nominally intact for several years, the Spanish installed Christianity and took control of the region.

Spain took over the silver- and gold-rich Mesoamerican and Andean territories, and the Caribbean islands where sugar became an important cash crop. Thus developed mercantilism, whereby the colonizing or mother country took raw materials from the territories they controlled for the colonizers' own benefit. Governments amassed wealth through protectionism and increasing exports at the expense of other rising colonial powers. This eventually involved developing goods and then selling them back to those colonized lands at an inflated price. The encomienda system granted European landowners the "right" to hold lands in the Americas and demand labor and tribute from the local inhabitants. Spreading Christianity was another important reason for European expansion. Local civilizations and resources were exploited and destroyed.

> **QUICK REVIEW**
>
> What was destructive about the *encomienda* system?

The **Columbian Exchange** enabled mercantilism to flourish. Conflict and illness brought by the Europeans—especially smallpox—decimated the Native Americans, and the Europeans were left without labor to mine the silver and gold or to work the land. African slavery was their solution.

Slavery was an ancient institution in many societies worldwide; however, with the Columbian Exchange slavery came to be practiced on a mass scale the likes of which the world had never seen. Throughout Africa and especially on the West African coast, Europeans traded for slaves with some African kingdoms and also raided the land, kidnapping people. European slavers took captured Africans in horrific conditions to the Americas; those who survived were enslaved and forced to work in mining or agriculture for the benefit of expanding European imperial powers.

The Columbian Exchange described the **triangular trade** across the Atlantic: European slavers kidnapped African people and took them to the Americas, sold them at auction and exchanged them for sugar and raw materials; these materials were traded in Europe for consumer goods, which were then exchanged in Africa for slaves (and also sold in the colonies), and so on.

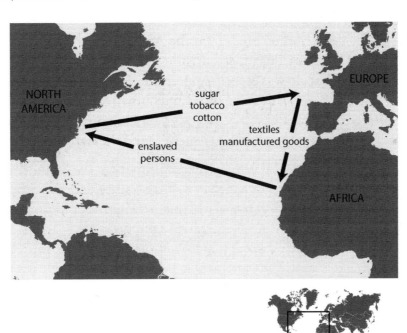

Figure 3.6. Triangular Trade

Throughout this period, Africans did resist both on ships and later, in the Americas; **maroon communities** of escaped slaves formed throughout the Western Hemisphere, the **Underground Railroad** in the nineteenth-century United States helped enslaved persons escape the South, and **Toussaint L'Ouverture** led a successful slave rebellion in Haiti, winning independence from the French for that country in 1791.

However, the slave trade continued for centuries. The colonies and later independent countries of the Western Hemisphere continued to practice slavery until the nineteenth century; oppressive legal and social restrictions based on race continue to affect the descendants of slaves to this day throughout the hemisphere.

During the eighteenth century, Spain and Portugal were preeminent powers in global trade thanks to colonization and **imperialism**, the possession and exploitation of land overseas. Later, Great Britain became an important presence in North America and on the seas; it would later dominate the oceans and amass colonies worldwide throughout the nineteenth century. Likewise, France gained territory in North America and in the West Indies; despite losses to Britain in the eighteenth century, that country would also expand its own global empire in the nineteenth century.

QUICK REVIEW

Explain the Columbian Exchange.

SAMPLE QUESTIONS

12) **Slaves were originally brought to the Americas as part of the triangular trade in order to do all of the following EXCEPT**

   A.   work on cotton plantations.

   B.   work on sugar plantations.

   C.   work in colonists' homes.

   D.   work in textile factories.

   Answers:

   A.   Incorrect. Many thousands of enslaved persons from Africa and of African origin were forced to harvest cotton.

   B.   Incorrect. Many thousands of slaves from Africa and of African origin were forced to work on sugar plantations.

   C.   Incorrect. Some slaves were forced to do housework.

   D.   Correct. Factories developed during the Industrial Revolution, and so were not present in the colonies while the slave trade was active.

13) **In South America, how was the Inca Empire able to consolidate its power?**

   A.   The Inca used advanced military technology to conquer neighboring peoples.

   B.   The Inca converted people to their own religion, gaining followers and loyal subjects.

   C.   The Inca used their mastery of high altitude transportation to expand their empire.

   D.   The Inca grew their empire by bringing in migrants from other parts of South America.

Answers:

A. Incorrect. Military technology was not the primary reason the Inca Empire became so large.

B. Incorrect. The Inca did not focus on mass conversion as a reason for empire building.

C. Correct. Advanced transportation in high altitude terrain enabled the Inca military to range widely throughout the Andes.

D. Incorrect. The Inca did not encourage migration into the areas they controlled.

REFORMATION AND NEW EUROPE

While Spain and Portugal consolidated their hold over territories in the Americas, conflict ensued in Europe. With the cultural changes of the Renaissance, the power of the Catholic Church was threatened; new scientific discoveries and secular Renaissance thought were at odds with many teachings of the church. The Catholic monk **Martin Luther** wrote a letter of protest to the pope in 1517 known as the **Ninety-Five Theses**, outlining ways he believed the church should reform; his ideas gained support, especially among rulers who wanted more power from the church. Triggering the **Reformation**, or movement for reform of the church, Luther's ideas led to offshoots of new versions of Christianity in Western Europe, separate from the Orthodox churches in Russia and Greece.

The English **King Henry VIII** developed the Protestant **Church of England,** further consolidating his own power, famously allowing divorce and marrying several times himself. His reign initiated a chain of events leading to the consolidation of Protestantism in England, and eventually civil war and the empowerment of Parliament.

Conflict between Protestants and Catholics was fierce on the Continent as well. The **Thirty Years' War** (1618–1648) began in Central Europe between Protestant nobles in the Holy Roman Empire who disagreed with the Catholic Holy Roman Emperor, Ferdinand II. Ferdinand was a leader of the 1619 **Counter-Reformation**, attempts at reinforcing Catholic dominance throughout Europe during and after the Reformation in the wake of the Renaissance and related social change. Ferdinand was also closely allied with the Catholic **Hapsburg Dynasty**, which ruled Austria and Spain.

At the same time, despite France's status as a Catholic country, it came into conflict with its Hapsburg-ruled neighbors Spain and Austria. As part of the Counter-Reformation, Spain had defeated Protestant powers in Central Europe in 1634, dominating the region. Thus the Hapsburgs controlled territory surrounding France, representing a military threat. As a result, despite their religious commonalities, France declared war on Spain in 1635 and shortly after on the Hapsburg-supported Holy Roman Empire. This political tactic represented a break from the prioritization of religious alliances and a movement toward emphasis on state sovereignty.

The tangled alliances among European powers resulted in war between not only France and Spain, but also Sweden and Austria, with the small states of the weakening Holy Roman Empire caught in the middle. The war had been centered on alliances and concerns about the nature of Christianity within different European countries. However, upon signing the 1648 **Treaty of Westphalia**, the European powers agreed to recognize state sovereignty and practice non-interference in each other's matters—at the expense of family and religious allegiances. 1648 marked a transition into modern international relations when politics and religion would no longer be inexorably intertwined.

The end of the Thirty Years' War represented the end of domination of the Catholic Church over Europe and the concept of religious regional dominance, rather than ethnic state divisions. Over the next several centuries, the church and religious empires like the Ottomans would eventually lose control over ethnic groups and their lands, later giving way to smaller nation-states.

As state sovereignty became entrenched in European notions of politics, so too did conflict among states. Conflict over control of the Hapsburg territories led to the **Seven Years' War** in 1756. In Europe, this war further cemented concepts of state sovereignty and delineated rivalries between European powers engaged in colonial adventure and overseas imperialism—especially Britain and France. It would kick-start British dominance in Asia and also lead to Britain's loss of its North American colonies.

European concepts of social and political organization became constructed around national sovereignty and nation-states. European economies had become dependent upon colonies and were starting to industrialize, enriching Europe at the expense of its imperial possessions in the Americas, in Africa, and increasingly in Asia.

Industrialization and political organization allowed improved militaries, which put Asian governments at a disadvantage. The major Asian powers—Mughal India, China, the Ottoman Empire, and Persia—would eventually succumb to European influence or come under direct European control.

SAMPLE QUESTIONS

14) **The power of the Catholic Church was diminished during the Reformation due to**

   A. its unwillingness to protect the indigenous peoples of the Americas.

   B. the discoveries of the Scientific Revolution.

   C. the growth of Islam in Western Europe.

   D. its failure to capture the Holy Land during the Crusades.

Answers:

   A. Incorrect. While some Catholic thinkers, like Bartolomé de las Casas, spoke out against atrocities committed against the indigenous peoples of the Americas, this was not a central issue for most Europeans.

B. **Correct.** The Scientific Revolution, humanism, and logic brought into question Church teachings long regarded as fact, undermining Church power.

C. Incorrect. Islam did not have a significant presence in Western Europe during the Reformation, and did not challenge the power of the Catholic Church there.

D. Incorrect. The Church had encouraged the Crusades, but was not directly responsible for them; European failure to permanently control the Holy Land did not cause the Church to lose legitimacy.

15) **Which of the following best describes the motivation for the reformer Martin Luther?**

A. He originally sought to develop a new form of Christianity separate from the Catholic Church.

B. He tried to reform the Catholic Church because he was unhappy with its teachings and its corruption.

C. He was influenced by European political leaders, who used him to limit the power of the Church.

D. He tried to topple the Catholic Church, believing it to have become too corrupt.

Answers:

A. Incorrect. Martin Luther was a Catholic monk; he originally sought reform within the Catholic Church.

B. **Correct.** Martin Luther and his followers opposed corruption in the Church and wanted changes.

C. Incorrect. The Reformation was not originally a political movement.

D. Incorrect. Martin Luther initially wanted reform; he did not want to overthrow the papacy or the Church.

THE AGE OF REVOLUTIONS

Monarchies in Europe had been weakened by the conflicts between Catholicism and Protestant faiths; despite European presence and increasing power overseas, as well as its dominance in the Americas, instability on the continent and in the British Isles made the old order vulnerable. Enlightenment ideals like democracy and republicanism, coupled with political instability, would trigger revolution against **absolute monarchy**. Revolutionary actors drew on the philosophies of enlightenment thinkers like John Locke, Jean-Jacques Rousseau, and Montesquieu, whose beliefs, such as republicanism, the social contract, the separation of powers, and the rights of man would drive the Age of Revolutions.

In 1642, the **English Civil War** broke out between the Royalists, who supported the monarchy, and the Parliamentarians, who wanted a republic. Eventually, the

Royalists succumbed to the Parliamentarians. The **1689 English Bill of Rights** established constitutional monarchy, in the spirit of the Magna Carta.

The American Revolution heavily influenced by **Locke**, broke out a century later. (Please see the section on U.S. history for details.)

The French Revolution was the precursor to the end of the feudal order in most of Europe. **King Louis XIV**, the *Sun King* (1643–1715), had consolidated the monarchy in France, taking true political and military power from the nobility. Meanwhile, French Enlightenment thinkers like **Rousseau**, **Montesquieu**, and **Voltaire** criticized absolute monarchy and the repression of freedom of speech and thought; in 1789, the French Revolution broke out.

DID YOU KNOW?

Louis XIV built the palace of Versailles, to centralize the monarchy—and also to contain and monitor the nobility.

The power of the Catholic Church had weakened and the Scientific Revolution and the Enlightenment had fostered social and intellectual change. Colonialism and mercantilism were fueling the growth of an early middle class: people who were not traditionally nobility or landowners under the feudal system were becoming wealthier and more powerful thanks to early capitalism. This class, the **bourgeoisie**, chafed under the rule of the nobility, which had generally inherited land and wealth (while the bourgeoisie earned their wealth in business).

In France, the problem was most acute as France had the largest population in Europe at the time. At the same time, France had one of the most centralized monarchies in Europe and entrenched nobilities. With a growing bourgeoisie and peasant class paying increasingly higher taxes to the nobility, resentment was brewing.

The French government was struggling financially and proposed taxing the nobility. In 1787, an unwilling council of nobles instead called for the **Estates-General** to be convened. This weak representative assembly reflected French society: the clergy, the nobility, and the **Third Estate**—the middle class and the poor peasants, or *commoners*. The burden of taxation traditionally fell on the Third Estate. In fact, peasants had to **tithe**, paying ten percent of their earnings to the nobles.

The Third Estate eventually declared itself the National Constituent Assembly. At the same time, panic over dwindling food supplies and suspicion over a conspiracy against the Third Estate triggered the **Great Fear** among the peasants in July 1789. Suspicion turned to action when the king sent troops to Paris, and on July 16 the people stormed the **Bastille** prison in an event still celebrated in France symbolic of the overthrow of tyranny. The peasantry then revolted in the countryside; consequently the National Constituent Assembly officially abolished the feudal system and tithing. Furthermore, the Assembly issued the **Declaration of the Rights of Man and the Citizen**, the precursor to the French constitution assuring liberty and equality, in the model of Enlightenment thought.

The French Revolution inspired revolutionary movements throughout Europe and beyond; indeed, the revolutionary principle of self-determination drove revolutionary France to support its ideals abroad. The country declared war on Austria in 1792, but following severe defeats the people became suspicious of the unpopular queen **Marie Antoinette**. The people imprisoned the royal family and the republic was established later that year. The monarchy was abolished.

Fearful of counterrevolutionaries in France and instability abroad, the republican government created the Committee for Public Safety in 1793 and the Reign of Terror began. Thousands of people were executed by **guillotine**, including the king and Marie Antoinette.

In 1804 **Napoleon Bonaparte** emerged as emperor of France, and proceeded to conquer much of Europe throughout the **Napoleonic Wars**, changing the face of Europe. French occupation of Spain weakened that country enough that revolutionary movements in its colonies strengthened; eventually Latin American colonies, inspired by the Enlightenment and revolution in Europe, won their freedom. **Simón Bolivar** led or influenced independence movements in Venezuela, Colombia (including what is today Panama), Ecuador, Peru, and Bolivia in the early part of the nineteenth century.

> **DID YOU KNOW?**
>
> An important tenet of the revolutionary ethos in France was the concept of self-determination, or the right of a people to rule themselves, which threatened other rulers fearing revolution in their own countries.

Napoleon's movement eastward also triggered the collapse of the Holy Roman Empire. However, the powerful state of Prussia emerged in its wake, and a strong sense of militarism and Germanic nationalism took root in the face of opposition to seemingly unstoppable France.

Nationalism is a sentiment of loyalty to one's own cultural or ethnic group above others. This was a new concept in a Europe that had previously been dominated by religious affiliation (Catholic and Protestant) and empires, where a ruler may have been from a different linguistic or cultural group (for instance, the Hapsburgs had ruled both in Central Europe and Spain; the Austro-Hungarian Empire controlled parts of the Balkans where neither German nor Hungarian was spoken).

> **HELPFUL HINT**
>
> Prussia had a particular rivalry with France, having lost several key territories during the Napoleonic Wars. In 1870, the militarily powerful kingdom went to war against France in the **Franco-Prussian War**, during which Prussia took control of Alsace-Lorraine, mineral rich and later essential for industrial development.

Nationalism triggered a sense of local identity; people did not identify with a power based in a faraway capital. Likewise, nationalism could be a unifying factor; numerous smaller German-speaking states in Central Europe connected with

Prussia, empowering that country. A **nation-state** is a sovereign territory ruled by an ethnic majority, in contrast to previous models of imperial rule in which one ethic group governed many others. Under the concept of a nation-state, individuals with shared experience (including ethnicity, language, religion, and cultural practices) should be unified under one government.

Prussia had come to dominate the German-speaking states that once comprised the Holy Roman Empire. Prussia, a distinct kingdom within the Holy Roman Empire since the thirteenth century, had become a powerful Central European state by the eighteenth century. It had become the main rival of Austria for influence in the Germanic lands of Central Europe. By the nineteenth century and due in part to emphasis on military prowess, Prussia became an important military power and a key ally in the efforts against Napoleon.

Napoleon was finally defeated in Russia in 1812 and was forced by the European powers to abdicate in 1813. He escaped from prison on the Mediterranean island of Elba and raised an army again, overthrowing the restored monarch Louis XVIII. Defeated at Waterloo by the British, he was once again exiled, this time to St. Helena in the southern Atlantic Ocean.

By 1815, other European powers had managed to halt his expansion; at the **Congress of Vienna** in 1815, European powers including the unified Prussia, the Austro-Hungarian Empire, Russia, and Britain agreed on a balance of power in Europe. Despite Napoleon's brief reemergence, the Congress of Vienna was the first real international peace conference and set the precedent for European political organization.

Following the Franco-Prussian War, **Otto von Bismarck** unified those linguistically and culturally German states of Central Europe. In 1871, the German Empire emerged as a unified power.

SAMPLE QUESTION

16) **Which of the following led to the French Revolution?**

   A. food shortages, heavy taxation of the peasants and bourgeoisie, and Enlightenment thought

   B. the rise of Napoleon and militarization of French culture

   C. the Congress of Vienna and shifting diplomatic alliances in Europe

   D. the concentration of power under the monarchy that resulted from the reign of Louis XIV

Answers:

   A. **Correct.** The peasants and bourgeoisie were dissatisfied with bearing the brunt of a heavy tax burden; meanwhile, poor harvests led to food shortages and panic in rural areas. These factors, along with Enlightenment thought and recent revolutions elsewhere, spurred the French Revolution.

B.   Incorrect. Napoleon came to power after the French Revolution, providing stability in a chaotic period.

C.   Incorrect. The Congress of Vienna was a conference held after the initial defeat of Napoleon to determine the future of Europe. It occurred after the French Revolution.

D.   Incorrect. The reign of Louis XIV weakened the nobility and centralized power under the king. However, his reign alone did not cause the Revolution, and he was long dead by the time it began.

IMPERIALISM

As colonialism in the fifteenth and sixteenth centuries had been driven by mercantilism, conquest, and Christian conversion, so was seventeenth, eighteenth, and nineteenth century imperialism driven by capitalism, European competition, and conceptions of racial superiority.

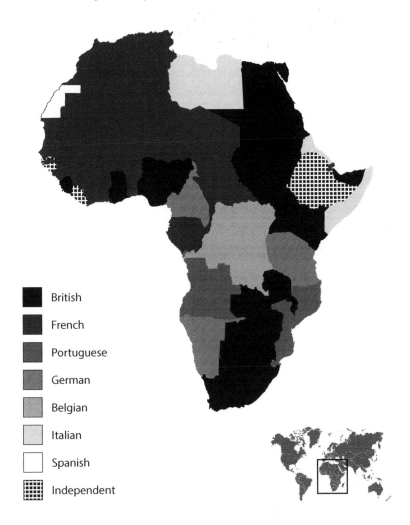

Figure 3.7. Imperial Africa

Despite its loss of the Thirteen Colonies, at the dawn of the nineteenth century Britain retained control of Canada, rich in natural resources like beaver pelts and timber. In addition, it controlled the resource-rich and strategically important Indian Subcontinent. Britain would become the strongest naval power in the world and continue to expand its empire, especially in the search for new markets for its manufactured goods to support its industrial economy.

During the reign of **Queen Victoria** (1837 – 1901) the British Empire would expand greatly, taking over India, Australia, and large parts of Africa. The concept of the **white man's burden,** wherein white Europeans were "obligated" to bring their "superior" culture to other civilizations around the globe, also drove imperialist adventure, popularizing it at home in Britain and elsewhere in Europe.

The European powers were immersed in became known as the **Scramble for Africa**; the industrial economies of Europe would profit from the natural resources abundant in that continent, and the "white man's burden" continued to fuel colonization. At the **1884 Berlin Conference**, control over Africa was divided among European powers (Africans were not consulted in this process). In the early twentieth century Britain also gained control of South Africa, and whites would rule the country until the end of **Apartheid** in the early 1990s. France controlled West Africa and eventually North Africa; Belgium controlled the resource-rich Congo.

However, not all non-European countries fell to European imperialism. During the **Meiji Restoration** in Japan in 1868, the Emperor promoted modernization of technology, especially the military. Japan emerged as a world power when it defeated Russia in the **Russo-Japanese War** in 1905, and would play a central role in twentieth century conflict.

SAMPLE QUESTIONS

17) **During the 1884 Berlin Conference, European imperial powers**

    A.   negotiated trade agreements with important Chinese cities.

    B.   established Apartheid in South Africa.

    C.   determined which parts of Africa would be controlled by which European powers.

    D.   formed the Triple Alliance.

Answers:

    A.   Incorrect. The 1884 Berlin Conference focused on Africa, not China.

    B.   Incorrect. The Apartheid system was not formally established until the early twentieth century.

    C.   **Correct.** The 1884 Berlin Conference determined the division of Africa among the European imperial powers. This was done without regard for or consultation with Africans.

    D.   Incorrect. The Triple Alliance was established by Germany, Austria-Hungary, and Italy.

18) **The Meiji Restoration was**

   A.   a Japanese attempt to restore traditional Japanese cultural practices.

   B.   a period of modernization and westernization in Japan.

   C.   the early stage of Japanese imperialism in Asia, when it invaded Korea.

   D.   a cultural movement in Japan to restore Shintoism and traditional poetry.

Answers:

   A.   Incorrect. During the Meiji Restoration, Japan abolished traditional institutions and began pursuing Western-style development.

   B.   Correct. The Meiji Restoration was a period of industrialization and westernization in Japan.

   C.   Incorrect. The Meiji Restoration occurred prior to its imperial incursions throughout Asia.

   D.   Incorrect. The Meiji Restoration was a socioeconomic movement, not a return to traditional cultural practices.

INDUSTRIAL REVOLUTION

Meanwhile, raw goods from the Americas fueled European economic growth and development, leading to the **Industrial Revolution** in the nineteenth century. This economic revolution began with textile production in Britain, fueled by cotton from its overseas territories in North America, and later India and Egypt. The first factories were in Manchester, where **urbanization** began as poor people from rural areas flocked to cities in search of higher-paying unskilled jobs in factories.

Early industrial technology sped up the harvesting and transport of crops and their conversion to textiles. This accelerated manufacturing was based on **capitalism**, the *laissez-faire* (or free market) theory developed by **Adam Smith**, who believed that an *invisible hand* should guide the marketplace—that government should stay out of the economy, as the market would eventually automatically correct for inequalities, price problems, and any other problematic issues.

Technology exponentially increased the amount of cotton that workers could process into yarn and thread. The **steam engine** efficiently powered mills and ironworks; factories no longer had to be built near running water to access power. Advances in iron technology allowed for stronger machinery and would support the later **Second Industrial Revolution** in the late nineteenth and early twentieth centuries, which was based on heavy industry, railroads, and weapons.

To access the raw materials needed to produce manufactured goods, Britain and other industrializing countries in Western Europe needed resources, driving imperialism. Cotton was harvested in India and Egypt for textile mills; minerals mined in South Africa and the Congo to power metallurgy.

Furthermore, as industrialization and urbanization led to the development of early middle classes in Europe and North America, imports of luxury goods like tea, spices, silk, precious metals, and other items from Asia increased to meet consumer demand. Colonial powers also gained by selling manufactured goods back to the colonies from which they had harvested raw materials in the first place, for considerable profit.

Largely unbridled capitalism had led to the conditions of the early Industrial Revolution; workers suffered from abusive treatment, overly long hours, low wages or none at all, and unsafe conditions, including pollution. The German philosophers **Karl Marx** and **Friedrich Engels**, horrified by conditions suffered by industrial workers, developed **socialism**, the philosophy that workers, or the proletariat, should own the means of production and reap the profits, rather than the bourgeoisie, who had no interest in the rights of the workers at the expense of profit and who did not experience the same conditions.

Marx argued for the abolition of the class system, wages, and private property. He argued instead for collective ownership of both the means of production and products, with equal distribution of income to satisfy the needs of all. Later, Marx and Engels wrote the ***Communist Manifesto***, a pamphlet laying out their ideas and calling for revolution. It inspired the formation of socialist groups worldwide.

A different version of socialism would later help Russia become a major world power. The Russian intellectuals **Vladimir Lenin** and **Leon Trotsky** would take Marx and Engels' theories further, developing **Marxism-Leninism**. They embraced socialist ideals and believed in revolution; however, they felt that **communism** could not be maintained under a democratic governing structure. Lenin supported dictatorship, more precisely the *dictatorship of the proletariat*, paving the way for the political and economic organization of the Soviet Union.

SAMPLE QUESTION

19) **According to Adam Smith, in a free market**

    A.   the government does not interfere with the economy.

    B.   workers own the means of production.

    C.   wages and private property have been abolished.

    D.   a dictatorship is necessary to maintain a strong economy.

Answers:

    A.   **Correct.** In *laissez-faire* (or free market) theory, the government lets the invisible hand of the market correct problems in the economy.

    B.   Incorrect. In socialism, not free market capitalism, workers own the means of production.

    C.   Incorrect. Both wages and private property are important elements of free market capitalism.

    D.   Incorrect. Lenin believed that dictatorship was necessary to maintain a communist society. In a free market, the government does not have to work to maintain the economy.

TWENTIETH CENTURY

Elementary-level students should also be aware of major twentieth- and twenty-first-century developments such as the world wars, the Cold War, and globalization.

Instability and tensions in Europe culminated with the assassination of the Austro-Hungarian Archduke Franz Ferdinand in Sarajevo on June 28, 1914, igniting the system of alliances that had been in place among European powers.

Austria-Hungary declared war on Serbia, and Russia came to Serbia's aid. As an ally of Austria-Hungary as part of the **Triple Alliance**, Germany declared war on Russia. Russia's ally France prepared for war; as Germany traversed Belgium to invade France, Belgium pleaded for aid from other European countries, and so Britain declared war on Germany.

Germany had been emphasizing military growth since the consolidation and militarization of the empire under Bismarck in the mid-nineteenth century. Now, under **Kaiser Wilhelm II**, who sought expanded territories in Europe and overseas for Germany, Germany was a militarized state and important European power in its own right.

Britain's imperial power allowed it to call on troops from all over the globe—Indians, Canadians, Australians, South Africans, and New Zealanders all fought in Europe. France, too, imported colonial fighters from North Africa.

In Europe, the 1914 Battle of the Marne between Germany and French and British forces defending France resulted in **trench warfare** that would continue for years, marking the Western Front. At Gallipoli in 1915, Australian and New Zealander troops fought the Ottoman Empire, allies of Germany, near Istanbul. Later that year, a German submarine, or U-boat, sank the *Lusitania*, a passenger ship in the Atlantic, killing many American civilians. In 1916, the Battle of Verdun, the longest battle of the war, ended in the failure of the Germans to defeat the French army. On July 1, 1916, the Battle of the Somme became part of an allied effort to repel Germany using artillery to end the stalemate on the Western Front; after four months, however, the front moved only 5 miles.

Finally, in 1917, the United States discovered that Germany secretly proposed an alliance with Mexico to attack the US. This finally spurred US intervention in the war; despite Russian withdrawal after the Bolshevik Revolution in October 1917, Germany was forced to surrender in the face of invasion by the US-supported allies.

According to the Schlieffen Plan, Germany had planned to fight a war on two fronts against both Russia and France. However, Russian forces stretched the German army too thin on the Eastern Front, while it became bogged down in trench warfare on the Western Front against the British, the French, and later the Americans.

Germany lost the war and was punished with the harsh **Treaty of Versailles**, which held it accountable for the entirety of the war. The Treaty brought economic hardship on the country by forcing it to pay **reparations**. German military failure and consequent economic collapse due to the Treaty of Versailles and later worldwide economic depression set the stage for the rise of Adolf Hitler.

The Treaty also created the **League of Nations**, an international organization designed to prevent future outbreaks of international war; however, it was largely toothless, especially because the powerful United States did not join. However, it would be the model for the stronger United Nations.

Instability between the First and Second World Wars resulted from the worldwide **Great Depression**. Growing nationalism in Germany, Italy, and Japan added to political uncertainty.

In Asia, Japan invaded Manchuria, northern China, in 1931. It already controlled Korea, Taiwan, and other Asian territories and began expanding its control farther into Southeast Asia and throughout the Pacific.

In Germany, Hitler's popular platform—to cancel the Treaty of Versailles—allowed him to rise. In 1934 he became the *Führer*, or leader, of Germany, and took total control of the country. He and the Nazis set into motion their agenda of racism and genocide against "non-Aryan" (non-Germanic) or "racially impure" people.

Jewish people were especially targeted. Throughout the 1930s, the Nazis began restricting Jewish rights. In 1938, an organized series of attacks on Jewish businesses, homes, and places of worship called **Kristallnacht** took place, so called because the windows of these places were smashed. In 1939, Jews were forced from their homes into **ghettoes**, isolated and overcrowded urban neighborhoods; in 1941, they were forced to wear **yellow stars** identifying them as Jewish.

Millions of Jewish people were sent to **concentration camps**, where many were murdered through forced labor and systematic gassing. At least six million European Jews were murdered by the Nazis in the **Holocaust**, as were Roma, Slavic people, homosexuals, disabled people, people of color, prisoners of war, communists, and others not considered "Aryan."

Meanwhile, Hitler sought to restore Germany's power and expand its reach by annexing and invading various countries. Germany's 1939 invasion of Poland is commonly considered the beginning of the **Second World War**. In 1940, Germany took Paris. The Battle of Britain began in July of that year; however, Germany suffered its first defeat and was unable to take Britain.

When Japan joined the **Axis** powers of Germany and Italy, the war officially spread to Asia, which was already in conflict. The **Chinese Civil War** was interrupted when Japan invaded China past Manchuria. In response, the Chinese factions joined forces against Japan; the communists became powerful. In June of 1941, Japan attacked the United States at **Pearl Harbor**. Consequently, the US joined the war in Europe and in the Pacific.

Back in Europe, having broken a promise made to the Soviet Union in 1939, Hitler invaded the USSR; however Germany was defeated at the Battle of Stalingrad, a turning point in the war. In 1944, the Allies invaded France on D-Day. While they liberated Paris in August, the costly Battle of the Bulge extended into 1945. Despite thousands of American casualties, Hitler's forces were pushed back. In the spring of 1945, the US crossed the Rhine while the USSR invaded Berlin; Hitler killed himself, and the Allies accepted German surrender.

The war in the Pacific would continue, however. Strategic battles were fought throughout the islands. **President Truman**, who had succeeded Roosevelt, elected to use the nuclear bomb on Japan to force its surrender rather than invade that country. In 1945, the war ended with Japanese surrender after the US bombed the Japanese cities Hiroshima and Nagasaki. That year in China, the Chinese Civil War recommenced; by 1949 the communists had emerged victorious.

Because of the widespread violence of the war and the millions of soldiers and civilians who died, especially those killed because of genocide, the **United Nations** was formed to prevent another world war. It was based on the League of Nations, and its mission is to champion human rights and uphold international security.

Allied forces took the lead in rebuilding efforts: the US occupied areas in East Asia and Germany, while the Soviet Union remained in Eastern Europe. The Allies had planned to rebuild Europe according to the Marshall Plan; however, the USSR occupied Eastern Europe. The **Cold War** had begun.

The US, Britain, and the USSR had originally agreed to divide Germany and to hold free elections in Eastern Europe, but by 1945, things had changed. The USSR felt betrayed by the US's use of the nuclear bomb; likewise, the US and Britain felt betrayed by the Soviet Union, which had occupied Eastern Europe and prevented democratic elections in order to establish a buffer zone following its extraordinarily heavy casualties in WWII—around twenty million. An *iron curtain* had come down across Europe, dividing east from west.

> **DID YOU KNOW?**
>
> Perhaps the most famous proposal in weapons technology during this time was the Strategic Defense Initiative; popularly known as *Star Wars*, this outer space based system would have intercepted Soviet intercontinental ballistic missiles.

The United States adopted a policy of containment, the idea that communism should be *contained*. Therefore, the United States became involved in the **Korean War** in 1950 and later the controversial **Vietnam War** throughout the 1960s and early 1970s.

Toward the end of the 1960s and into the 1970s, the Cold War began to thaw. The US and USSR signed a series of treaties to limit nuclear weapons. In 1972, President Richard Nixon visited China, establishing relations between the communist government and the United States.

However, the climate would change again in the 1970s and 1980s. The **arms race** was underway. President Ronald Reagan pursued a militaristic policy, prioritizing weapons development with the goal of outspending the USSR on weapons technology.

In 1991, the Soviet Union fell thanks in part to reforms like *glasnost* and *perestroika* (or openness and transparency). After a coup overthrowing Premier Mikhail Gorbachev, the Soviet leader, the USSR was dissolved. A Soviet war in Afghanistan and military overspending in an effort to keep up with the United States had weakened the USSR to the point of collapse, and the Cold War ended.

SAMPLE QUESTIONS

20) While the beginning of the Second World War is usually understood to be Hitler's invasion of Poland, some scholars date it even earlier. Which of the following events do some scholars identify as the beginning of World War II?

   A. the Rape of Nanjing

   B. the Japanese takeover of Korea

   C. the Japanese invasion of Manchuria

   D. the Chinese Civil War

   Answers:

   A. Incorrect. Some scholars date the beginning of World War II to Japan's invasion of Manchuria, which occurred before the 1937 Rape of Nanjing.

   B. Incorrect. Japan annexed Korea in 1910 following the growth of its influence in East Asia after the Russo-Japanese War and other developments. This was before the First World War.

   C. Correct. Given Japan's role as an Axis power and the conflict in East Asia, some historians believe that WWII began with Japan's invasion of Manchuria in 1931.

   D. Incorrect. The Chinese Civil War took place throughout the 1930s and after World War II; it was not a cause of the Second World War.

21) Which of the following happened to Jewish people under the Nazi regime?

   A. Their homes and businesses were attacked and destroyed.

   B. They were forced to live in ghettoes, overcrowded neighborhoods with poor living conditions.

   C. They were sent to concentration camps and murdered.

   D. All of the above

   Answers:

   D. Correct. Under the Nazis, Jewish people were forced to live in ghettoes; their businesses and homes were destroyed; and they suffered other persecution. Jews, communists, Roma, homosexuals, and others were also forced into slave labor in concentration camps, and millions were murdered.

GLOBALIZATION

Globalization is increasing economic, political, and cultural interdependence and interaction throughout the world. At its core, globalization is an economic trend; **multinational corporations (MNCs)** are the primary driving forces of globalization. However, globalization has significant cultural and political impacts as well. For example, the exportation of American fast food restaurants, like McDonald's (one example of an MNC), to other parts of the world reflects the capitalist drive to find new markets. Furthermore, the introduction of this type of food has a significant impact on one of the major distinguishing cultural traits of other countries—their cuisine.

Another example is language; English continues to spread throughout the world as the main language used in business and on the Internet. Spanish, French, Arabic, and Chinese are also widely spoken and used as second or third languages by millions of people in business, in pop culture, and to disseminate news. Looking at causes and events in history is another way to make **cross-cultural comparisons**. For example, students could analyze different holiday traditions from various countries.

In this era of globalization, international markets became increasingly open through free-trade agreements among countries, making international business easier. Technological advances like improvements in transportation and the Internet made international trade and communication faster, easier, and cheaper. Political cooperation like the formation of the European Union and other groups all make globalization possible.

The **European Union**, as it is known today, was formed in 1992 after the Cold War. Former communist countries became democratic societies and joined it; as of 2015, twenty-eight countries are members, with more on the path to membership. EU countries cooperate politically; many also share a common currency, the **euro**, and some EU countries even have open borders. In Africa, the **African Union**, similar to the EU, is a forum for African countries to organize and cooperate politically, militarily, and economically. The **G-20**, the world's twenty most important economic and political powers, includes many former colonies and non-European countries.

However, more open borders, reliable international transportation, and faster, easier worldwide communication brought risks, too. In the early twenty-first century, the United States was attacked by terrorists on **September 11, 2001,** resulting in thousands of civilian casualties. Consequently, the US launched a major land war in Afghanistan and another later in Iraq.

→ Go on

22) **Which of the following is an example of a cross-cultural comparison?**

    A.   A chef studies variations in a recipe that are based on the diner's preference for sweets.

    B.   A Thai husband learns different holiday traditions from his wife, who is Chinese.

    C.   Students compare the prices of groceries in different cities.

    D.   A career coach helps clients determine their goals.

Answers:

    A.   Incorrect. Personal preferences are not an example of culture.

    B.   **Correct.** Reviewing different holiday celebrations exemplifies studying different cultures.

    C.   Incorrect. Studying different prices is economic, not cultural, study.

    D.   Incorrect. Determining career goals relates to personal preferences.

United States History

NATIVE AMERICAN SOCIETIES

Prior to European colonization, diverse Native American societies controlled the continent; they would later come into economic and diplomatic contact, and military conflict, with European colonizers and United States forces and settlers.

Major civilizations that would play an important and ongoing role in North American history included the **Iroquois** in the Northeast, known for longhouses and farming in the Three Sisters tradition; they consisted of a confederation of six tribes. The **Algonquin** were another important northeastern civilization; rivals of the Iroquois, the Algonquin were important in the fur trade. Algonquin languages were spoken throughout the Great Lakes region.

Farther west, the **Shawnee** were an Algonquin-speaking people based in the Ohio Valley; however their presence extended as far south and east as the present-day Carolinas and Georgia. While socially organized under a matrilineal system, the Shawnee had male kings and only men could inherit property. Also matrilineal and Algonquin-speaking, the **Lenape** were considered by the Shawnee to be their "grandfathers" and thus accorded respect. Another Algonquin-speaking tribe, the **Kickapoo** were originally from the Great Lakes region and moved west. The Algonquin-speaking **Miami** moved from Wisconsin to the Ohio Valley region, forming settled societies and farming maize. They too took part in the fur trade as it developed during European colonial times. These tribes later formed the Northwest Confederacy to fight US westward expansion.

In the South, major tribes included the **Creek**, **Chickasaw**, and **Choctaw**, the descendants of the **Mississippi Mound Builders** or Mississippian cultures, societies which built mounds from around 2100 to 1800 years ago as burial tombs or the bases for temples. Sharing similar languages, all the tribes would later participate in an alliance—the Muscogee Confederacy—to engage the United States. The Chickasaw and Choctaw were matrilineal; the former also engaged in Three Sisters agriculture like the Iroquois.

Another major southern tribe, the **Cherokee** spoke (and speak) a language of the Iroquoian family. It is thought that they migrated south to their homeland in present-day Georgia sometime long before European contact, where they remained until they were forcibly removed in 1832. Organized into seven clans, the Cherokee were also hunters and farmers like other tribes in the region and would later come into contact—and conflict—with European colonizers and the United States of America.

The nomadic tribes of the Great Plains like the **Sioux**, **Cheyenne**, **Apache**, **Comanche**, and **Arapaho** lived farther west. These tribes depended on the **buffalo** for food and materials to create clothing, tools, and domestic items; therefore they followed the herds. While widely known for their equestrian skill, horses were introduced by Europeans and so Native American tribes living on the Great Plains did not access them until after European contact. Horseback riding facilitated the hunt; previously, hunters surrounded buffalo or frightened them off of cliffs.

In the Southwest, the **Navajo** controlled territory in present-day Arizona, New Mexico, and Utah. Pastoralists, they had a less hierarchical structure than other Native American societies. The Navajo were descendants of the **Ancestral Pueblo** or **Anasazi**, who practiced Three Sisters agriculture and stone construction, building cliff dwellings.

In the Pacific Northwest, Native American peoples depended on fishing, using canoes. Totem poles depicted histories. The **Coast Salish**, whose language was widely spoken throughout the region, dominated the Puget Sound and Olympic Peninsula area. Farther south, the **Chinook** controlled the coast at the Columbia River.

Ultimately, through both violent conflict and political means, Native American civilizations lost control of most of their territories and were forced onto reservations by the United States. Negotiations continue today over rights to land and opportunities and reparations for past injustices.

SAMPLE QUESTION

23) **All of the following contributed to the destruction of Native American populations in North America except:**

    A.   colonists overuse of natural resources such as bison and timber

    B.   transfer of smallpox from Europeans to Native Americans

    C.   violent conflict over land and resources between Europeans and Native Americans

    D.   geographical displacement by colonists

Answers:

A.   **Correct.** Colonists use of natural resources had little impact on the size of the Native American population.

B.   Incorrect. Smallpox decimated Native American populations, which had never been exposed to the disease.

C.   Incorrect. Ongoing violent conflict between European colonizers and Native Americans over hundreds of years caused thousands of deaths and led to social breakdown among some Native American societies.

D.   Incorrect. Colonization and related conflict forced tribes to move from their traditional lands.

THE AMERICAN REVOLUTION

European powers had begun colonizing North America in the sixteenth century to access fur and agricultural resources; by the eighteenth century, Britain controlled most of the east coast of the continent, including the Thirteen Colonies, which became the original United States. France and Britain battled for control of northeastern North America, and following the **French and Indian War**, Great Britain consolidated its control over much of the continent.

Despite British victory in the French and Indian War, it had gone greatly into debt. Furthermore, there were concerns that the colonies required a stronger military presence following Native American attacks and uprisings like **Pontiac's Rebellion** in 1763. Consequently, **King George III** signed the **Proclamation of 1763**, an agreement not to settle land west of the Appalachians, in an effort to make peace; however much settlement continued in practice.

King George III enforced heavy taxes and restrictive acts in the colonies to generate income for the Crown and eventually to punish disobedience. England expanded the **Molasses Act** of 1733, passing the **Sugar Act** in 1764 to raise revenue by taxing sugar and molasses, which were widely consumed in the colonies. In 1765, Britain enforced the **Quartering Act**, forcing colonists to provide shelter to British troops stationed in the region.

The 1765 **Stamp Act**, the first direct tax on the colonists, triggered more tensions. Any document required a costly stamp, the revenue reverting to the British government. Colonists felt the tax violated their rights, given that they did not have direct representation in British Parliament. As a result, they began boycotting British goods and engaging in violent protest. **Samuel Adams** led the **Sons and Daughters of Liberty** in violent acts against tax collectors and stirred up rebellion with his **Committees of Correspondence**, which distributed anti-British propaganda.

Protests against the Quartering Act in Boston led to the **Boston Massacre** in 1770, when British troops fired on a crowd of protestors. By 1773, in a climate of continued unrest driven by the Committees of Correspondence, colonists protested the latest taxes on tea levied by the **Tea Act** in the famous **Boston Tea**

Party by dressing as Native Americans and tossing tea off a ship in Boston Harbor. In response, the government passed the **Intolerable Acts**, closing Boston Harbor and bringing Massachusetts back under direct royal control.

In response to the Intolerable Acts, colonial leaders met in Philadelphia at the **First Continental Congress** in 1774 and presented colonial concerns to the king, who ignored them. However, violent conflict began in 1775 at **Lexington and Concord**, when American militiamen (**minutemen**) gathered to resist British efforts to seize weapons and arrest rebels in Concord. On June 17, 1775, the Americans fought the British at the **Battle of Bunker Hill**; despite American losses, the number of casualties the rebels inflicted caused the king to declare that the colonies were in rebellion. Troops were deployed to the colonies; the Siege of Boston began.

In May 1775, the **Second Continental Congress** met at Philadelphia to debate the way forward. Debate among leaders like Benjamin Franklin, John Adams, Thomas Jefferson, and James Madison centered between the wisdom of continued efforts at compromise and negotiations, and declaring independence. Again, the king ignored them. By the summer of 1776, the Continental Congress agreed on the need to break from Britain; on July 4, 1776, it declared the independence of the United States of America and issued the **Declaration of Independence**.

> When in the Course of human events, it becomes necessary for one people to dissolve the political bands which have connected them with another, and to assume among the powers of the earth, the separate and equal station to which the Laws of Nature and of Nature's God entitle them, a decent respect to the opinions of mankind requires that they should declare the causes which impel them to the separation.

> We hold these truths to be self-evident, that all men are created equal, that they are endowed by their Creator with certain unalienable Rights, that among these are Life, Liberty and the pursuit of Happiness. That to secure these rights, Governments are instituted among Men, deriving their just powers from the consent of the governed, that whenever any Form of Government becomes destructive of these ends, it is the Right of the People to alter or to abolish it, and to institute new Government, laying its foundation on such principles and organizing its powers in such form, as to them shall seem most likely to effect their Safety and Happiness. Prudence, indeed, will dictate that Governments long established should not be changed for light and transient causes; and accordingly all experience hath shewn, that mankind are more disposed to suffer, while evils are sufferable, than to right themselves by abolishing the forms to which they are accustomed. But when a long train of abuses and usurpations, pursuing invariably the same Object evinces a design to reduce them under absolute Despotism, it is their right, it is their duty, to throw off such Government, and to provide new Guards for their future security. Such has been the patient sufferance of these Colonies; and such is now the necessity which constrains them to

alter their former Systems of Government. The history of the present King of Great Britain is a history of repeated injuries and usurpations, all having in direct object the establishment of an absolute Tyranny over these States. To prove this, let Facts be submitted to a candid world.

Preamble to the Declaration of Independence

Americans were still divided over independence; **Patriots** favored independence while those still loyal to Britain were known as **Tories**. **George Washington** had been appointed head of the Continental Army and led a largely unpaid and unprofessional army; despite early losses, Washington gained ground due to strong leadership, superior knowledge of the land, and support from France.

Initially, the British seemed to have many advantages in the war, including more resources and troops. Britain won the **Battle of Brooklyn** (Battle of Long Island) in August 1776 and captured New York City. The tide turned in 1777 at **Valley Forge**, when Washington and his army survived the bitterly cold winter and managed to overcome British military forces.

A victory at **Saratoga** led the French to help the rebels in 1778. Now fighting shifted south. Britain captured Georgia and Charleston, South Carolina; however, British forces could not adequately control the country as they proceeded to Yorktown, Virginia, in 1781. At the **Battle of Yorktown**, British forces were defeated by the Continental Army with support from France and were forced to surrender.

Meanwhile, the British people did not favor the war and voted the Tories out of Parliament; the incoming Whig party sought to end the war. After troops fought for two more years, the **Treaty of Paris** ended the revolution in September 1783. In 1787, the first draft of the Constitution was written, and George Washington became the first president of the United States two years later. The American Revolution would go on to inspire revolutions around the world.

SAMPLE QUESTIONS

24) **The Intolerable Acts included all of the following except**

   A.   the Boston Port Act.

   B.   the Quartering Act.

   C.   the Alien and Sedition Acts.

   D.   the Massachusetts Government Act.

   Answers:

   A.   Incorrect. Closing the Port of Boston was a major blow to the colonies and one of the Intolerable Acts.

   B.   Incorrect. Forcing colonists to take British soldiers into their homes outraged colonial subjects.

   C.   Correct. The Alien and Sedition Acts were implemented during John

Adams' administration.

D.   Incorrect. The Massachusetts Government Act punished the colonists by revoking local control of Massachusetts.

25)   **What advantage did the colonists have over the British in the American Revolution?**

A.   vast financial wealth

B.   superior weaponry

C.   strong leadership and knowledge of the terrain

D.   a professional military and access to mercenaries

Answers:

A.   Incorrect. While some colonists were quite wealthy, colonial wealth paled in the face of British wealth.

B.   Incorrect. The colonists did not have superior weaponry.

C.   **Correct.** The colonial military did have strong leaders, and an intimate knowledge of the terrain, many having been born there.

D.   Incorrect. Britain had an experienced military with substantial experience fighting in Europe and elsewhere. In addition, King George III hired Hessian mercenaries from Germany to supplement British troops.

Manifest Destiny

In the nineteenth century, the idea of **Manifest Destiny**, or the sense that it was the fate of the United States to expand westward and settle the continent, pervaded. In 1803 President Thomas Jefferson oversaw the **Louisiana Purchase**, which nearly doubled the size of the United States. **Meriwether Lewis** and **William Clark** were dispatched to explore the western frontier of the territory: Jefferson hoped to find an all-water route to the Pacific Ocean (via the Missouri River). While this route did not exist, Lewis and Clark returned with a deeper knowledge of the territory the US had come to control.

Later, British provocation at sea and in the northwest led to the **War of 1812** between the United States and Britain, which was allied with the Shawnee-led Northwest Confederacy. Growing nationalism in the United States pressured Madison into pushing for war; Congress declared war under President Madison with the intent to defend the United States, end unfair trade practices and poor treatment of Americans on the high seas, and penetrate British Canada. Despite the Confederacy's alliance with Britain, the United States prevailed.

The war resulted in no real gains or losses for either the Americans or the British, yet at the war's end, the United States had successfully defended itself as a country and reaffirmed its independence. Patriotism ran high, strengthening the idea of Manifest Destiny. In 1819, following the Seminole War the United States purchased Florida from Spain in the **Adams-Onis Treaty** (conflict with the Seminole would continue). The **Monroe Doctrine**, President James Monroe's policy that the Western Hemisphere was "closed" to any further European colonization or exploration, asserted US power in the region.

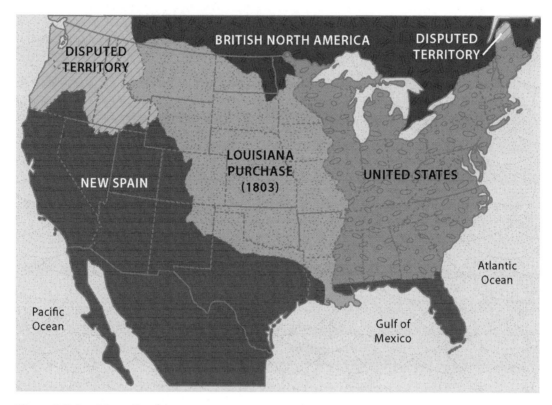

Figure 3.8. Louisiana Purchase

With westward expansion came questions over the expansion of slavery. In 1820, the **Missouri Compromise** allowed Missouri to join the union as a slave state but provided that any other states north of the thirty-sixth parallel (36°30') would be free. However, more tension and compromises over the nature of slavery in the West were to come.

With continental expansion came more conflict with Native Americans. Despite legal resistance by the Cherokee, President Andrew Jackson enforced the 1830 **Indian Removal Act**, forcing Cherokee, Creek, Chickasaw, Choctaw, and others from their lands in the Southeast. Thousands of people were forced to travel to Indian Territory (today, Oklahoma) on the infamous **Trail of Tears** to make way for white settlers.

The United States continued to grow throughout the nineteenth century. In 1845, the United States annexed Texas, which contributed to the outbreak of the Mexican-American War the next year. As a result, it gained California and the Utah and New Mexico territories in the 1848 Treaty of Guadalupe Hidalgo. In 1846, the United States and Britain agreed on the Oregon Treaty, which established a border at the forty-ninth parallel.

Meanwhile, social change in the Northeast and growing Midwest continued. As the market economy and early industry developed, so did an early **middle class**. Women asserted their rights: activists like **Susan B. Anthony** and **Elizabeth Cady Stanton** worked for women's suffrage, culminating in the 1848 **Seneca Falls Convention**.

The country was increasingly divided over slavery; **sectionalism** grew, strengthening disunity between the North and the South. Reform movements continued to include **abolitionism**, the ending of slavery. The former slave **Frederick Douglass** advocated abolition. An activist leader and writer, Douglass publicized the movement along with the American Anti-Slavery Society and publications like Harriet Beecher Stowe's *Uncle Tom's Cabin*. He and other activists like **Harriet Tubman** helped free slaves using the **Underground Railroad**. An estimated 100,000 slaves escaped the South between 1810 and 1850 through a system of safe houses, even though these actions violated state laws. The radical abolitionist **John Brown** led violent protests against slavery. Abolitionism became a key social and political issue in the mid-nineteenth century; slavery was the main cause of the Civil War.

Antislavery factions in Congress had attempted to halt the extension of slavery to the new territories obtained from Mexico, but they were unsuccessful; in the Compromise of 1850, Congress decided that the voters in some new territories would be allowed to decide whether slavery should be legal or determined by popular sovereignty. In 1854, Congress passed the Kansas-Nebraska Act, effectively repealing the Missouri Compromise, allowing those territories to decide slavery by popular sovereignty as well. In response, the new **Republican Party** emerged. One of its members, **Abraham Lincoln**, was elected president in 1860 on an antislavery platform.

SAMPLE QUESTIONS

26) **What did the Missouri Compromise accomplish?**

   A.   It admitted Missouri as a free state.

   B.   It admitted California as a free state.

   C.   It allowed slavery in New Mexico and Utah to be decided by popular sovereignty.

   D.   It banned slavery north of the thirty-sixth parallel.

Answers:

   A.   Incorrect. The Missouri Compromise allowed slavery in Missouri.

   B.   Incorrect. California was not admitted as a state until 1850.

   C.   Incorrect. This was a feature of the Compromise of 1850.

   D.   **Correct.** The Missouri Compromise prohibited slavery north of the thirty-sixth parallel in new US territories, permitting slavery in Missouri.

27) **Which of the following effectively repealed the Missouri Compromise?**

    A.   the Dred Scott decision

    B.   the Compromise of 1850

    C.   the Kansas-Nebraska Act

    D.   the Fugitive Slave Act

Answers:

    A.   Incorrect. The Dred Scott decision upheld the Fugitive Slave Act.

    B.   Incorrect. The Compromise of 1850 only permitted the possibility of slavery in a small section of land north of the thirty-sixth parallel in the far West (parts of Utah).

    C.   **Correct.** The Kansas-Nebraska Act allowed slavery north of the thirty-sixth parallel throughout the plains and the Western territories which the Missouri Compromise had previously forbidden.

    D.   Incorrect. The Fugitive Slave Act did not determine where slavery was legal.

CIVIL WAR

Following Lincoln's election, South Carolina immediately seceded, followed by Mississippi, Alabama, Florida, Louisiana, Georgia, and Texas. They formed the Confederate States of America, or the **Confederacy**, on February 1, 1861, under the leadership of **Jefferson Davis**, a senator from Mississippi.

Shortly after the South's secession, Confederate forces attacked Union troops in Sumter, South Carolina; the **Battle of Fort Sumter** sparked the Civil War. As a result, Virginia, Tennessee, North Carolina, and Arkansas seceded and joined the Confederacy. West Virginia was formed when the western part of Virginia refused to join the Confederacy.

Both sides believed the conflict would be short-lived; however, after the First Battle of Bull Run when the Union failed to route the Confederacy, it became clear that the war would not end quickly. Realizing how difficult it would be to defeat the Confederacy, the Union developed the **Anaconda Plan**, a plan to "squeeze" the Confederacy, including a naval blockade and taking control of the Mississippi River. Since the South depended on international trade in cotton for much of its income, a naval blockade would have serious economic ramifications for the Confederacy.

However, the Second Battle of Bull Run was a tactical Confederate victory led by General Robert E. Lee and Stonewall Jackson. The Union army remained intact, but the loss was a heavy blow to morale. The Battle of Antietam was the first battle to be fought on Union soil. Union General George B. McClellan halted General Lee's invasion of Maryland but failed to defeat Confederate forces. Undaunted, on January 1, 1863, President Lincoln decreed the end of slavery in the rebel states with the **Emancipation Proclamation**. The Battle of Gettysburg was a major Union victory.

It was the bloodiest battle in American history up to this point; the Confederate army would not recover.

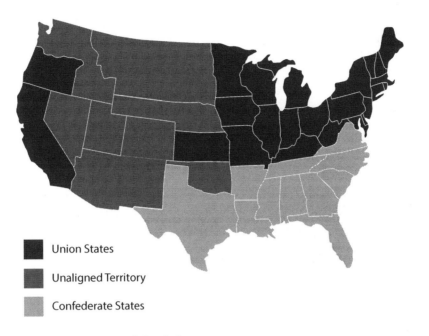

Figure 3.9. Union and Confederacy

Meanwhile, following the Siege of Vicksburg, Mississippi, Union forces led by General Ulysses S. Grant gained control over the Mississippi River, completing the Anaconda Plan. The Battle of Atlanta was the final major battle of the Civil War; victorious, the Union proceeded into the South, and the Confederacy fell. In April 1865, General Lee surrendered to General Grant at Appomattox, Virginia, and the war ended.

SAMPLE QUESTIONS

28) **What assets did the Confederacy have during the Civil War?**

   A. The Confederacy had superior weaponry and production resources.

   B. The Confederacy maintained brisk trade with Europe, enabling it to fund the war.

   C. The Confederacy benefitted from strong military leadership and high morale among the population.

   D. The Confederacy's strong infrastructure allowed it to transport supplies and people efficiently throughout the South.

Answers:

   A. Incorrect. The South's technological resources were inferior to those of the North.

   B. Incorrect. European countries ceased trade with the South, finding alternative sources of cotton in protest of slavery.

C.   **Correct.** The Confederacy had excellent military leaders, and much of the population strongly believed in the right of states to make decisions without federal interference.

D.   Incorrect. The Confederacy had limited infrastructure.

29) **In the Emancipation Proclamation, President Lincoln declared an end to slavery**

A.   in Kentucky and Missouri.

B.   in the Union only.

C.   in slave states that had not seceded from the Union.

D.   in the rebel states.

Answers:

A.   Incorrect. The Emancipation Proclamation applied to rebel states; Missouri and Kentucky did not secede.

B.   Incorrect. Lincoln freed the slaves in the Confederacy with the Emancipation Proclamation, not in the Union.

C.   Incorrect. The Emancipation Proclamation applied to the rebel states.

D.   **Correct.** The Emancipation Proclamation freed the slaves in the Confederacy.

RECONSTRUCTION AND INDUSTRIALIZATION

Reconstruction after the war would bring huge changes in the South and redefine how blacks fit into American society. The South was in economic ruins; many Southerners, especially newly freed slaves and other African Americans, sought better economic opportunities by moving to the North. Congress passed the Civil Rights Act in 1866 recognizing the rights of former slaves as US citizens; it also passed the Reconstruction Acts the next year, enforcing military occupation of the South. These acts laid out the process for readmission to the Union: among other requirements, states had to ratify the Thirteenth, Fourteenth, and Fifteenth Amendments. These made slavery illegal, recognized equal rights, and permitted African American males to vote, respectively.

Still, agriculture and infrastructure were ruined, and many were bitter over Northern occupation and involvement. Even though the South was forced to accept the end of slavery, Southern states created "black codes" which restricted black Americans' rights. African Americans faced ongoing discrimination and violence in the South, including segregation and threats from hate groups.

The end of the Civil War also brought on an increase in **industrialization**. A British phenomenon, industrialization made its way to the United States. Machines replaced hand labor as the main way of manufacturing, exponentially increasing production capacities. Later in the nineteenth century, the US began developing heavy industry.

The **assembly line** developed by Henry Ford enabled **mass production**. Factors that contributed to this boom included the invention of new products (e.g., the automobile, the telephone, and the electric light), improvement of production methods, an abundance of natural resources and infrastructure (railways opened the West further and connected factories and markets to raw materials), and banking (more people wanted to invest in booming businesses, and banks were financing them).

New cities and towns became larger as people started to live and work in urban areas, attracted by employment opportunities. Unfortunately, lack of planning for this phenomenon—**urbanization**—led to inadequate sanitation (which contributed to cholera and typhoid epidemics), pollution, and crime. However, overall, the United States' economy was growing, the middle class was becoming larger, and industry and technology were developing.

SAMPLE QUESTIONS

30) **The Reconstruction Acts**

    A. immediately improved conditions for African Americans in the South.

    B. immediately benefitted the Southern economy.

    C. were widely considered fair in Congress and by Southerners.

    D. imposed Northern military control over the South.

Answers:

    A. Incorrect. Conditions for most freed slaves did not immediately improve; they continued to face widespread violence and discrimination.

    B. Incorrect. With damage to agricultural land and existing infrastructure, the Southern economy and many Southerners suffered; Reconstruction programs did not immediately take effect.

    C. Incorrect. Radical Republicans felt that the Reconstruction Acts did not go far enough in punishing the South; others in Congress felt they were too harsh. Likewise, many in the South felt they were unfair.

    D. Correct. The Reconstruction Acts effectively placed the South under martial law.

31) **Even after the end of slavery, African Americans in the rural South still suffered due to**

    A. sharecropping, which kept them in heavy debt, often to their former "masters."

    B. the Colored Farmers' Alliance, which was organized to limit their efforts to become independent farmers.

    C. the Reconstruction Acts, which specifically punished Southern blacks who did not join the Union army.

    D. labor unions, which advocated for white workers' rights in factories in urban areas and ignored rural issues.

Answers:

- **A.** **Correct.** Sharecropping perpetuated racial inequality in the South.

- B.   Incorrect. The Colored Farmers' Alliance assisted African American farmers.

- C.   Incorrect. The Reconstruction Acts did not include this provision.

- D.   Incorrect. While labor unions championed urban workers, most of whom were white, this was not in direct opposition to efforts to advance African Americans in the South.

World War and Cold War

While the United States became increasingly prosperous and stable, Europe was becoming increasingly unstable. Americans were divided over whether the US should intervene in international matters. This debate became more pronounced with the outbreak of **World War I** in Europe.

Inflammatory events like German submarine warfare (*U-boats*) in the Atlantic Ocean, the sinking of the *Lusitania*, which resulted in many American civilian deaths, the embarrassing Zimmerman Telegram (in which Germany promised to help Mexico in an attack on the US), and growing American nationalism, or pride in and identification with one's country, triggered US intervention in the war. On December 7, 1917, the US declared war. With victory in 1918, the US had proven itself a superior military and industrial power. Interventionist President **Woodrow Wilson** played an important role in negotiating the peace; his Fourteen Points laid out an idealistic international vision, including an international security organization.

However, European powers negotiated and won the harsh **Treaty of Versailles**, which placed the blame for the war entirely on Germany and demanded crippling reparations from it, one contributing factor to **World War II** later in the twentieth century. The League of Nations, a collective security organization, was formed, but a divided US Congress refused to ratify the Treaty, so the US did not join it. Consequently the League was weak and largely ineffective.

After the war ended, the US suffered from a slight recession. It wasn't until 1929 that the stock market crashed, which triggered the **Great Depression**. Millions of investors saw their fortunes disappear and consumer spending and investing continued to drop, which led to large unemployment rates. Approximately half the banks closed, and upward of 15 million people were unemployed.

Franklin Delano Roosevelt was elected to the presidency in 1932. FDR offered Americans a **New Deal**: a plan to bring the country out of the Depression. During the **First Hundred Days** of FDR's administration, he stabilized the economy through a series of emergency acts for the immediate repair of the banking system. FDR did not only address economic issues; a number of acts provided long-term relief to the poor and unemployed. The New Deal especially generated jobs through programs that developed infrastructure and provided construction jobs for the unemployed. The economy truly rebounded during the Second World War.

FDR was increasingly concerned about the rise of fascism in Europe, seeing it as a global threat. Thus the United States provided support to Great Britain before entering the war. FDR spoke publicly about the **Four Freedoms**: freedom of speech, freedom of religion, freedom from want, and freedom from fear.

However after the Japanese attack on **Pearl Harbor** on December 7, 1941, the US entered the war. While directly attacked by Japan, which was allied with the fascist Axis powers of Italy and Germany, the United States focused first on the European theater. On June 6, 1944, or **D-Day**, the US led the invasion of Normandy, invading Europe. After months of fighting, following the deadly and drawn-out Battle of the Bulge, the Allies were able to enter Germany and end the war in Europe.

The United States was then able to focus more effectively on the war in the Pacific. President **Harry Truman** had taken power following FDR's death in 1945. Rather than force a US invasion of Japan, which would have resulted in huge numbers of casualties, he authorized the bombing of Hiroshima and Nagasaki in Japan, the only times that **nuclear weapons** have been used in conflict. The war ended with Japanese surrender on September 2, 1945.

With most of Europe destroyed, the victorious US and the Soviet Union emerged as the two global **superpowers**. Although the Soviet Union and the United States were allies during the war, the relationship between them grew tense as the war ended. When the Soviet Union occupied Eastern European countries, suppressing democracy there, the **Cold War** effectively began.

During the Cold War, the US and the USSR never came into direct conflict; rather, there were alternating periods of tension and relaxed relations, or détente. During the **Cuban Missile Crisis** (1962), Soviet missiles were discovered in Cuba, and military crisis was narrowly averted thanks to the diplomacy of the Soviet leader Nikita Khrushchev and the popular US president John F. Kennedy. The two countries also supported opposing sides in wars throughout the world—the Korean War, the **Vietnam War**, the Soviet-Afghan War, and many more. Finally, the two superpowers both possessed **nuclear weapons**; thankfully, both sides developed a series of agreements placing limitations on those weapons, and they were never used.

The Cold War extended to **space exploration**, also known as the space race. The Soviets launched the first artificial satellite on October 4, 1957, known as Sputnik. The US launched its own satellite called Explorer 1 the following year. While the US created the National Aeronautics and Space Administration (NASA) to further space exploration, on April 1961 the Soviets launched the first person, Yuri Gargarin, into space. However, the American Neil Armstrong was the first person to set foot on the moon during NASA's Apollo 11 mission on July 20, 1969.

The Cold War ended with the collapse of the Soviet Union in 1991; without two superpowers, the world entered a period of globalization (see the section on world history for details).

32) **The US entered World War I largely because of which of the following?**

A. the Zimmerman Telegram

B. the rise of Nazi Germany

C. the assassination of Franz Ferdinand

D. the attack on the *Lusitania*

Answers:

A. **Correct.** The Zimmerman Telegram, a German offer to assist Mexico in attacking the US, forced the United States to enter World War I, following a series of other German provocations.

B. Incorrect. Nazi Germany did not exist until the 1930s.

C. Incorrect. While the assassination of Franz Ferdinand triggered the First World War in Europe, the United States did not enter the conflict until later.

D. Incorrect. The attack on the *Lusitania* angered many Americans but was not sufficient to trigger US entry into the conflict.

33) **During FDR's terms in office, which of the following was created?**

A. Medicare

B. Social Security

C. the Federal Reserve

D. all of the above

Answers:

A. Incorrect. The Medicare Act was passed under the Johnson administration.

B. **Correct.** The Social Security Act was part of the New Deal.

C. Incorrect. The Federal Reserve Act was passed in 1913 following the Panic of 1907.

D. Incorrect. Only answer choice B is correct.

CIVIL RIGHTS

During the 1960s, the US experienced social and political change. The **Civil Rights Movement**, led by activists like the **Rev. Dr. Martin Luther King, Jr.** and **Malcolm X**, fought for African American rights in the South, including the abolition of segregation, and also for better living standards for blacks in northern cities. In Montgomery, Alabama, **Rosa Parks**, an African American woman, was arrested for refusing to give up her seat to a white man on a bus. Buses were segregated at the time, and leaders including Dr. King organized the Montgomery Bus Boycott to challenge segregation; the effort was ultimately successful. Building on their success, civil rights activists led peaceful protests and boycotts to protest segregation at lunch counters, in stores, at public pools, and in other public places.

The movement grew to include voter registration campaigns supported by students and other activists (both black and white) from around the country—the **Freedom Riders**, so-called because they rode buses from around the country to join the movement in the Deep South. Civil rights workers organized the March on Washington in 1963, when Dr. King delivered his famous *I Have a Dream* speech. In 1964, Congress passed the Civil Rights Act, which outlawed segregation.

The Civil Rights Movement extended beyond the Deep South. **Cesar Chavez** founded the **United Farm Workers**, which organized Hispanic migrant farm workers in California and the Southwest who faced racial discrimination, poor treatment, and low pay. The UFW used boycotts and nonviolent tactics similar to those used by civil rights activists in the South. The **American Indian Movement (AIM)** brought attention to injustices and discrimination suffered by Native Americans nationwide. **Feminist** activists fought for fairer treatment of women in the workplace and for women's reproductive rights. Finally, activists in New York and San Francisco began openly fighting for the civil rights of gays and lesbians.

SAMPLE QUESTIONS

34) **Segregation was found unconstitutional by which of the following Supreme Court decisions?**

A.   *Brown v. Board of Education*

B.   *Plessy v. Ferguson*

C.   *Scott v. Sandford*

D.   *Korematsu v. US*

Answers:

A.   **Correct.** *Brown v. Board of Education* found that keeping races separate (in this case, in segregated schools) could not ensure that all people would receive equal treatment, and that segregation was therefore unconstitutional.

B.   Incorrect. *Plessy v. Ferguson* upheld segregation.

C.   Incorrect. *Scott v. Sandford* upheld and strengthened the Fugitive Slave Act, thereby upholding the Kansas-Nebraska Act and effectively abolishing the Missouri Compromise.

D.   Incorrect. *Korematsu v. US* ruled the constitutionality of the Japanese internment camps during World War II.

Go on →

35) **How did Martin Luther King and other activists achieve civil rights for black Americans?**

   A.   through violent uprisings

   B.   using nonviolence

   C.   with the help of the Soviet Union

   D.   by lobbying Congress only

Answers:

   A.   Incorrect. For the most part, civil rights activists took a nonviolent approach in their work.

   B.   Correct. Nonviolence was a defining characteristic of the mainstream Civil Rights Movement.

   C.   Incorrect. The Civil Rights Movement was a domestic phenomenon.

   D.   Incorrect. Civil rights activists did eventually succeed in getting civil rights legislation passed by working with the government; however, the movement was based in grassroots activism and protest.

THE TWENTY-FIRST CENTURY

By the end of the twentieth century, the United States had established itself as the dominant global economic, military, and political power. It had established military bases and a military presence worldwide, in Europe, Asia, the Pacific, and the Middle East. However, its global power did not prevent conflict. After the terrorist attacks on September 11, 2001, the United States began a war in Afghanistan, and later one in Iraq.

Still, the US dominated global trade: American corporations established themselves globally. American culture was widely popular: since the early twentieth century, American pop culture like music, movies, television shows, and fashion was enjoyed by millions of people around the world. Domestically, society became increasingly liberal. In 2008, the country elected the first African American president, **Barack Obama**. Technology like the **Internet** facilitated national and global communication, media, and business; minority groups like the LGBT community engaged in more advocacy; and environmental issues became more visible. The country continues to evolve.

SAMPLE QUESTION

36) **Which of the following is an example of a social liberal policy enacted during the presidency of Barack Obama?**

   A.   the passage of an Equal Rights Amendment to the Constitution

   B.   the legalization of same-sex marriage throughout the United States

   C.   reduction in rates of imprisonment

   D.   a more equitable, progressive income tax

Answers:

A.   Incorrect. The Equal Rights Amendment was never ratified.

B.   Correct. Same-sex marriage became legal in the United States in 2015.

C.   Incorrect. The United States has one of the highest rates of incarceration in the world.

D.   Incorrect. The United States does not have a progressive income tax.

United States Government, Civics, and Democracy

Students should understand and be aware of the purpose of US government and its major principles; the three branches of government; federalism; major speeches and key documents; and the rights and responsibilities of US citizens.

In 1776, colonial leaders including John Adams and Thomas Jefferson began drafting a formal statement of the colonies' intentions for independence from the British government. The Continental Congress adopted the **Declaration of Independence** on the fourth of July of that year, now celebrated as Independence Day in the United States. According to the document, independence from Britain was necessary: it outlined grievances against the British Crown, and it asserted that "all men are created equal; that they are endowed by their Creator with certain unalienable rights; that among these are Life, Liberty and the pursuit of Happiness."

Dominating American political thought since the American Revolution, **republicanism** stresses liberties and rights as central values, opposes corruption, rejects inherited political power, and encourages citizens to be civic minded and independent. It is based on **popular sovereignty**, that is, the concept that the people are the source of political power. These ideas helped to form not only the Declaration of Independence but also the Constitution.

The colonies had broken away from Britain because of what they viewed as an oppressive, overbearing central government. As a result, the first government they created, whose framework was called the **Articles of Confederation**, was an intentionally weak, democratic government. Called a "firm league of friendship," it was designed to create a loose confederation between the colonies (now states) while allowing them to retain much of their individual sovereignty.

As a result, the Articles established a weak government with extremely limited authority: it did not have the power to levy taxes or raise an army. The legislature was intentionally and clearly subordinate to the states. Representatives were selected and paid by state legislatures.

It quickly became clear that this government was too weak to be effective, and by 1787, the new government of the United States was already in crisis. Without the power to levy taxes, the federal government had no way to alleviate its debt burden from the war. In addition, without an organizing authority, states began issuing their own currencies and crafting their own competing trade agreements with foreign nations, halting trade and sending inflation through the roof. Without a national judicial system, there was no mechanism to solve the inevitable economic disputes. Furthermore, there were uprisings in the country.

A convention of the states was called to address problems in the young United States. At the **Constitutional Convention** in 1787, a decision was made to completely throw out the old Articles and write a new governing document from scratch.

The states did not want a central government that was so strong that it would oppress the states or the people, so they decided to prevent the concentration of power by dividing it. **Separation of powers** limited the powers within the federal government, dividing power among three branches: the executive, the legislative, and the judicial. In addition, each branch was given powers that would limit the power of the other branches in a system called **checks and balances**.

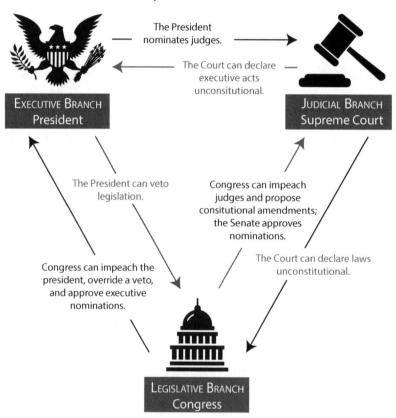

Figure 3.10. Checks and Balances

The executive branch—via the role of president—has the power to veto (reject) laws passed by the legislature. The legislative branch, consisting of Congress, can override the president's veto (with a two-thirds vote) and pass the law anyway. Finally, the judicial branch, consisting of the Supreme Court and other courts, can determine the constitutionality of laws (**judicial review**).

At the writing of the Constitution, the branch of the federal government endowed with the most power was the legislative branch, which makes laws. Simply called **Congress**, this branch is composed of a bicameral legislature (two houses).

While this structure was not originally adopted under the Articles of Confederation, the framers chose it when reorganizing the government, mainly due to a dispute at the convention over the structure of the legislative body—specifically the voting power of each state.

Small states advocated equal representation, with each state having the same number of representatives, each with one vote. However, the more populous states argued for a plan based on **proportional representation**. Each state would be assigned a number of representatives based on its population (enslaved people deprived of their rights would even be counted among the population, benefiting those states with large slave populations). In the end, the **Great Compromise** was reached. There would be two houses: the **House of Representatives** (the lower house) would have proportional representation, and the **Senate** (the upper house) would have equal representation.

This system had two other advantages. The House of Representatives would also be directly elected by the people, and the Senate by the state legislatures. This supported the federal structure of the government: one house would serve the needs of the people directly, and the other would serve the needs of the states. Also, it curbed federal power by fragmenting it and slowing down the legislative process. Today, senators are also directly elected by the people.

Under the Constitution, the federal government is charged with matters that concern the population at large, such as managing federal lands, coining money, and maintaining an army and navy. It also handles conflicts between the states via the federal judiciary and by regulating interstate trade. Matters of regional or local concern are handled by state or local governments. This relationship is best codified in the Tenth Amendment, which states that any powers not explicitly given to the federal government are reserved for the states. The written Constitution can only be amended by a super majority.

State governments are generally modeled after these three branches, with the executive branch headed by the governor, the legislative branch headed by elected representatives, and the judicial branch headed by the state supreme court. **Local governments** have elected officials and generally follow charters that state constitutions have adopted. As they do with the federal government, the people vote for their state and local government representatives.

It took three years for all states to ratify the Constitution, with Rhode Island being the last to ratify on May 29, 1790. Much of the debate was over the lack of guarantees of basic civil rights in the Constitution. As a solution, James Madison in 1789 introduced twelve amendments to the Constitution. Ten of these twelve are known as the Bill of Rights.

The First Amendment protects **freedom of speech**. Congress may not pass laws that prohibit people from exercising freedom of religion, the press, assembly, or the right to petition against the government.

The Second Amendment allows citizens to bear arms.

The Third Amendment stops the government from quartering troops in private homes.

The Fourth Amendment protects citizens from searches and seizures without a warrant.

The Fifth Amendment ensures that citizens cannot be punished or subject to criminal prosecution without due process. Citizens also have the power of eminent domain, which means that private property cannot be seized for public use without proper compensation.

The Sixth Amendment gives citizens a right to a fair and fast trial by jury, the right to know the crimes for which they are charged, and the right to confront witnesses. Citizens also have the right to legal representation and to gather testimonies from witnesses.

The Seventh Amendment allows civil cases to be tried by jury (in the Articles of Confederation, only criminal trials could be tried by jury).

The Eighth Amendment disallows excessive bail or fines; it also prohibits cruel and unusual punishment.

The Ninth Amendment gives all rights not specifically enumerated in the Constitution to the people; it provides that the list of rights is not exhaustive.

The Tenth Amendment provides that all other powers not provided to the federal government in the Constitution belong to the states.

In the **Gettysburg Address**, Abraham Lincoln referred to the Constitution and the Declaration of Independence, asserting that the Civil War was a test of the survival of the Union as established in 1776. Declaring that the people must ensure that the "government of the people, by the people, for the people, shall not perish from the earth," he claimed that the Declaration of Independence was the ultimate expression of the original democratic intentions for the United States. Using the founding document as a basis for his speech, he pointed out that the Civil War was a "new birth of freedom," bringing equality to US citizens.

With citizenship comes responsibility. Today, US citizens maintain their government by **voting** for public officials at the local, state, and national levels. They also must pay **taxes** in order to provide the revenue the government requires to carry out its functions. The federal, state, and local governments all levy taxes of different kinds: income taxes, sales taxes, property taxes, and others. This money supports everything from installing stop signs to maintaining military aircraft.

US citizens are free to join **civic groups** that lobby government for legislation that works in their interest or that carry out public service in their communities. Some of these groups include the ACLU, which defends individual liberties, the NAACP, which works for African American rights, and AARP, which supports the interests of the elderly. Citizens can also join groups that carry out **community**

service such as the Boy Scouts and the Girl Scouts, or they may do such work through their church, mosque, synagogue, or other place of worship. Some students may already be doing community service themselves.

SAMPLE QUESTIONS

37) **Which of the following is NOT one of the amendments in the Bill of Rights?**

    A.   Citizens have the right to bear arms.

    B.   The Senate must have equal representation.

    C.   Citizens have the power of eminent domain.

    D.   The government cannot quarter troops in private homes.

Answers:

    A.   Incorrect. According to the Second Amendment, US citizens have the right to bear arms.

    B.   **Correct.** The Bill of Rights does not determine representation in Congress.

    C.   Incorrect. The Fifth Amendment states that private property cannot be seized for public use without proper compensation.

    D.   Incorrect. The Third Amendment prohibits the government from quartering troops in private homes.

38) **Implied powers are powers that**

    A.   are specifically listed in the Constitution.

    B.   belong to the states.

    C.   are not specifically listed but are needed to perform other listed duties.

    D.   exist because the United States is a sovereign nation.

Answers:

    A.   Incorrect. Powers specifically listed in the Constitution are called expressed powers.

    B.   Incorrect. Powers that belong to the states are called reserved powers.

    C.   **Correct.** Powers that are not listed but are necessary for the functioning of the government are called implied powers. They are made possible by the elastic clause.

    D.   Incorrect. Powers that are derived from US sovereignty are called inherent powers.

Economics

Elementary-level students should understand the basic concepts of supply and demand, scarcity, opportunity cost, how and why people generate wealth, how technology affects the economy, and the government's role in the economy.

The study of economics is the study of the production and consumption of products as well as how people produce and obtain these goods. It explains how people interact with the market; studying economics usually explains the behavior of people or the government.

One of the most important concepts in economics is **supply and demand**. Supply refers to how much the market can actually offer, and demand is how much desire there is for a product or service. The demand is the relationship between price and quantity, which is how much people are willing to pay for the product. The supply simply means how much product producers are willing to supply at a certain price. This relationship between price and how much product is offered to the market is known as the supply relationship.

Figure 3.11. Equilibrium Price

Price is used to show the relationship between supply and demand. When the demand is high for a product, the price generally goes up. When the demand is low, price falls. However, if the price is considered too high by the public, there may be excess supply because people will purchase less. Causes of excess supply include other price changes, including the price of alternative goods, and public preferences. Likewise, there might be excess demand if the price is set too low and many people want the product, but there may not be enough supply. This might happen if there is a government ban on the product, the government imposes a price ceiling, or suppliers decide to not raise prices.

For example, before Halloween, prices of Halloween candy are high because consumers are willing to pay high prices. They want to purchase enough candy to celebrate the holiday at parties and to distribute to trick-or-treaters, even if it is expensive. However, after Halloween, leftover candy is usually on sale. This is because demand for candy is low: the holiday is over and so people do not need it. That leftover candy represents excess supply. In order to get rid of it, suppliers drop prices to entice consumers with a sweet tooth to buy it even though Halloween is past.

When supply and demand are equal, the economy is at equilibrium. However, that is not always the case. When there is insufficient supply to meet demand, the result is **scarcity**. People need to choose which want to satisfy. For example, if there is a low supply of chocolate, chocolate prices will be high. Consequently, a consumer must decide whether to spend more money than usual on chocolate or not to buy any at all.

Every choice has a value. **Opportunity cost** is when a consumer makes a choice at the cost of another choice or the value of an opportunity. For example, imagine that someone must choose between eating chocolate cake or apple pie. If that person chose the chocolate cake, he or she gave up the opportunity to eat the apple pie. The opportunity cost is the apple pie. Decisions made by an individual or the government based on opportunity cost are driven by needs, wants, income, and time.

When making economic choices both parts of the value (costs and benefits) should be considered. The ideal choice will have the greatest benefits at the lowest cost. For example, there are two stores that sell chocolate, but the first store sells it at $35 a box and the second store sells it at $40 a box. However, it takes an hour to drive to the first store and it will cost about $10 in gas to get there and back, while it takes 15 minutes and $2.50 in gas to reach the second store. Economically speaking, it is not worthwhile to drive to the first store. Choosing to pay more for the chocolate at the second store is the cost, and the benefit is the time and cost of gas saved by rejecting the first store.

People use resources in order to create **wealth** and enhance their lives. These resources are either goods or services people provide in exchange for money. People provide labor, creating goods and services available for purchase. Labor refers to people who work in almost any job: on farms, in factories, as computer programmers, etc. The goods and services produced enhance people's lives. For example, not everyone owns a farm or can grow a variety of produce, so consumers depend on farmers around the world to grow various agricultural products in order to obtain them. Those farmers use resources such as water and land in order to generate wealth. Likewise, not everyone can fix a computer, so a consumer can bring his or her computer to an expert to be repaired. The owner of a computer repair service would be compensated with cash, and he or she similarly builds wealth by using that cash to invest in the business, buy property, invest in the stock market, or for other purposes.

Technological innovation is also driven by the economy (and vice versa). For example, more efficient transportation has increased trade and the exchange of wealth. Railroads enabled US businesses to transport raw materials to their production facilities, thereby increasing production of goods. These areas then will need more people to provide labor, helping companies and individuals generate more wealth and providing jobs and salaries to workers, who themselves were thus able to generate more wealth in cash. More recently, computers and the Internet have sped up communication and commerce, opening new ways of doing business.

When population increases, people consume more resources, generating more demand for products to meet their needs. In addition, as companies generate more wealth, they can invest in innovation and even more new technology.

The federal government helps to regulate the economy. **Government regulation** falls into either economic regulation or social regulation. Economic regulation controls prices directly or indirectly. The government works to prevent monopolies: the control of a market for a good or service by one company or group. For example, the government may prohibit utility companies from raising their prices beyond a certain point. Antitrust law is another type of economic regulation. It strengthens market forces to protect consumers from businesses and to eliminate or minimize the need for direct regulation. These laws are intended to ensure fair competition in the US economy.

Social regulation encourages businesses to behave responsibly and prohibits harmful behavior. For example, the US Occupational Safety and Health Administration enforces workplace regulations to protect worker safety, and the Environmental Protection Agency regulates industry by upholding environmental standards for emissions and waste.

Finally, the government collects **taxes** not only to cover its expenses but also to help fuel the economy. Federal taxes pay for costs like federal employee salaries and retirement programs, government programs, and the military. Other government programs that are financed through taxes include veterans' benefits and NASA. Payroll taxes help **finance** the Medicare and Social Security programs which provide assistance for the elderly and those with low incomes. Government spending helps to increase the wealth of businesses and individuals. For example, if the government spends money to build bridges and highways, construction businesses generate more income. If an individual is retired or cannot work for health reasons, Social Security will provide assistance.

SAMPLE QUESTIONS

39) Which of the following terms best describes a situation in which the federal government prevents the only Internet service company in a local community from raising its prices?

A. economic regulation

B. social regulation

C. opportunity cost

D. scarcity

Answers:

A.   **Correct.** In this instance of economic regulation, the government is controlling prices by preventing a monopoly.

B.   Incorrect. Social regulation works to ensure ethical business practices. In this example, the government is only concerned with prices.

C.   Incorrect. Opportunity cost describes making one choice at the expense of another; it does not apply to this situation.

D.   Incorrect. If the supply of a product cannot meet demand for it, the result is scarcity; that concept does not apply in this situation.

40)   **Which of the following cannot shift a demand curve?**

A.   changes in income

B.   price of related goods

C.   production costs

D.   consumer tastes

Answers:

A.   Incorrect. Change in income is a determinant of demand. As buyers are able to buy more, the real price of goods changes based on the income effect.

B.   Incorrect. As the price of related goods increases, overall demand can increase.

C.   **Correct.** Production costs can impact the supply curve, but not the demand curve.

D.   Incorrect. If consumers lose interest in a product or gain a new interest in it, the demand curve can shift accordingly.

Social Studies Skills and Processes

Social studies encourages students to investigate questions about people, their values, and the choices they make. In other words, students engage in **inquiry**: they seek information, knowledge, or the truth. Inquiry-based learning in social studies is a process in which students gather information by identifying relevant questions and uncovering sources in order to interpret information and report their findings.

Teachers can help students develop critical thinking skills by encouraging **questioning**. The more questions students ask, the more carefully they evaluate sources and actively research information that helps them to draw conclusions.

Using research and resource materials is a critical component in social studies processes. There are two main types of sources: primary and secondary. **Primary sources** are original records and have information from a person who experienced the event firsthand. Primary sources include original documents like the US Constitution and Declaration of Independence, journals, speeches, physical artifacts, and some first-person accounts in places such as newspapers or historical documents.

Secondary sources are texts created by people who did not personally experience or witness the event. They are based on primary sources. Examples of secondary sources include books, research papers and analyses, and some reports or features in newspapers and magazines written by journalists and other writers.

Using a variety of sources is essential when conducting research. Analyzing the relationship between primary and secondary sources relating to the same subject matter gives students a deeper understanding of the topic being studied. Understanding the advantages and disadvantages of each source also helps students understand and actively engage in **data interpretation**: assessing whether their sources are valid or appropriate.

Using primary sources permits students to draw **conclusions** based on their own interpretations of those sources, rather than relying on secondary interpretations. Primary sources also allow students to more directly address the topic and usually provide information found nowhere else. However, certain primary sources may not have any objective information or accurate facts. Moreover, these types of sources can be difficult to find and analyze.

Secondary sources enrich study by providing different perspectives and expert conclusions. Furthermore, using reputable sources may be more efficient; they may be more accessible or easier to understand. However, secondary sources may focus on issues beyond the topic under study; they may be outdated; or they may be tainted by the author's bias.

Students must think critically when reading or using any source. They should understand how to distinguish between **fact** and **opinion**. Facts are statements that can be proven, and opinions are statements that reflect someone's view; they cannot be proven. Understanding these differences helps students evaluate sources. If students can distinguish between fact and opinion, then they can determine the validity of the source in question.

When interpreting information, students should be aware of variables involved. A **variable** is anything that can take on a different value. For example, age is considered a variable; so is place of origin. There are many kinds of variables, but they mainly fall into dependent and independent variables. Independent variables are manipulated or controlled by the researcher; they are not changed by any other factors. Dependent variables rely on the independent variable; they may be changed by other factors.

Understanding variables helps students interpret information and draw conclusions. For example, a student writing an essay arguing that westward expansion had a positive effect on the US would need to gather sources such as first-hand accounts of people who moved to the West for opportunities, charts demonstrating population growth, and information about the types of jobs available during those times.

When drawing conclusions, students should demonstrate an ability to address arguments and provide explanations. When constructing their conclusions, they should provide relevant information. They may even offer new perspectives on the research problem. For example, students can find ways to address local community problems. No matter what, they should all demonstrate an understanding of the problem being researched and thoughtful use of the tools available in social studies.

SAMPLE QUESTIONS

41) **Which of the following best describes an independent variable?**

A.   the amount of paint a painter needs to paint a room

B.   the number of errors a student gets on a test

C.   the dosage and timing of an anti-inflammatory drug to test its impact

D.   how much time it will take to drive between Houston and San Antonio

Answers:

A.   Incorrect. The amount of paint required for a room is a dependent variable; it is determined not by the painter but by the room size.

B.   Incorrect. Test scores depend on a number of factors, such as the time the student devoted to studying or the student's confidence level.

C.   **Correct.** The doctor or scientist who carries out the experiment controls the timing and dose.

D.   Incorrect. While it is possible to estimate how long a trip between the two cities will take, factors like traffic and weather can change and will affect timing. Here, length of time is a dependent variable.

42) **Which of the following are examples of primary sources?**

A.   original photographs, first-hand newspaper reports, textbooks, and interviews

B.   memoirs, original photographs, first-hand newspaper reports, and diary entries

C.   speeches, newspaper reports, essays, and reviews

D.   essays, reviews, textbooks, and analytical papers

Answers:

A.   Incorrect. Textbooks are not primary resources.

B.   **Correct.** All of these are examples of primary resources.

C.   Incorrect. While speeches are primary sources, only first-hand newspaper reports count as primary resources. If they are reported, then they are considered secondary resources. Essays and reviews are secondary sources.

D.   Incorrect. These are all examples of secondary resources.

Terms

abolitionism: the ending of slavery

Abraham Lincoln: first Republican president, an abolitionist elected in 1860; his election triggered Southern secession. He led the country through the Civil War, but he was assassinated in 1865 before Reconstruction truly began

absolute location: a location identifiable by specific geographic coordinates

absolute monarchy: unrestricted rule by a king or queen

Adam Smith: economic theorist who espoused capitalism

Algonquin: northeastern Native American civilization in the Great Lakes region

ancient Egyptians: emerged as early as 5000 BCE in the Nile Valley; known for their pyramids, art, use of papyrus as paper, and pictorial writing (hieroglyphs); united under one monarch, or pharaoh

anthropology: the study of humans and their cultures

Apartheid: oppressive social system in South Africa that separated people by race in public places; led to structural inequalities and lowered standard of living for people of color; lasted for most of the twentieth century

arms race: competitive weapons development between the US and the USSR during the 1980s; the US intended to outspend the USSR, thereby weakening it

Articles of Confederation: the original framework of the US government, designed to create a loose confederation between the colonies (now states) while allowing them to retain much of their individual sovereignty; created an intentionally weak, democratic government

assembly line: a labor-intensive method of production developed by Henry Ford in which workers repetitively execute separate key tasks in production, expediting the product's completion

Assyria: Sumerian-based civilization in the Near East; established military dominance and played an important role in regional trade

Atahuallpa: the last independent Inca emperor, defeated by Francisco Pizarro in 1533

Athens: ancient Greek city-state that became a revolutionary democracy controlled by the poor and working classes around 460 BCE; the first known democracy

Augustus Caesar: Julius Caesar's nephew Octavian who gained control of Rome in 27 BCE and became the first Roman emperor

Axis: the alliance of Germany, Italy, and Japan during WWII

Aztecs: militaristic Mesoamerican civilization that dominated Mexico and Central America before European contact

Babylonia: Sumerian-based civilization in Mesopotamia; developed courts and an early codified rule of law—the Code of Hammurabi—"an eye for an eye, a tooth for a tooth"

Barack Obama: first African American president, elected in 2008; ended wars in Afghanistan and Iraq; halted the Great Recession; developed programs to provide healthcare to uninsured Americans

Bastille: Paris prison stormed on July 16, 1789, when the king sent troops to Paris; symbolic of tyranny

Battle of Bunker Hill: took place on June 17, 1775; caused King George III to declare that the colonies were in rebellion

Battle of Fort Sumter: 1861 attack on Union troops in Sumter, South Carolina, by Confederate forces shortly after South Carolina seceded from the Union; this battle sparked the Civil War

Battle of Lexington and Concord: beginning of violent conflict between American rebel militiamen (minutemen) and the British in 1775

Battle of Tours (or Poitiers): victory by Charles Martel in 732 CE that stopped Islamic incursions into Europe

Battle of Yorktown: 1781 defeat of British forces by the Continental Army with support from France, ending the Revolutionary War

Berlin Conference: 1884 conference in Berlin where Africa was divided up into colonies controlled by European powers as part of the *scramble for Africa*, without regard for Africans

Bill of Rights: the first ten amendments to the US Constitution; a set of guarantees of certain rights enjoyed by Americans

Boston Massacre: 1770 event in which British troops fired on a crowd of American protestors

Boston Tea Party: 1773 protest of the Tea Act in which American colonial protestors disguised as Native Americans tossed tea off a ship in Boston Harbor

bourgeoisie (communism and socialism): the class that owns the means of production and profits from the labor of the workers (proletariat); in communism, the proletariat are encouraged to overthrow the bourgeoisie

bourgeoisie (French Revolution): in eighteenth-century France, the emergent middle class growing powerful thanks to early capitalism, but not traditionally nobles or landowners under the feudal system; along with peasants, bore the brunt of taxation

Bubonic (Black) Plague: bacterial infection with global effects that killed a third of Europeans in the fourteenth century; led to broader social change

capitalism: the *laissez-faire* (or free market) theory of economics in which government should not interfere with trade; problems in the market like monopolies would lead to inefficiencies and thus correct themselves

cardinal directions: north, south, east, and west

Cesar Chavez: civil rights activist; led the United Farm Workers, who advocated for Hispanic farm workers who faced racial discrimination, poor treatment, and low pay

Charlemagne: Frankish (French) leader who united much of Western Europe in the Middle Ages following a chaotic period after the fall of the Roman Empire, leading to more organization and strengthening of the feudal system; crowned emperor in 800 CE

Charles Martel: Frankish (French) leader who stopped Islamic incursions into Europe from Iberia (al Andalus)

checks and balances: each branch of government has certain powers that limit the power of the other branches

Cherokee: Southeastern Native American civilization thought to be descended from the Iroquois; emerged in present-day Georgia; forced during the Trail of Tears to leave their land and migrate to Indian Territory (Oklahoma)

Christopher Columbus: explorer who arrived in the Americas while seeking a sea route west from Europe to Asia

Church of England: Protestant church founded by King Henry VIII; after years of conflict, would become the dominant religion in England

Civil Rights Movement: social and political movement for the rights of African Americans and other disenfranchised people in the 1960s

Cold War: period of ongoing tension and conflict between the US and the USSR, the post-WWII global superpowers; remained "cold" because the two countries never engaged in direct military confrontation

Columbian Exchange: describes the broad exchange of people, ideas, organisms, and technology across the Atlantic (encompassing *triangular trade*)

Committees of Correspondence: colonial rebel protest group that distributed anti-British propaganda

communism: Marxist theory that revolution (class war) is needed to achieve a socialist society

Communist Manifesto: nineteenth-century pamphlet written by Marx and Engels about socialism; called for revolution against the capitalist system; inspired the formation of socialist groups worldwide

concentration camps: forced labor and death camps where the Nazis imprisoned and killed Jews, Roma, Slavic people, homosexuals, disabled people, people of color, prisoners of war, communists, and others as part of the Holocaust

conflict: the process of disagreement, usually resolved when one of the parties receives either the entirety or a satisfactory amount of the desired goal

Congress: the branch of the federal government that makes laws (the legislative branch); technically, it has the most power in government

Congress of Vienna: following defeat of Napoleon in 1815, the conference where Prussia, the Austro-Hungarian Empire, Russia, and Britain agreed on balance of power in Europe; the first real international peace conference; set the precedent for European political organization

Constitution: the document that provides the framework for the US government

Constitutional Convention: 1787 meeting of the states to resolve problems arising from limitations on federal power. A decision was made to completely throw out the old Articles and write a new governing document from scratch— the Constitution

cooperation: the process of working together to achieve similar goals; often leads to positive outcomes

Counter-Reformation: attempts at reinforcing Catholic dominance throughout Europe during and after the Reformation in the wake of the Renaissance and related social change

Creek, **Chickasaw**, and **Choctaw**: major Muskogean-speaking southeastern Native American civilizations; descendants of the Mississippi Mound Builders

Crusade: holy war launched by Christian Europeans against Muslims in the Holy Land following decline of Christian Byzantine Empire; several crusades occurred for varying political reasons

cuneiform: a Sumerian development; the earliest known example of writing using characters to form words (not pictographs)

D-Day: June 6, 1944, when the US led the invasion of Normandy, invading Europe during WWII

Declaration of Independence: issued on July 4, 1776, this document, written in great part by Thomas Jefferson and signed by the leaders of the Second Continental Congress, asserted US independence from Britain

Declaration of the Rights of Man and the Citizen: precursor to the revolutionary French constitution assuring liberty and equality; written in the model of Enlightenment thought

demand: how much desire there is for a product or service

demokratia: ancient Greek word meaning "people power"

desert: a climate located in the low latitudes north and south of the savannah; the hottest and driest parts of the earth; receives less than 10 inches of rainfall a year

East African slave trade: Arabs, Asians, and other Africans kidnapped African people and enslaved them throughout the Arab world and South Asia; later, Europeans did the same in African, Asian, and Indian Ocean colonies

economic regulation: indirect or direct price control by the government

Elizabeth Cady Stanton: women's rights activist; founded the National Woman Suffrage Association and led the 1848 Seneca Falls Convention on women's rights

Emancipation Proclamation: January 1, 1863, declaration by President Lincoln abolishing slavery in the US rebel states *encomienda*: Spanish political and economic system in which the king granted European landowners the "right" to hold lands in the Americas and demand labor and tribute from the local inhabitants

English Bill of Rights: established constitutional monarchy in England in 1689

English Civil War: 1642 conflict between the Royalists, who supported the monarchy, and the Parliamentarians, who wanted a republic

Enlightenment: the basis for reinvigorated European culture and political thought beginning around the eighteenth century that would drive its development

Estates-General: the weak representative governing assembly under the French king; included the clergy, the nobility, and the Third Estate (the middle class and the poor peasants); convened in an unsuccessful effort to resolve fiscal crisis prior to the outbreak of the French Revolution

euro: a common currency shared by some European countries

European Union: a forum for European countries to organize and cooperate politically, militarily, and economically; formed after the Cold War to promote European unity

exchange: the process of giving one thing and receiving another (usually with similar value) in return

feudalism: socio-economic organization in medieval Europe; a hierarchy where land and protection were offered in exchange for loyalty

fiefs: territory granted by lords to their vassals in exchange for loyalty under the feudal system

First Continental Congress: meeting of colonial leaders in Philadelphia in 1774, organized in response to the Intolerable Acts; colonial leaders later presented concerns to the king and were rebuffed

First Crusade: invasion of the Holy Land and capture of Jerusalem by European Christians in 1099 in an effort to take the region from Islamic control

Forbidden City: imposing home of the Chinese emperor; constructed under the Ming dynasty

Four Freedoms: in the context of the rise of fascism, FDR defined these as freedom of speech, freedom of religion, freedom from want, and freedom from fear

Francisco Pizzaro: Spanish conquistador who defeated the Inca king Atahuallpa, effectively beginning Spanish rule in the Andean region

Franco-Prussian War: 1870 conflict when Prussia began to assert its military power and took control of mineral-rich Alsace-Lorraine from France; outcome helped fuel Prussian industrial development

Franklin Delano Roosevelt: elected to the presidency in 1932; developed the New Deal, rescuing the United States from the Great Depression, and led the country through WWII

Friedrich Engels: nineteenth-century German economist and philosopher who, with Karl Marx, developed socialism

Genghis Khan: Mongol leader who led expansion of the Mongol Empire in the twelfth and thirteenth centuries

genocide: killing people based on their ethnicity

geographic features: physical features of place like continents, bodies of water, plains, plateaus, mountains, and valleys

George Washington: colonial military leader, general of the Continental Army, first US president; his able military leadership helped the colonies eventually secure independence, and his political leadership helped keep the young country united

glasnost: Soviet reform meaning "openness"

government regulation: government involvement in the economy to effect an economic or social outcome

Great Depression: the global economic collapse that resulted in widespread poverty and unemployment in the United States and the world

Great Fear: terror among French peasants in 1789 over food shortages and a suspected conspiracy against the Third Estate

guillotine: device used by the republican government to execute counter-revolutionaries in post-revolutionary France; symbolic of chaotic period during the Reign of Terror

Hapsburg Dynasty: powerful Catholic European ruling family that controlled Austria and Spain throughout Thirty Years' War and beyond

Hernan Cortés: Spanish explorer who captured Aztec ruler Montezuma II and invaded Mexico

hieroglyphs: ancient Egyptian writing (unlike cuneiform, pictographs, or pictorial writing)

high latitudes: latitudes from 66.5° north and south to the poles

Holocaust: the dispossession, imprisonment, and murder of at least six million Jews, Roma, Slavic people, homosexuals, disabled people, people of color, prisoners of war, communists, and others by the Nazis

Holy Land: term to describe the Levant, location of holy cities and sites important to the three major monotheistic religions (Judaism, Christianity, and Islam); often used in reference to the Crusades

Holy Roman Empire: collection of disparate Germanic lands in Central Europe from 962 CE to 1806

House of Representatives (the lower house of Congress): the body of lawmakers in Congress with proportional representation reflecting the population of each state

human geography: the study of the impact of people on the physical world

humanism: a mode of thought emphasizing human nature, creativity, and an overarching concept of truth; emerged during the European Renaissance

humid continental climate: located in the middle latitudes, the agriculturally productive, true four-season climate

humid subtropical climate: located in the middle latitudes, a warm and moist climate on coastal areas north and south of the tropics that receive warm ocean currents and warm winds year round

Hundred Years' War: ongoing conflict in Europe during the fourteenth and fifteenth century, particularly between England and France; period of political disorganization

imperialism: the possession and exploitation of land overseas

Incas: Andean civilization dominant in western South America before European contact; constructed mountain transportation and agricultural infrastructure

Indian Removal Act: 1830 law that forced Cherokee, Creek, Chickasaw, Choctaw, and others from their lands in the Southeast to Indian Territory (Oklahoma)

indulgences: promises that knights who fought in the Crusades would be forgiven for any sins committed and go to heaven

Industrial Revolution: nineteenth-century economic revolution beginning in Europe marked by mechanization in agriculture and transportation and the emergence of factories

industrialization: the process of manufacturing; the process of an economy transforming from dependence on agricultural to industrial production; replacement of hand labor by machines as the main way of manufacturing, exponentially increasing production capacities

institutions: extensions of core social values created in response to varying individual and group needs; include government, private enterprise, religious institutions, academic institutions, local communities, and the family unit

intermediate directions: the directions between the cardinal directions

Intolerable Acts: 1774 Acts enforced by Britain in response to tensions and violence in the colonies, including closing Boston Harbor and bringing Massachusetts back under direct royal control

iron curtain: a metaphor for the concept of a post-WWII Europe divided between east (with communist governments generally aligned with the USSR) and west (with democratic capitalist governments generally aligned with the US)

Iroquois: northeastern Native American civilization in New York and southern Ontario/Quebec; a confederation of six tribes

Ivan the Great: Russian leader and monarch who defeated the Mongols to return Moscow and Slavic lands to Russian control in 1480; consolidated early Russian Empire

Ivan the Terrible: Russian monarch who expanded Russian territory into Europe; strengthened government and Russian Orthodox Christianity

Joan of Arc: French leader in the 1429 Battle of Orléans; inspired French resistance to English incursions

John Adams: colonial leader, member of the Continental Congress, federalist, second US president, cousin to the radical Samuel Adams; Adams supported a strong federal government and expanded executive power

John Locke: Enlightenment thinker who believed in the social contract: in exchange for protection and to enjoy social benefits, people relinquish some sovereignty to a republican government; influenced the American Revolution

Julius Caesar: a popular Roman military leader who forced the corrupt Senate to give him control and who began transitioning Rome from a republic to what would become an empire; assassinated in 44 BCE

Karl Marx: nineteenth-century German economist and philosopher who, with Friedrich Engels, developed socialism

King Henry VIII: sixteenth-century English monarch; rejected Catholicism; founder of the Church of England

King Louis XIV: seventeenth-century French monarch who consolidated the monarchy and disempowered the nobility; known as *the Sun King*

Kingdom of Ghana: gold-rich kingdom in West Africa; important trading partner of North African Muslims on the Trans-Saharan trade routes

knights: warriors who fought for lords; were usually rewarded with land and often became lords themselves

League of Nations: a largely toothless international organization established after WWI and designed to prevent future outbreaks of international war; the basis for the later United Nations

Leon Trotsky: revolutionary Russian socialist; ally of Lenin; a founder of the Soviet Union and leader of the Russian Revolution

Louisiana Purchase: 1803 purchase of French-controlled territory in North America by the United States, authorized, controversially, by President Jefferson; nearly doubled the size of the country

low latitudes: the region located from the equator to latitudes 23.5° north and south

Machu Picchu: Inca citadel in the Andes

Magna Carta: English document that protected the property and rights of individuals; the basis for today's parliamentary system in that country; early version of a constitution

Malcolm X: civil rights leader who championed better living standards for blacks in northern cities and the empowerment of African American communities

Mali Empire: powerful African Islamic empire based at Timbuktu; rich in salt and gold

Manifest Destiny: the concept that it was the mission and fate of the United States to expand westward and settle the continent

Mansa Musa: emperor of the Mali Empire; made pilgrimage to Mecca in 1324, showing influence of the empire

Marie Antoinette: unpopular French queen during the French Revolution; symbolic of the nobility's disconnection with and abuse of the people; came under suspicion for her Austrian origins; ultimately arrested and assassinated

marine climate: the warm and rainy climate located in the middle latitudes in areas that are near or surrounded by water

maroon communities: settlements of escaped slaves in the Western Hemisphere

Martin Luther: Catholic monk who wrote a letter of protest to the pope in 1517 known as the Ninety-Five Theses

Martin Luther King, Jr.: civil rights leader who fought for equal rights for African Americans; embraced peaceful protest as a means to achieve legislative and social change to end segregation between black and white Americans

Marxism-Leninism: revolutionary concept of socialism developed by Vladimir Lenin and inspiration for the Soviet Union

mass production: large-scale production of consumer products (enabled by the assembly line and factories)

Maya: dominated the Yucatan peninsula around 300 CE; had a complex spiritual belief system; detailed calendar, written language, and pyramidal temples; studied astronomy and mathematics

Mecca: birthplace of Muhammad; holy city of Islam

Mediterranean climate: a climate located in the middle latitudes between latitudes 30° and 40° north and south characterized by wet, mild winters and dry, warm summers

Mehmed the Conqueror: fifteenth-century Ottoman caliph who expanded the empire from Hungary through Mesopotamia

Meiji Restoration: period of technological and military modernization in Japan beginning in 1868; helped Japan become an important military power

mercantilism: economic system in which the colonizing country took raw materials from colonies for its own benefit, amassing wealth through protectionism and increasing exports at the expense of other rising colonial powers

Middle Ages: time period from the fall of Rome to around the tenth century in Europe

middle latitudes: the region located from latitudes 23.5° to 66.5° north and south

migration: patterns of movement from one place to another, with the intention of settling permanently at the new location

Ming Dynasty: reestablished ethnic Han Chinese control in fourteenth-century China following the Yuan period; oversaw expansion of Chinese power; fostered cultural development

Missouri Compromise: 1820 legislation that allowed Missouri to join the union as a slave state but provided that any other states north of the thirty-sixth parallel (36°30') would be free

Mongol Empire: Central Asian empire that dominated most of Eurasia thanks to the Mongols' equestrian and archery skills and lack of a dominant regional power

monopoly: the control of a market for a good or service by one company or group

Montesquieu: French Enlightenment thinker who introduced the idea of the separation of powers, an important element of the American democracy

Montezuma II: Aztec leader when Europeans arrived in Mesoamerica; captured by Spanish explorer Hernan Cortés

Moors: North African Muslims who invaded and settled Iberia (al Andalus)

Mughal Empire: composed of small kingdoms in Indian Subcontinent from the sixteenth century until British rule; influential in Indian Ocean trade routes

Muhammad: Arab leader who introduced Islam and led conquest of Arabian Peninsula

multinational corporations (MNCs): companies based in one country with operations in one or more other countries; the primary driving forces of globalization

Napoleon Bonaparte: nineteenth-century French emperor who conquered much of Europe, changing political balance of power on the continent

Napoleonic Wars: series of early-nineteenth-century wars between Napoleonic France and various European powers; ultimately resulting in new balance of power in Europe

nation-state: sovereign territory ruled by an ethnic majority

nationalism: sentiment of loyalty to one's own cultural or ethnic group above others; premise for independence movements among ethnic groups under imperial control in Europe during Age of Revolutions

natural resources: fresh water, arable land, fuel, livestock, and game

Navajo: a pastoral people that controlled territory in present-day Arizona, New Mexico, and Utah; descendants of the Ancestral Pueblo or Anasazi, who built cliff dwellings

New Deal: plan presented by FDR to rescue the United States from the Great Depression; included emergency acts to save the banking system and long-term relief for the poor and unemployed

Nile Valley: the fertile land on the banks of the Nile River conducive to agriculture and irrigation

Ninety-Five Theses: letter of protest written in 1517 to the pope by the monk Martin Luther; expressed dissatisfaction with the state of the Catholic Church; ideas at the heart of the Protestant Reformation

nuclear weapons: very powerful weapons that can destroy entire cities; possessed by only a few world powers; first developed by the United States and the Soviet Union

opportunity cost: when a consumer makes a choice at the cost of another choice or the value of an opportunity

Otto von Bismarck: Prussian leader who consolidated the linguistically and culturally Germanic, Central European states of Prussia into the German Empire in 1871

Ottoman Empire: Turkic empire that controlled Anatolia, the Balkans, and eventually the Middle East and much of the Mediterranean world; Ottomans captured Istanbul, capital of the Ottoman Empire, in 1453

Pax Romana: a period of stability in the Mediterranean region under the Roman Empire

Pearl Harbor: US military base in Hawaii; on December 7, 1941, Japan attacked Pearl Harbor, causing the US to enter WWII

perestroika: a term meaning "transparency" referring to Soviet reform

pharaoh: ancient Egyptian monarch

physical geography: the study of the natural processes of the earth

Plains tribes: included the Sioux, Cheyenne, Apache, Comanche, and Arapaho who lived in the Great Plains area; nomadic peoples; depended mainly on the buffalo for sustenance

polis: ancient Greek word meaning "city-state" or "community"

political features: towns and cities; county, state, or national borders

pope: the leader of the Catholic Church; in medieval Europe, also a powerful political leader

president: the head of state and head of the executive branch; has the power to appoint federal officials and judges, sign or veto laws (approve or deny them), and make foreign policy; he or she is also the commander-in-chief of the US armed forces

primary socialization: when a child learns the values, actions, and attitudes that are appropriate for members of his or her particular culture

printing press: device enabled the rapid production and distribution of written manuscripts, thereby spreading information more widely

pyramids: Egyptian burial tombs for pharaohs

Quartering Act: a 1765 law that forced American colonists to provide shelter, even in their homes, to British troops stationed in the region

Queen Victoria: eighteenth-century British monarch who oversaw imperial expansion throughout India, Australia, and large parts of Africa

Qur'an: the holy book of Islam

Reconquista: Christian raids of Islamic Spain (al-Andalus); expulsion of Islamic powers from Iberia; and unification of Christian kingdoms in Spain into one Christian kingdom

Reformation: movement for reform of the Catholic Church; resulted in new factions of Christianity in Europe

regions: parts of the world with definable and identifiable characteristics

relative location: where a place is situated in relation to another place or places

Renaissance: revival of learning, art, architecture, and philosophy in Europe, especially influenced by work from ancient Greece and Rome; triggered social change and backlash against the church

reparations: costly financial compensation charged of Germany by the victors of WWI to cover the cost of the war

Rousseau: French Enlightenment thinker who believed in the social contract and the concept of the rule of law, which would bring stability to a republic founded on the social contract; influenced the American and French Revolutions

Russo-Japanese War: 1905 defeat of Russia by Japan that cemented Japan's status as an emerging industrial and military world power; signaled decline of imperial Russia

Samuel Adams: radical colonial American rebel; leader of the Sons and Daughters of Liberty and Committees of Correspondence

savannah: climate located in the low latitudes north and south of the rainforest; dry in the winter and wet in the summer, experiencing an average of 10 to 30 inches of rain

scarcity: insufficient supply to meet demand

Scientific Revolution: time of scientific exploration and discoveries based in Islamic and ancient Greek and Roman scholarship; threatened the power of the Catholic Church

Scramble for Africa: term used to describe rapid nineteenth-century European colonization of Africa; African colonization symbolized power and prestige among European countries

Second Continental Congress: meeting of colonial leaders in Philadelphia in 1775 when colonial leaders agreed on declaring independence and forming the United States of America

Second Industrial Revolution: occurred in the late nineteenth and early twentieth century; based on heavy industry, railroads, and weapons

secondary socialization: occurs when an individual learns the appropriate values, actions, attitudes, and behaviors as a member of a smaller group within a larger society

Senate: the body of lawmakers in Congress with equal representation—two senators are elected to represent each state (the upper house of Congress); governing body of republican ancient Rome as of 509 BCE

separation of powers: limits the powers within the federal government by dividing power among three branches: the executive, the legislative, and the judicial

September 11, 2001: the date that the United States was attacked by terrorists, resulting in thousands of civilian casualties and major land wars in Afghanistan and Iraq

serfs: peasants who remained on fiefs ("tied to the land") under feudalism; farmed for lords and granted small plots of land for personal use; were entitled to the lords' protection but not obligated to fight; not slaves, but not truly free persons

Seven Years' War: first true global conflict (1756–1763); conflict among Europeans over control of Hapsburg territories; conflict between England and France in North America and Asia for colonial power

Shawnee: an Algonquin-speaking people based in the Ohio Valley; Shawnee leader Tecumseh led the Northwest Confederacy against the United States in 1812

Silk Road: term to describe trade routes stretching from Europe to China through Central Asia; spurred global exchange of goods and information

Simón Bolivar: nineteenth-century revolutionary Latin American leader

social regulation: government regulation that encourages businesses to behave responsibly and prohibits harmful behavior

social structures: (as relates to geography) the organization of a society and how social events relate to and affect places, etc.

socialism: philosophy that workers (proletariat) should own the means of production and directly benefit from profits of their labor rather than the bourgeoisie, who could not be trusted to put the interests of the proletariat over profit

socialization: a process whereby individuals learn skills, beliefs, values, and behavior patterns of society and how these can influence their own norms and customs

sociology: the study of groups, institutions, and society

Songhai Empire: west-central African empire; succeeded the Mali Empire; rich in salt

Sons and Daughters of Liberty: colonial rebel protest group that carried out violent acts against tax collectors

Sparta: ancient Greek military city-state

spatial relationships: how one place is located in relation to another place

Stamp Act: controversial 1765 tax on all published documentation in the colonies; the first direct tax on the colonists

steam engine: important machine for Industrial Revolution; powered factories allowing them to be built anywhere

steppes or prairie: a climate located in the middle latitudes far from the ocean, characterized by flatlands and minimal rainfall

suburbanization: the movement of urban dwellers from cities to live in growing suburbs, semi-rural areas at the outskirts of cities

Suleiman the Magnificent: sixteenth-century Ottoman caliph who consolidated Ottoman rule throughout the Mediterranean world

Sumerians: ancient Near Eastern people who emerged around 2500 BCE; developed irrigation, agriculture, education, math, astronomy, religion, art and literature, city-states, governance, and administration

supply: how much of a product the market can actually offer

Susan B. Anthony: women's rights activist and leader in women's suffrage movement; leader at 1848 Seneca Falls Convention

system of alliances: the complicated diplomatic and military alliances among European powers that led to the outbreak and magnitude of WWI

taiga: a cold climate located in the high latitudes south of the tundra; contains the world's largest forest-lands, extreme mineral wealth, and many swamps and marshes

taxes: money paid by the people, organizations, and companies to the government. This money covers government expenses like federal employee salaries and retirement programs, government programs, and the military. It also helps fuel the economy

Tea Act: controversial 1773 tax on colonial tea that triggered the Boston Tea Party

Tenochtitlan: capital of Aztec Empire near modern Mexico City

Third Estate: the middle class (bourgeoisie) and peasants (commoners) of pre-revolutionary France; those who bore the brunt of taxation

Thirty Years' War: European conflict (1618–1648) based on rifts between Protestant and Catholic Christianities and related alliances; outcome reinforced concept of state sovereignty in Europe

Thomas Jefferson: colonial leader, architect of the Declaration of Independence; third US president; Jefferson was antifederalist and disapproved of a strong US Constitution

tithe: percentage of earnings (10 percent) owed as taxes to the nobility by peasants in pre-revolutionary France

Toussaint L'Ouverture: leader of slave rebellion in Haiti, ultimately winning Haitian independence from France in 1791

Trail of Tears: the forced migration of Cherokee and others from their land in the Southeast to Indian Territory (today, Oklahoma) to make way for white settlers following the Indian Removal Act; the term describes the suffering, poor conditions, and death suffered by many during the migration

Treaty of Versailles: the treaty that ended WWI, held Germany accountable for the entirety of the war, and brought economic hardship to the country by forcing it to pay reparations to the other powers

Treaty of Westphalia: ended the Thirty Years' War in 1648; established the concept of state sovereignty and non-interference; considered the foundation of modern international relations

trench warfare: bloody, long-term fighting in fortified trenches on the Western Front during WWI

triangular trade: pattern of trade in the Atlantic world: Europeans purchased or kidnapped Africans in West Africa to be enslaved, taken to the Americas, and traded for raw materials like sugar; these materials were taken to Europe and traded for consumer goods; and these goods were exchanged in Africa for slaves (and sometimes also in the colonies)

Triple Alliance: alliance of Austria-Hungary, Germany, and Italy in the First World War (against Russia, the United Kingdom, and France, the *Triple Entente*)

tropical rainforests: moist forests exhibiting high biodiversity, located mainly in the equatorial lowlands in Central Africa, Southeast Asia, and the Amazon basin

tundra: a cold climate located in the high latitudes north of the taiga; with extremely cold and long winters, the ground is frozen for most of the year and becomes mushy during the short summer

Underground Railroad: a secret network of safe houses and connections to help Southern slaves escape to the North and to Canada

United Nations: an international organization formed after WWII to prevent another world war, to champion human rights, and to uphold international security

urban planning: managing the development and use of cities

urbanization: the development of cities; became a feature of human development at the advent of the nineteenth-century Industrial Revolution, when unskilled jobs in factories attracted rural workers to cities, offering them higher wages than an agricultural lifestyle did

vassals: swore loyalty (fealty) to lords under the feudal system; were rewarded with land; shared yield

vice president: fulfills the duties of the president when he or she is unable; becomes president in the event of the president's death; also serves as president of the Senate

Vikings: Scandinavian seafaring civilization that explored the North Atlantic and northern Europe; evidence indicates the Vikings traveled as far as the eastern Mediterranean

Vladimir Lenin: revolutionary Russian socialist; believed in the *dictatorship of the proletariat*, or that socialism could not be maintained democratically; developed Marxism-Leninism; led the Russian Revolution; founder of the Soviet Union

Voltaire: French Enlightenment thinker critical of absolute monarchy, the Catholic Church, and censorship; influenced the French Revolution

War of 1812: conflict between the US, Britain, and the British-allied Northwest Confederacy (led by the Shawnee leader Tecumseh). The US maintained its territorial integrity despite British incursions from Canada; meanwhile, the US gained power in the Northwest (present-day Ohio Valley region), facilitating westward expansion despite resistance from the Shawnee and other tribes allied with the Confederacy

white man's burden: concept that drove nineteenth-century European imperialism; idea that white Europeans were justified in oppressing other peoples to "improve" them as European culture was "superior"

William the Conqueror: Norman leader who invaded England in 1066, bringing more organization and feudal economy

Yuan Dynasty: Mongol dynasty in China; upended local hierarchy, but maintained some traditional administrative and other functions

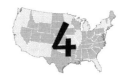

Science

Earth and Space Science

ASTRONOMY

Astronomy is the study of space. Earth is just one of a group of **planets** that orbit the **sun**, which is the star at the center of Earth's **solar system**. The planets in the solar system are Mercury, Venus, Earth, Mars, Jupiter, Saturn, Uranus, and Neptune. Every planet, except Mercury and Venus, has **moons**, or naturally occurring satellites that orbit a planet. The solar system also includes **asteroids** and **comets**, small rocky or icy objects that orbit the sun. Many of these are clustered in the asteroid belt, which is located between the orbits of Mars and Jupiter.

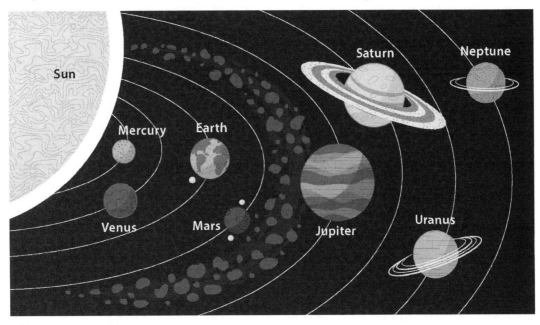

Figure 4.1. Solar System

The solar system is a small part of a bigger star system called a galaxy. (The galaxy that is home to Earth is called the Milky Way.) **Galaxies** consist of gas, dust, and hundreds of billions of **stars**, which are hot balls of plasma and gases, all held together by gravity. The universe has many types of stars, including supergiants, giants, white dwarfs, and neutron stars. Stars form in nebulas, which are large clouds of dust and gas. When very large stars collapse, they create **black holes**, which have a gravitational force so strong that even light cannot escape.

HELPFUL HINT:

The phrase **My Very Educated Mother Just Served Us Noodles** can help students remember the order of the planets: Mercury, Venus, Earth, Mars, Jupiter, Saturn, Uranus, Neptune.

Earth, the moon, and the sun interact in a number of ways that impact the planet. When the positions of the three align, **eclipses** occur. A **lunar eclipse** occurs when Earth lines up between the moon and the sun: the moon moves into the shadow of Earth and appears dark in color. A **solar eclipse** occurs when the moon lines up between Earth and the sun: the moon covers the sun, blocking sunlight.

The cycle of day and night and the seasonal cycle are determined by the earth's motion around the sun. It takes approximately 365 days, or one year, for Earth to revolve around the sun. While Earth is revolving around the sun, it is also rotating on its axis, which takes approximately 24 hours, or one day. As the planet rotates, different areas alternately face toward the sun and away from the sun, creating night and day.

The earth's axis is not directly perpendicular to its orbit, meaning the planet is tilted. The seasons are caused by this tilt. When the Northern Hemisphere is tilted toward the sun, it receives more sunlight and experiences summer. At the same time that the Northern Hemisphere experiences summer, the Southern Hemisphere, which receives less direct sunlight, experiences winter. As the earth revolves, the Northern Hemisphere tilts away from the sun and moves into winter, while the Southern Hemisphere tilts toward the sun and moves into summer.

SAMPLE QUESTION

1) **What term is used when the moon moves between the earth and the sun?**

   A. aurora

   B. lunar eclipse

   C. black hole

   D. solar eclipse

   Answers:

   A. Incorrect. An aurora occurs when particles from the solar wind are trapped in the earth's magnetic field.

B. Incorrect. A lunar eclipse is when the earth moves between the moon and the sun, blocking moonlight.

C. Incorrect. A black hole is a massive star with a gravitational field so strong that even light cannot escape.

D. Correct. When the moon moves between the earth and the sun, a solar eclipse occurs, blocking sunlight from the planet.

GEOLOGY

Geology is the study of the minerals and rocks that make up the earth. A **mineral** is a naturally occurring, solid, inorganic substance with a crystalline structure. There are several properties that help identify a mineral, including color, luster, hardness, and density. Examples of minerals include talc, diamonds, and topaz.

Although a **rock** is also a naturally occurring solid, it can be either organic or inorganic and is composed of one or more minerals. Rocks are classified based on how they were formed. The three types of rocks are igneous, sedimentary, and metamorphic. **Igneous rocks** are the result of tectonic processes that bring **magma**, or melted rock, to the earth's surface; they can form either above or below the surface. **Sedimentary rocks** are formed when rock fragments are compacted as a result of weathering and erosion. Lastly, **metamorphic rocks** form when extreme temperature and pressure change the structure of preexisting rocks.

> **HELPFUL HINT:**
>
> Luster describes how light reflects off the surface of a mineral. Terms to describe luster include dull, metallic, pearly, and waxy.

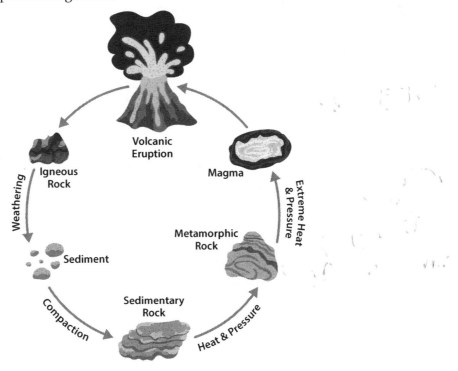

Figure 4.2. The Rock Cycle

The rock cycle describes how rocks form and break down. Typically, the cooling and solidification of magma as it rises to the surface creates igneous rocks. These rocks are then subject to **weathering**, the mechanical and/or chemical processes by which rocks break down. During **erosion** the resulting sediment is deposited in a new location. This **deposition** creates new sedimentary rocks. As new layers are added, rocks and minerals are forced closer to the earth's core where they are subject to heat and pressure, resulting in metamorphic rock. Eventually, they will reach their melting point and return to magma, starting the cycle over again. This process takes place over hundreds of thousands or even millions of years.

The outermost layer of Earth is called the **crust**, a very thin and broken surface layer. Beneath the crust is the **mantle**, a dense layer of rock. The mantle has an upper layer that is cooler and more rigid, and a deep mantle that is hotter and more liquid. Under the mantle is the **core**, which also includes two parts: a liquid outer core and an inner core composed of solid iron. Scientists believe the inner core spins at a rate slightly different from the rest of the planet, which creates Earth's magnetic field.

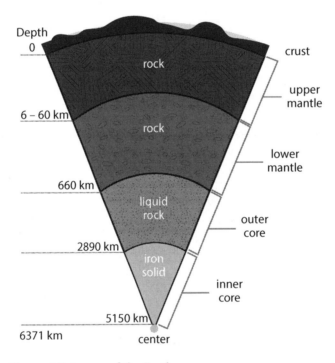

Figure 4.3. Layers of the Earth

The crust and upper layer of the mantle make up the **lithosphere**, the planet's surface layer. Under the lithosphere is a hot, semisolid part of the mantle called the **asthenosphere**. The lithosphere includes **tectonic plates**, which are the broken pieces of Earth's solid outer crust. The tectonic plates float on top of the more liquid asthenosphere that flows very slowly beneath them.

Earth's surface is divided into seven large land masses called **continents**, which are often separated by oceans. Scientists believe that over 200 million years ago the continents were joined together in one giant landmass called Pangaea. Due to **con-**

tinental drift, the slow movement of the tectonic plates, the continents gradually shifted to their current positions, and are still moving.

Many geologic features and events are located along the boundaries where Earth's tectonic plates meet. There are three types of plate boundaries: divergent, convergent, and transform. A **divergent plate boundary** occurs when tectonic plates are moving away from one another and can form new ridges or ocean basins. A **convergent plate boundary** is where two tectonic plates collide and one plate is pushed upward on top of the other forming mountains, or one is pushed downward forming a trench. A **transform plate boundary** is formed when plates move in opposite directions along a boundary.

Earthquakes happen along plate boundaries as the tectonic plates crash into each other or scrape together when they move and cause violent shaking of the ground. **Volcanoes**, which are vents in the earth's crust that allow molten rock to reach the surface, frequently occur along the edges of tectonic plates. However, they can also occur at hotspots located far from plate boundaries. There are three types of volcanoes: composite, shield, and cinder cone. A **composite volcano**, or strato-volcano, is cone-shaped, with steep sides, and is made of layers of solid lava, ash, and rock. A **shield volcano** is more dome-shaped, with gently sloping sides, and is made mostly of fluid lava flows. A **cinder cone volcano** is a small, steep hill formed by ash and debris surrounding a single lava vent and often has a crater at the top.

Paleontology, the study of the history of life on Earth, is sometimes also considered part of geology. Paleontologists study the **rock record**, which retains biological history in the form of **fossils**, the preserved remains and traces of ancient life. Fossils can be used to learn about the evolution of life on the planet, including bacteria, plants, and animals that have gone extinct. Throughout Earth's history, there have been five documented catastrophic events that caused major extinctions. For each mass extinction, there are several theories about the cause but no definitive answers. Theories about what triggered mass extinctions include climate change, ice ages, asteroid and comet impacts, and volcanic activity.

Scientists believe that the earth is about 4.5 billion years old. They have divided Earth's history into stages based on geological or paleontological events that happened during each time period. There are four major time periods: the Precambrian era, the Paleozoic era, the Mesozoic era, and the Cenozoic era. The Precambrian era is the period from the earth's formation until life began to appear. Plants and animals developed during the Paleozic era, but about 95 percent of all life on Earth became extinct at the end of this period. The Mesozoic era was the age of the dinosaurs, but their extinction by the end of this period is believed to have been caused by a large asteroid that hit the earth. The Cenozoic era began after the dinosaurs became extinct and is the current time period. Birds, flowering plants, and mammals—including humans—developed during this period.

SAMPLE QUESTIONS

2) **Which process within the rock cycle creates metamorphic rock?**

   A. compaction

   B. heat and pressure

   C. crystallization

   D. weathering

   Answers:

   A. Incorrect. Compaction is the process through which sediment is compressed to create sedimentary rock.

   B. **Correct.** Heat and pressure change the composition of sedimentary rock to create metamorphic rock.

   C. Incorrect. Crystallization occurs when hot flowing magma develops mineral crystals as it cools and hardens.

   D. Incorrect. Weathering is the process responsible for the wearing away of rocks, minerals, and soils.

3) **Which is NOT a characteristic of a mineral?**

   A. naturally occurring

   B. organic

   C. solids

   D. a crystalline structure

   Answers:

   A. Incorrect. A mineral is a naturally occurring substance.

   B. **Correct.** A mineral is inorganic; only a rock may be composed of organic material.

   C. Incorrect. A mineral is a solid.

   D. Incorrect. A mineral has a crystalline structure.

4) **The magnitude of an earthquake refers to its**

   A. power.

   B. energy release.

   C. destructive ability.

   D. depth.

   Answers:

   A. Incorrect. The magnitude of an earthquake does not directly refer to its power; rather, it refers to the energy released during the earthquake.

   B. **Correct.** The magnitude of an earthquake refers to the energy released during the earthquake.

C.   Incorrect. The magnitude of an earthquake does not directly refer to its destructive ability; however, this is indirectly related due to the impact of the energy released during the earthquake.

D.   Incorrect. The magnitude of an earthquake does not directly refer to its depth, though the depth of an earthquake can affect its magnitude.

HYDROLOGY

Earth's surface includes many bodies of water that together form the **hydrosphere; the study of water on Earth is called hydrology**. The largest of these are the bodies of salt water called **oceans**. There are five oceans: the Arctic, Atlantic, Indian, Pacific, and Southern. Together, the oceans account for 71 percent of Earth's surface and 97 percent of Earth's water.

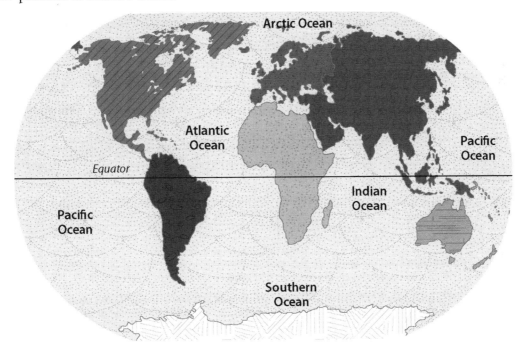

Figure 4.4. Earth's Oceans

Oceans are subject to **tides,** cyclic rising and falling water levels at shorelines, which are the result of the gravitational pull of the moon and sun. **Currents** are movements of the ocean water caused by differences in salt content or temperature and winds. **Waves** carry energy through the water and are caused by wind blowing across the surface of the ocean.

Other bodies of water include **lakes**, usually fresh water, and **seas**, mainly saltwater. Rain that falls on the land flows into **rivers** and **streams**, which are moving bodies of water that flow into lakes, seas, and oceans. When all the rain that falls on a given area of land flows into a single body of water, that land area is called a **watershed** or **drainage basin**. The earth also contains **groundwater**, or water that is stored underground in rock formations called aquifers.

Much of Earth's water is stored as ice. The North and South Poles are usually covered in large sheets of ice called **polar ice**. **Glaciers** are large masses of ice and snow that move. Over long periods of time, they scour Earth's surface, creating features such as lakes and valleys. Large chunks of ice that break off from glaciers are called **icebergs**.

The **water cycle** is the circulation of water throughout the earth's surface, atmosphere, and hydrosphere. Water on the earth's surface **evaporates**, or changes from a liquid to a gas, and becomes water vapor. Water vapor in the air then comes together to form **clouds**. When it cools, this water vapor condenses into a liquid and falls from the sky as **precipitation**, which includes rain, sleet, snow, and hail. Precipitation replenishes groundwater and the water found in features such as lakes and rivers, starting the cycle over again.

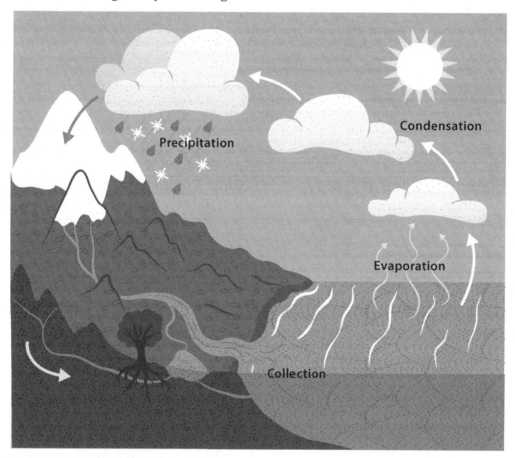

Figure 4.5. The Water Cycle

SAMPLE QUESTION

5) **The rhythmic movements of water caused by the gravitational pull of the moon and sun are called**

A. tides.

B. currents.

C. glaciers.

D. waves.

Answers:

A. **Correct.** Tides, the rise and fall of the ocean level at shorelines, are caused by the moon and sun.

B. Incorrect. Currents are movements within bodies of water caused by differences in temperature.

C. Incorrect. Glaciers are large masses of ice and water.

D. Incorrect. Waves are caused by wind blowing across the surface of the ocean.

METEOROLOGY

Above the surface of Earth is the mass of gases called the **atmosphere**. The atmosphere includes the troposphere, which is closest to Earth, followed by the stratosphere, mesosphere, and thermosphere. The outermost layer of the atmosphere is the exosphere, which extends to 6,200 miles above Earth's surface. Generally, temperature in the atmosphere decreases with altitude. The **ozone layer**, which captures harmful radiation from the sun, is located in the stratosphere.

The humidity, or amount of water vapor in the air, and temperature are two major atmospheric conditions that determine **weather**, the day-to-day changes in atmospheric conditions. The study of weather is known as **meteorology**. A warm front occurs when warm air moves over and replaces a cold air mass, causing the air at the front to feel warmer and more humid. A cold front occurs when cold air moves under and replaces a warm air mass, causing a drop in temperature.

> **HELPFUL HINT:**
>
> Between each layer is a boundary where conditions change. This boundary takes the first part of the name of the lower layer followed by the suffix –*pause*. For example, the boundary between the troposphere and stratosphere is called the tropopause.

As warm air rises, the water vapor in it condenses around tiny pieces of dust, forming a water droplet or ice crystal. A **cloud** is made up of billions of these tiny water droplets or ice crystals. Clouds are defined by their locations in the sky and their shapes. Clouds that appear highest in the sky are called **cirrus clouds**, and are usually thin and wispy and do not produce precipitation. **Stratus clouds** are flat, wispy, white or gray clouds found in the lower level of the sky. **Cumulus clouds** are tall, puffy clouds that are often dark at the bottom and whiter toward the top. Clouds with the prefix *alto-* (altocumulus, altostratus) are located in the middle level of the sky and produce precipitation that does not reach the ground. **Nimbus clouds** such as nimbostratus and cumulonimbus have a lot of water vapor in them and are likely to produce precipitation.

Sometimes, weather turns violent. Tropical cyclones, or **hurricanes**, originate over warm ocean water. Hurricanes have destructive winds of 74 miles per hour or more and create large storm surges, when sea water rises above the normal tide level, that can cause extensive damage along coastlines. Hurricanes, typhoons, and cyclones are all the same type of storm; they just have different names based on where the storm is located. Hurricanes originate in the Atlantic or Eastern Pacific Ocean, typhoons in the Western Pacific Ocean, and cyclones in the Indian Ocean. **Tornadoes** occur when unstable warm and cold air masses collide and a rotation is created by fast-moving winds.

The long-term weather conditions in a geographic location are called **climate**. A **climate zone** is a large area that experiences similar average temperature and precipitation. The three major climate zones, based on temperature, are the polar, temperate, and tropical zones. Each climate zone is divided into subclimates that have unique characteristics. The tropical climate zone (warm temperatures) can be divided into tropical wet, tropical wet and dry, semiarid, and arid. The temperate climate zones (moderate temperatures) include Mediterranean, humid subtropical, marine West Coast, humid continental, and subarctic. The polar climate zones (cold temperatures) include tundra, highlands, nonpermanent ice, and ice cap. Polar climates are cold and experience prolonged, dark winters due to the tilt of Earth's axis.

SAMPLE QUESTIONS

6) Which characteristic generally increases as altitude increases in the troposphere?

   A. temperature

   B. pressure

   C. density

   D. none of the above

   Answers:

   A. Incorrect. Temperature generally decreases with increasing altitude in the troposphere.

   B. Incorrect. Pressure generally decreases with increasing altitude in the troposphere.

   C. Incorrect. Density generally decreases with increasing altitude in the troposphere, as the molecules are spread farther apart with increasing elevation.

   D. Correct. Temperature, pressure, and density all decrease as altitude increases.

7) Which layer of the atmosphere absorbs harmful ultraviolet radiation from the sun?

   A. the mesosphere

   B. the stratosphere

   C. the troposphere

   D. the thermosphere

Answers:

A.   Incorrect. The mesosphere is the layer where the air becomes thin and has some of the coldest temperatures on Earth.

B.   **Correct.** The stratosphere contains a sublayer called the ozone layer, which absorbs harmful ultraviolet radiation from the sun.

C.   Incorrect. The troposphere is the layer closest to Earth's surface and is where most of Earth's weather occurs.

D.   Incorrect. The thermosphere contains molecules that are spread far apart and become super-heated.

Life Science

BIOMOLECULES

Life is made possible by a set of biological molecules that each serve a specific purpose. **Carbohydrates** are the sugars that act as a source of energy for all living things. **Lipids**, or fats, are a way for organisms to store energy, and they also help with cell functioning. **Proteins** serve a wide variety of biological functions, and are composed of building blocks called amino acids. **Enzymes** are a special type of protein that can cause or speed up a specific chemical reaction. Enzymes are important in the digestive system and help the body break down and extract energy from different kinds of foods.

Lastly, **nucleic acids**, such as DNA and RNA, store an organism's genetic code, which is all the information needed for the organism to function. Both DNA and RNA are made of small molecules called nucleotides. **DNA** has four types of nucleotides: adenine, cytosine, guanine, and thymine. **RNA** substitutes uracil for thymine. The nucleotides form pairs: adenine with thymine (or uracil) and cytosine with guanine. The pairs are linked by a backbone that forms a shape like two ropes twisted together called a double helix. In some cells, nucleic acids are stored inside a special area called a **nucleus**. Within the nucleus, DNA is packed into units called **chromosomes**.

SAMPLE QUESTION

8)   **Enzymes are an example of which type of macromolecule?**

A.   lipids
B.   nucleic acids
C.   carbohydrates
D.   proteins

Answers:

A.   Incorrect. An enzyme is not a lipid, which are fats.

B.   Incorrect. An enzyme is not a nucleic acid, which include DNA and RNA.

C.   Incorrect. Enzymes are not carbohydrates, which are sugars.

D.   Correct. An enzyme is a protein that catalyzes a reaction.

STRUCTURE AND FUNCTION OF CELLS

Organisms are living things consisting of at least one **cell**, which is the smallest unit of life that can reproduce on its own. Unicellular organisms, such as amoebas, are made up of only one cell, while multicellular organisms are composed of many cells. There are two basic types of cells: prokaryotic and eukaryotic. **Prokaryotic cells** do not have a nucleus, and some single-celled organisms like bacteria are prokaryotes. **Eukaryotic cells** contain a nucleus where the genetic material is stored and are found in multicellular organisms.

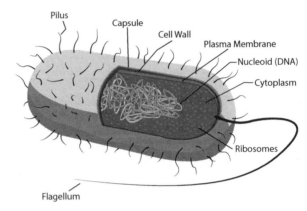

Figure 4.6. Prokaryotic Cell

A cell consists of cytoplasm and genetic material (DNA) inside a **cell membrane**, or protective covering. Separate from the cytoplasm in eukaryotic cells is the **nucleus**, which is the membrane-bound body that holds the cell's DNA. Within the cytoplasm of eukaryotic cells are a number of **organelles** that perform specific functions. These include **mitochondria**, which produce energy; **ribosomes**, which produce proteins; and **vacuoles**, which store water and other molecules.

Plant cells include a number of structures not found in animal cells. These include the **cell wall**, which provides the cell with a hard outer structure, and chloroplasts, where **photosynthesis** occurs. During photosynthesis, plants store energy from sunlight as sugars, which serve as the main source of energy for cell functions.

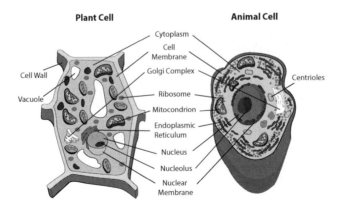

Figure 4.7. Animal Cell Versus Plant Cell

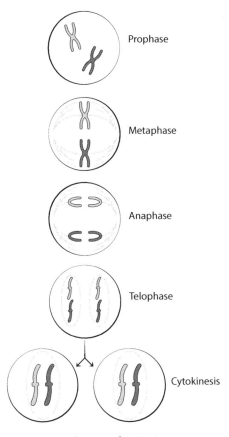

Prophase

Metaphase

Anaphase

Telophase

Cytokinesis

Figure 4.8. Phases of Mitosis

Cell division, or **mitosis**, produces two cells with the same DNA as the original cell. Mitosis has five steps: prophase, metaphase, anaphase, telophase, and interphase. Prophase is when the cell is getting ready to divide by duplicating its DNA. During metaphase, the chromosomes line up in pairs along the central axis of the cell. Anaphase is when the pairs begin to split, with one of the chromosomes moving toward one side of the cell and the other moving toward the opposite side. Once the chromosomes are at opposite sides of the cell, the cell moves into telophase: the cell membrane splits and two new cells are formed. After the division is completed, the two new cells return to a normal resting state, which is called interphase.

Meiosis is the formation of reproductive cells called gametes (eggs and sperm). Meiosis is a process that includes two cell divisions with phases similar to those of mitosis. In the first division, the chromosomes are duplicated and pairs of chromosomes align and exchange genetic material with one another during the prophase. Then metaphase, anaphase, and telophase proceed much like as in mitosis. The interphase between the two division processes is very short and the DNA is not duplicated before the second division cycle. The cell divides again using the same process as described for mitosis; however, the chromosomes are not duplicated. Instead, each chromosome divides in half and each new cell receives only half of the genetic material contained in the original parent cell.

> **HELPFUL HINT:**
>
> Phases of mitosis can be remembered using the phrase **I P**icked **M**y **A**pples **T**oday. The order is interphase, prophase, metaphase, anaphase, telophase.

When an egg is fertilized by the sperm to form a zygote, half of the new organism's chromosomes come from the egg (mother) and half come from the sperm (father). In humans, reproductive cells have twenty-three chromosomes and body cells have forty-six (one set of twenty-three from each parent).

SAMPLE QUESTIONS

9)   The chromosomes of a eukaryotic organism are found in the

A.   chloroplast.

B.   nucleus.

C.   ribosome.

D.   cytoplasm.

Answers:

A.   Incorrect. The structures and molecules needed to carry out photosynthesis are found in the chloroplast.

B.   Correct. The nucleus is the organelle that carries the DNA of eukaryotic organisms.

C.   Incorrect. Proteins are made at ribosomes.

D.   Incorrect. The bacterial chromosome is found in the cytoplasm.

10)   A distinct difference between a plant cell and an animal cell is the presence of

A.   ribosomes.

B.   mitochondria.

C.   a cell wall.

D.   a nucleus.

Answers:

A.   Incorrect. All eukaryotic cells possess ribosomes.

B.   Incorrect. Mitochondria are also found in all eukaryotic cells.

C.   Correct. A plant cell is enveloped by a cell wall, but animal cells do not possess cell walls.

D.   Incorrect. Both plant cells and animal cells carry a nucleus.

11)   Mitosis produces two daughter cells that each have _____ number of chromosomes in the parent cell.

A.   a quarter of the

B.   half of the

C.   the same

D.   double the

Answers:

A.   Incorrect. Mitosis does not quarter the number of chromosomes in the daughter cells.

B.   Incorrect. Meiosis produces daughter cells with half the number of chromosomes in the parent cell.

C. **Correct.** Mitosis creates daughter cells with the same number of chromosomes as the parent cell.

D. Incorrect. Mitosis does not double the number of chromosomes in the daughter cells.

Cellular Metabolism

Cellular metabolism, or cellular respiration, is how cells produce energy. Cells use oxygen to break down the sugar glucose and store the energy in the form of a chemical called adenosine triphosphate (ATP). ATP provides the energy for the cell to grow and reproduce.

Cellular respiration has three parts: glycolysis, the Krebs cycle, and the electron transport chain. Glycolysis is considered the preparatory phase in which one molecule of ATP is used to produce two molecules of pyruvate. It happens in the cell cytoplasm in both eukaryotes and prokaryotes and can happen with or without oxygen. When the process uses oxygen it is called aerobic, but it can also occur when there is no oxygen present. In that case, called anaerobic, one molecule of glucose is converted into two molecules of lactate and two molecules of ATP.

The second part of the respiration process is the Krebs cycle (also called the citric acid cycle), which happens inside the cytoplasm in prokaryotes and in the mitochondria in eukaryotes. The Krebs cycle is a multistep chemical process that converts the products of glycolysis into the energy-carrying molecules NADH and FADH2. The cycle also produces two ATP molecules for every molecule of glucose.

The final step in cellular respiration is the electron transport chain (ETC), which produces thirty to thirty-two molecules of ATP for every molecule of glucose. Electrons from NADH and FADH2 are transferred between a series of membrane-bound complexes, which in turn move hydrogen ions to create a proton gradient

Figure 4.9. Cellular Respiration

across the membrane. This proton gradient powers the synthesis of ATP. In aerobic respiration, oxygen acts as the final electron receptor at the end of the ETC.

Some plant, algae, and bacteria cells can make their own glucose from carbon dioxide and water using energy from sunlight through photosynthesis. Photosynthesis involves two processes. The first is called the light reaction because it depends on light from the sun for energy. In the first part of photosynthesis, a molecule of chlorophyll absorbs a tiny packet of energy from the sun called a photon. The photon causes the chlorophyll to donate one electron and begin a chain reaction that produces ATP and adds hydrogen to the energy-rich molecule NADPH to form NADPH2.

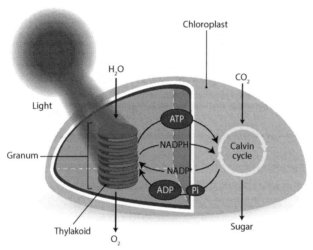

Figure 4.10. Photosynthesis

The second part of photosynthesis is called the Calvin cycle (also referred to as the Calvin-Benson-Bassham (CBB) cycle). The Calvin cycle uses the ATP and NADPH2 produced in the first step to make glucose from carbon dioxide (CO^2) in the air and water from the plant's roots. The glucose is stored, and when the plant needs energy, it is transformed into ATP by the Krebs cycle. This step is sometimes also called the dark or light-independent reaction because it can happen without light.

SAMPLE QUESTIONS

12) **Which of the following is true of cellular respiration?**

   A. Two molecules of ATP are produced during electron transport.

   B. Thirty-four molecules of ATP are produced during glycolysis.

   C. Thirty-four molecules of ATP are produced during the Krebs cycle.

   D. Thirty-eight molecules of ATP are produced during the entire process of cellular respiration.

Answers:

A.   Incorrect. Thirty-four molecules of ATP are usually produced during electron transport.

B.   Incorrect. Two molecules of ATP are usually produced during glycolysis.

C.   Incorrect. Two molecules of ATP are usually produced during the Krebs cycle.

D.   Correct. A total of thirty-eight molecules of ATP are produced: two molecules from glycolysis, two molecules from the Krebs cycle, and thirty-four molecules from electron transport.

13) **Photosynthesis takes place in which organelle of a photosynthetic, eukaryotic organism?**

A.   nucleus

B.   chloroplast

C.   ribosome

D.   endoplasmic reticulum

Answers:

A.   Incorrect. The genetic material of a eukaryotic cell is found in the nucleus.

B.   Correct. The chloroplast houses the photosynthetic machinery.

C.   Incorrect. Ribosomes foster protein synthesis.

D.   Incorrect. Proteins and lipids are synthesized by the endoplasmic reticulum.

GENETICS AND EVOLUTION

When organisms reproduce, **genetic** information is passed to the next generation through deoxyribonucleic acid, or DNA. Within DNA are blocks of nucleotides called **genes**, each of which contains the code needed to produce a specific protein. Genes are responsible for **traits**, or characteristics, in organisms such as eye color, height, and flower color. During sexual **reproduction**, the child receives two copies of each gene, one each from the mother and the father. Some of these genes will be **dominant**, meaning they are expressed, and some will be **recessive**, meaning they are not expressed. Each child will have a mix of its parents' traits.

> **HELPFUL HINT**
>
> Many of the rules of genetics were discovered by Gregor Mendel, a nineteenth-century abbot who used pea plants to show how traits are passed down through generations.

A special chart that shows all the possible genetic combinations from parents with given genotypes is called a **Punnett square**. A Punnett square is a grid with four squares, where the possible genes from one parent are written along the top and the possible genes from the other parent are written down the side. Each square is filled in with the corresponding letters from the top and side of the grid, with capital letters representing dominant genetic traits listed first, followed by lowercase letters representing recessive traits.

When an individual's genetic code is damaged, that organism may have a **genetic disorder**. For example, cystic fibrosis, which causes difficulty with basic bodily functions such as breathing and eating, results from damage to the gene which codes for a protein called CFTR. Down syndrome, which causes developmental delays, occurs when a person has three copies of chromosome twenty-one (meaning they received two copies from one parent as a result of an error in meiosis).

Cross Aa × Aa

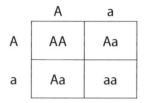

Figure 4.11. Punnett Square

Genes are not static. Over time, **mutations** or changes in the genetic code, occur that can affect an organism's ability to survive. Four common types of genetic mutations are substitution, insertion, deletion, and frameshift. Substitution mutations occur when one nucleotide is exchanged with another (such as switching the bases adenine and cytosine). Insertion mutations happen when extra nucleotide pairs are inserted into the DNA sequence. Removal of nucleotide pairs from the DNA sequence results in deletion mutations. Finally, frameshift mutations occur when the insertion or deletion of nucleotides causes the gene to be misread. Harmful mutations will appear less often in a population or be removed entirely because organisms with those mutations will be less likely to reproduce and thus will not pass on that trait.

CONSIDER THIS

Why might a harmful mutation continue to exist in a population?

Beneficial mutations may help an organism reproduce, and thus that trait will appear more often. Over time, this process, called **natural selection**, results in the **evolution** of new species. The theory of evolution was developed by naturalist Charles Darwin when he observed how finches on the Galapagos Islands had a variety of beak shapes and sizes that corresponded to different food sources, allowing the birds to coexist.

There are four basic types of speciation, based on the extent of isolation among populations: allopatric, peripatric, parapatric, and sympatric. Allopatric speciation happens when a population is divided by geographic features into two isolated populations. When small subpopulations form and become genetically isolated from the main population, peripatric speciation occurs. In parapatric speciation, two species that are partially isolated by geography develop characteristics that make them reproductively incompatible. Sympatric selection is the development of two different species from a single population occupying one geographic location.

14) The process of organisms with advantageous traits surviving more often and producing more offspring than organisms without these advantageous traits describes which basic mechanism of evolution?

    A.   gene flow

    B.   genetic drift

    C.   mutation

    D.   natural selection

Answers:

    A.   Incorrect. Gene flow is the transfer of alleles from one population to another.

    B.   Incorrect. Genetic drift is the increase or decrease in the presence of an allele due to chance.

    C.   Incorrect. A mutation is a change in the genetic code that leads to advantageous traits.

    D.   **Correct.** The mechanism of natural selection is rooted in the idea that there is variation in inherited traits among a population of organisms and that there is differential reproduction as a result.

15) Which of the following is NOT a form of reproductive isolation that could lead to sympatric speciation?

    A.   behavioral isolation

    B.   mechanical isolation

    C.   temporal isolation

    D.   habitat isolation

Answers:

    A.   Incorrect. Behavioral isolation is a mechanism that could lead to sympatric speciation.

    B.   Incorrect. Mechanical isolation is a mechanism that could lead to sympatric speciation.

    C.   Incorrect. Temporal isolation is a mechanism that could lead to sympatric speciation.

    D.   **Correct.** Sympatric speciation occurs to populations within the same habitat.

CLASSIFICATION OF ORGANISMS

Scientists use the characteristics of organisms to sort them into a variety of **classifications** using a system called taxonomy. The highest level of taxonomic classification is the **kingdom**, and each kingdom is then broken down into smaller categories.

The smallest level of classification is a **species**, which includes individuals with similar genetics that are capable of breeding. The entire system is given in table 4.1.

Table 4.1. Taxonomic Classification

- Kingdom
- Phylum
- Class
- Order
- Family
- Genus
- Species

All organisms are sorted into one of five kingdoms: Monera, Protista, Fungi, Plantae, and Animalia. The kingdom **Monera** includes bacteria, which are unicellular organisms that have no nucleus. **Protists** are also unicellular organisms, but they have a nucleus. Both monera and protists reproduce **asexually** by cellular division.

Fungi are a group of unicellular and multicellular organisms that have cell walls and reproduction strategies that differ from those in the other kingdoms. This kingdom includes common organisms like mushrooms and molds. Fungi can reproduce both asexually by cellular division and **sexually** through spores. Many species of fungi are decomposers and attain energy by breaking down organic matter in the environment.

Plants are a kingdom of organisms that use the energy from sunlight to make food (the sugar glucose) through the process of photosynthesis. (Plants are discussed in more detail below).

The kingdom **Animalia** contains multicellular organisms that can move around and must consume other organisms for energy. The kingdom includes several notable classifications that divide organisms based on important features. These include whether the organism has a backbone or spine: **vertebrates** do, while **invertebrates** do not. Animals are also classified based on whether they are **ectotherms**, meaning their source of body heat comes from the environment, or **endotherms**, meaning their body heat is derived from metabolic processes within the body. Ectothermic animals are sometimes known as cold-blooded, and endothermic animals as warm-blooded. Animal classification also looks at animal reproduction: some animals lay eggs, while others give birth to live young.

HELPFUL HINT

The phrase **K**ing **P**hillip **C**ame **O**ver **F**rom **G**reat **S**pain is a way to remember the order of taxonomic classification of organisms: kingdom, phylum, class, order, family, genus, species.

Amphibians are ectothermic vertebrates that have gills when they hatch from eggs but develop lungs as adults. Examples of amphibians include frogs, toads, newts, and salamanders. **Reptiles**, such as snakes, lizards, crocodiles, turtles, and tortoises, are cold-blooded vertebrates that have scales and lay eggs on land. **Birds** are endothermic vertebrate animals that have wings, feathers, scaly legs, beaks, and no teeth, and bear their young in a hard-shelled egg. **Mammals** are endothermic vertebrate animals that have hair, give live birth (with a few exceptions), and produce milk for the nourishment of their young.

All organisms have a **life cycle**, or stages of life. For example, when a frog lays eggs in water, the eggs hatch to become tadpoles with gills. The tadpoles eventually grow legs and develop lungs, and the tail is absorbed into the body. At this point, a tadpole has become an adult frog.

SAMPLE QUESTION

16) Which of the following taxonomic ranks is the most specific, consisting of organisms that can only interbreed with one another?

A. phylum

B. species

C. genus

D. population

Answers:

A. Incorrect. *Phylum* is a broad taxonomic rank that includes many different species of organisms.

B. Correct. *Species* is the principal taxonomic rank.

C. Incorrect. *Genus* is a rank higher than species and includes several groups of species that cannot interbreed.

D. Incorrect. *Population* is the ecological term for a group of individuals of the same species; it is not a taxonomic rank.

HUMAN BODY SYSTEMS

In a multicellular organism, cells are grouped together into **tissues**, and these tissues are grouped into **organs**, which perform specific **functions**. The heart, for example, is the organ that pumps blood throughout the body. Organs are further grouped into **organ systems**, such as the digestive or respiratory systems.

Anatomy is the study of the structure of organisms, and **physiology** is the study of how these structures function. Both disciplines study the systems that allow organisms to perform a number of crucial functions, including the exchange of energy, nutrients, and waste products with the environment. This exchange allows organisms to maintain **homeostasis**, or the stabilization of internal conditions.

HELPFUL HINT

In science, a **system** is a collection of interconnected parts that make up a complex whole with defined boundaries. Systems may be closed, meaning nothing passes in or out of them, or open, meaning they have inputs and outputs.

The human body has a number of systems that perform vital functions, including the digestive, excretory, respiratory, circulatory, skeletal, muscular, immune, nervous, endocrine, and reproductive systems.

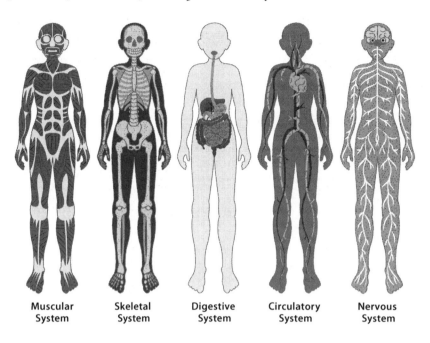

| Muscular System | Skeletal System | Digestive System | Circulatory System | Nervous System |

Figure 4.12. Body Systems

The **digestive system** breaks food down into nutrients for use by the body's cells. Food enters through the **mouth** and moves through the **esophagus** to the **stomach**, where it is physically and chemically broken down. The food particles then move into the **small intestine**, where the majority of nutrients are absorbed. Finally, the remaining particles enter the **large intestine**, which mostly absorbs water, and waste exits through the **rectum** and **anus**. This system also includes other organs, such as the **liver**, **gallbladder**, and **pancreas**, that manufacture substances needed for digestion.

The **excretory system** removes waste products from the body. Its organs include the liver, which breaks down harmful substances, and the **kidneys**, which filter waste from the bloodstream. The excretory system also includes the **bladder** and **urinary tract**,

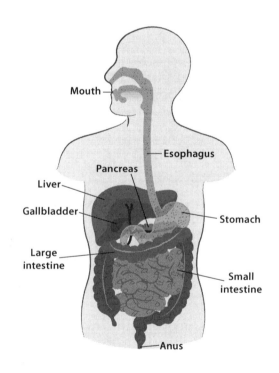

Figure 4.13. Digestive System

which expel the waste filtered by the kidneys; the lungs, which expel the carbon dioxide created by cellular metabolism; and the skin, which secretes salt in the form of perspiration.

The **respiratory system** takes in oxygen (which is needed for cellular functioning) and expels carbon dioxide. Humans take in air primarily through the nose but also through the mouth. This air travels down the **trachea** and **bronchi** into the **lungs**, which are composed of millions of small structures called alveoli that allow for the exchange of gases between the blood and the air.

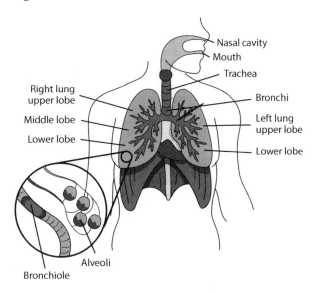

Figure 4.14. Respiratory System

The circulatory system carries oxygen, nutrients, and waste products in the blood to and from all the cells of the body. The **heart** is a four-chambered muscle

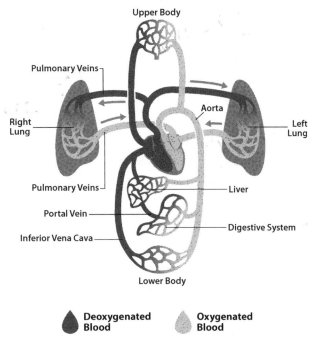

Figure 4.15. Circulatory System

that pumps blood throughout the body. The four chambers are the right atrium, right ventricle, left atrium, and left ventricle. Deoxygenated blood (blood from which all the oxygen has been extracted and used) enters the right atrium and then is sent from the right ventricle through the pulmonary artery to the lungs, where it collects oxygen. The oxygen-rich blood then returns to the left atrium of the heart and is pumped out the left ventricle to the rest of the body.

Blood travels through a system of vessels. **Arteries** branch directly off the heart and carry blood away from it. The largest artery is the aorta, which carries blood from the heart to the rest of the body. **Veins** carry blood back to the heart from other parts of the body. Most veins carry deoxygenated blood, but the pulmonary veins carry oxygenated blood from the lungs back to the heart to then be pumped to the rest of the body. Arteries and veins branch into smaller and smaller vessels until they become **capillaries**, which are the smallest vessels and the site where gas exchange occurs.

The **skeletal system**, which is composed of the body's **bones** and **joints**, provides support for the body and helps with movement. Bones also store some of the body's nutrients and produce specific types of cells. Humans are born with 237 bones. However, many of these bones fuse during childhood, and adults have only 206 bones. Bones can have rough or smooth texture and come in four basic shapes: long, flat, short, and irregular.

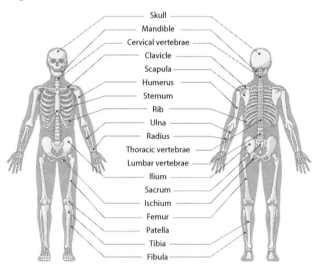

Figure 4.16. Important Bones of the Skeletal System

The **muscular system** allows the body to move and also moves blood and other substances through the body. The human body has three types of muscles. Skeletal muscles are voluntary muscles (meaning they can be controlled) that are attached to bones and move the body. Smooth muscles are involuntary muscles (meaning they cannot be controlled) that create movement in parts of the digestive tract, blood vessels, and reproduction system. Finally, cardiac muscle is the involuntary muscle that contracts the heart, pumping blood throughout the body.

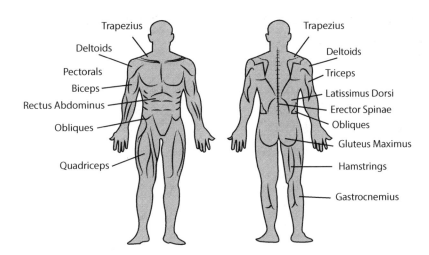

Figure 4.17. Major Muscles of the Body

The **immune system** protects the body from infection by foreign particles and organisms. It includes the **skin** and mucous membranes, which act as physical barriers, and a number of specialized cells that destroy foreign substances in the body. The human body has an adaptive immune system, meaning it can recognize and respond to foreign substances once it has been exposed to them. This is the underlying mechanism behind vaccines.

The immune system is composed of **B cells**, or B lymphocytes, that produce special proteins called **antibodies** that bind to foreign substances, called **antigens**, and neutralize them. **T cells**, or T lymphocytes, remove body cells that have been infected by foreign invaders like bacteria or viruses. **Helper T cells** coordinate production of antibodies by B cells and removal of infected cells by T cells. **Killer T cells** destroy body cells that have been infected by invaders after they are identified and removed by T cells. Finally, **memory cells** remember antigens that have been removed so the immune system can respond more quickly if they enter the body again.

The **nervous system** processes external stimuli and sends signals throughout the body. It is made up of two parts. The central nervous system (CNS) includes the brain and spinal cord and is where information is processed and stored. The brain has three parts: the cerebrum, cerebellum, and medulla. The **cerebrum** is the biggest part of the brain, the wrinkly gray part at the front and top, and controls different functions like thinking, vision, hearing, touch, and smell. The **cerebellum** is located at the back and bottom of the brain and controls motor movements. The **medulla**, or brain stem, is where the brain connects to the spinal cord and controls automatic body functions like breathing and heartbeat.

The peripheral nervous system (PNS) includes small cells called **neurons** that transmit information throughout the body using electrical signals. Neurons are made up of three basic parts: the cell body, dendrites, and axons. The cell body is the main part of the cell where the organelles are located. Dendrites are long arms that extend from the main cell body and communicate with dendrites from other cells through chemical messages passed across a space called a synapse. Axons are extensions from the cell body and transmit messages to the muscles.

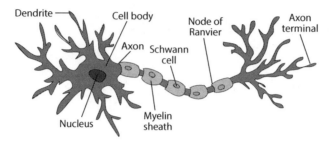

Figure 4.18. Neuron

The **endocrine system** is a collection of organs that produce **hormones**, which are chemicals that regulate bodily processes. These organs include the pituitary gland, hypothalamus, pineal gland, thyroid gland, parathyroid glands, adrenal glands, testes (in males), ovaries (in females), and the placenta (in pregnant females). Together, the hormones produced by these organs regulate a wide variety of bodily functions, including hunger, sleep, mood, reproduction, and temperature. Some organs that are part of other systems can also act as endocrine organs, including the pancreas and liver.

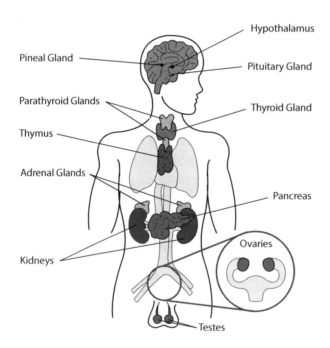

Figure 4.19. Endocrine System

The reproductive system includes the organs necessary for sexual reproduction. In males, sperm is produced in the **testes (also known as testicles)** and carried through a thin tube called the **vas deferens** to the **urethra**, which carries sperm through the **penis** and out of the body. The **prostate** is a muscular gland approximately the size of a walnut that is located between the male bladder and penis and produces a fluid that nourishes and protects sperm.

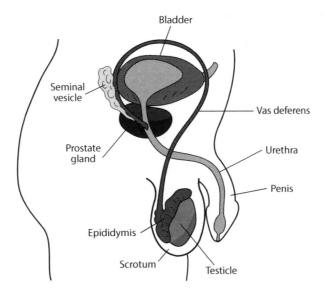

Figure 4.20. Male Reproductive System

In the female reproductive system, eggs are produced in the **ovaries** and released roughly once a month to move through the **fallopian tubes** to the **uterus**. If an egg is fertilized, the new embryo implants in the lining of the **uterus** and develops over the course of about nine months. At the end of **gestation**, the baby leaves the uterus through the **cervix**, and exits the body through the **vagina**. If the egg is not fertilized, the uterus will shed its lining.

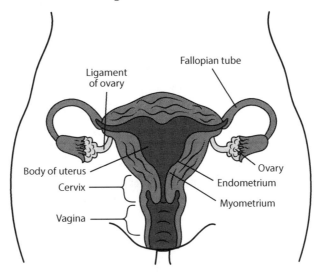

Figure 4.21. Female Reproductive System

SAMPLE QUESTIONS

17) **What is the primary function of the respiratory system?**

    A.   to create sound and speech

    B.   to take oxygen into the body while removing carbon dioxide

    C.   to transport nutrients to the cells and tissue of the body

    D.   to act as a barrier between the body's organs and foreign pathogens

Answers:

A.   Incorrect. The respiratory system helps create sound, but that is not its primary purpose.

B.   Correct. Oxygen intake and carbon dioxide disposal are the primary functions of the respiratory system.

C.   Incorrect. The circulatory system transports nutrients throughout the body.

D.   Incorrect. While parts of the respiratory system filter out foreign pathogens, this is not the system's primary purpose.

18)   **Which muscular organ processes food material into smaller pieces and helps mix it with saliva?**

A.   pharynx

B.   tongue

C.   diaphragm

D.   stomach

Answers:

A.   Incorrect. The pharynx connects the mouth to the esophagus and larynx.

B.   Correct. The tongue is the muscle that helps break apart food, mix it with saliva, and direct it toward the esophagus.

C.   Incorrect. The diaphragm is the muscle that moves the lungs.

D.   Incorrect. The stomach receives the bolus that passes through the esophagus from the mouth.

PLANTS

Plants are multicellular eukaryotic organisms that belong to the kingdom Plantae and produce energy primarily by photosynthesis. Photosynthesis is a process in which a chemical called **chlorophyll** uses energy from sunlight to convert water and carbon dioxide in the air into sugars. The chlorophyll is contained in special organelles called chloroplasts and is responsible for the green color of most plants' leaves.

One way plants are grouped is by how they transport water and nutrients throughout the plant. Some plants are vascular, which means that they have special tissues that transport water and nutrients, while others are nonvascular and distribute water and nutrients by passing them from cell to cell through osmosis or diffusion.

Vascular plants have three basic parts: leaves, a stem, and roots. **Leaves** are the organ where sunlight is captured and used by the chlorophyll to produce food for the plant through photosynthesis. They come in many different shapes and sizes, but are often broad and flat in order to capture as much sunlight as possible. Most leaves are green because of the chlorophyll they contain. The **stem** is the part of the plant that provides structure and supports the weight of the plant. The stem has special tissues that transport nutrients throughout the plant and is where plants store food. The special tissue that plants use to transport water and minerals is called **xylem**. **Phloem** is another special tissue that transports sugar and other nutrients throughout the plant. The **roots** anchor the plant and absorb water and nutrients from the soil.

Vascular plants are grouped as flowering or nonflowering based on how they reproduce. Flowering plants use flowers as their reproductive organs. Flowers are made from special brightly colored leaves called **petals** that together form the **corolla**. The petals are supported by other special leaves called **sepals** that together form the **calyx**. Inside the flower are both male and female reproductive organs. The male reproductive organ is called the **stamen** and has two parts, the **anther** and the **filament**. The male reproductive cells, called **pollen**, are produced in the stamen and stored in the anther. The anther is located at the end of a stalk called the filament.

The female reproductive organ is called the **pistil**, and is usually located in the center of the flower. The pistil has two parts, the **carpel** and the **stigma**. The carpel is the ovary of the flower, where **ova** (eggs), the female reproductive cells, are produced. The stigma is where the pollen (the male reproductive cell) is received and is sometimes extended on a stalk called the **style**. Flowering plants are brightly colored to attract insects that move pollen from the anther to the stigma to fertilize the eggs.

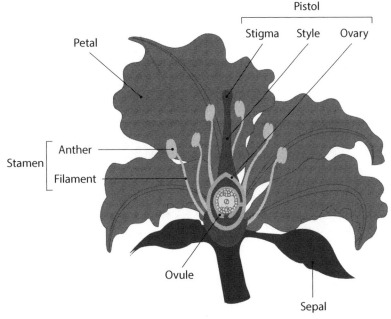

Figure 4.22. Flower with Male and Female Reproductive Structures

After **fertilization** occurs, the flower forms a fruit that contains the seeds that grow from the fertilized eggs. **Seeds** are the plant embryo and come in a variety of shapes, sizes, and colors. The **fruit** provides nutrients and protects the seeds as they grow. It also attracts birds and animals that help distribute the seeds away from the plant. Seeds can also be distributed by air and water. The seeds are protected by a waxy layer called the seed coat.

Once the seed is distributed, it needs air, water, and soil to grow. When seeds begin to grow, it is called **germination**. The seed begins to form small roots and uses nutrients stored in a special organ called the **endosperm** for energy until it can form leaves and generate energy through photosynthesis. Flowering plants are also divided based on the number of embryos, or **cotyledons**, in their seeds. Plants with only one embryo in each seed, like corn or wheat, are called **monocots**. Those with two embryos in each seed, like beans, are called **dicots**. When the seed develops leaves, it is called a sprout or seedling. It continues to grow until it becomes a mature plant and can reproduce again by growing flowers.

Non-flowering plants are divided into two groups: those that use seeds to reproduce and those that use spores to reproduce. Non-flowering plants that use seeds to reproduce are called **gymnosperms**, which literally means *naked seeds*. These plants produce seeds that do not have a covering like the fruits produced by flowering plants. **Conifers** are a major group of gymnosperm plants that use woody cones to protect their seeds. Most conifers are trees like pine, cedar, or redwood. Conifers produce male and female cones. The male cones produce pollen that is distributed by the wind, and if the pollen falls on a female cone, the female cone produces seed that are protected by the cone. The seeds produced by conifers have winged structures on them that allow them to be carried by the wind. Once they reach the ground, the seeds germinate and grow.

Plants that produce spores include ferns and mosses. **Spores** are usually a single cell and the plant produces them in large numbers. Because they are small and lightweight, they are distributed by the wind. Once the spores are distributed and land in a hospitable environment, they begin to divide and produce a new plant.

SAMPLE QUESTIONS

19) **The primary function of the root system is to**

    A.   anchor the plant.

    B.   prevent water loss.

    C.   deliver nutrients to all parts of the plant.

    D.   absorb water and nutrients from the soil.

Answers:

    A.   Incorrect. This is an important function of the root system, but not the primary function.

B. Incorrect. This describes one of the functions of the stomata in the shoot system of the plant.

C. Incorrect. While the root system is an essential contributor to this process, this is primarily the function of the vascular tissue of the plant.

D. **Correct.** The roots primarily exist to continually grow towards water and absorb it and other nutrients.

20) **Which of the following is an evolutionary advantage of the angiosperms, giving them the competitive edge over other groups of plants?**

A. broad leaves that absorb more sunlight for photosynthesis

B. the ability to be perennial, living and growing year after year

C. fruit that nourishes the developing seed

D. flowers that attract pollinators, ensuring more successful plant fertilization

Answers:

A. Incorrect. Broad leaves are found among pteridophytes, gymnosperms, and angiosperms.

B. Incorrect. Angiosperms can be perennial or annual; gymnosperms are almost always perennial.

C. Incorrect. This is not the role of the fruit but rather the role of the endosperm, which is found in all seeds.

D. **Correct.** The attractive nature of the flower encourages animals to pollinate the plant.

ECOLOGY

Ecology is the study of organisms' interactions with each other and the environment. As with the study of organisms, ecology includes a classification hierarchy. Groups of organisms of the same species living in the same geographic area are called **populations**. These organisms compete with each other for resources and mates and display characteristic patterns in growth related to their interactions with the environment. For example, many populations exhibit a **carrying capacity**, which is the highest number of individuals the resources in a given environment can support. Populations that outgrow their carrying capacity are likely to experience increased death rates until the population reaches a stable level again.

> **HELPFUL HINT**
>
> The five levels of ecology, from smallest to largest (organisms, populations, communities, ecosystems, biosphere), can be remembered using the phrase **O**ld **P**eople **C**atch **E**asy **B**reaks.

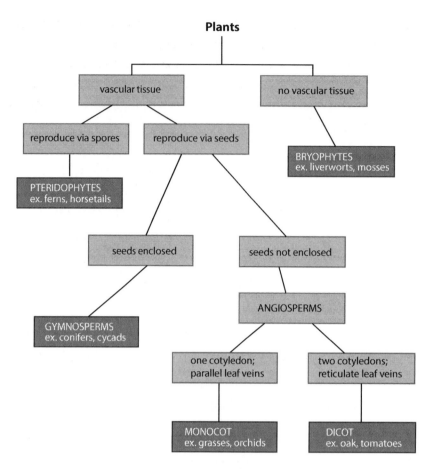

Figure 4.23. Plant Taxonomy

Populations of different species living together in the same geographic region are called **communities**. Within a community many different interactions among species occur. **Predators** consume **prey** for food, and some species are in **competition** for the same limited pool of resources. Two species may also have a **parasitic** relationship in which one organism benefits to the detriment of the other, such as ticks feeding off a dog.

Within a community, a species exists in a **food web** where every species either consumes or is consumed by another (or others). An organism's place in the food web is called its trophic level. The lowest trophic level in the web is occupied by **producers**, which include plants and algae that produce energy directly from the sun. The next level are **primary consumers** (herbivores), which consume plant matter. The next trophic level includes **secondary consumers** (carnivores), which consume herbivores. A food web may also contain another level of **tertiary consumers** (carnivores that consume other carnivores). In a real community, these webs can be extremely complex, with species existing on multiple trophic levels. Communities also include **decomposers**, which are organisms that break down dead matter.

The collection of biotic (living) and abiotic (nonliving) features in a geographic area is called an **ecosystem**. For example, in a forest, the ecosystem consists of all the organisms (animals, plants, fungi, bacteria, etc.) in addition to the soil, groundwater, rocks, and other abiotic features. Ecosystems are constantly developing and changing through a process called **ecological succession.** There are two types of ecological succession: primary and secondary. **Primary succession** describes the development and changes that occur during colonization of a new habitat such as newly exposed rock. **Secondary succession** describes changes to previously colonized habitats that have been disrupted by events such as forest fires.

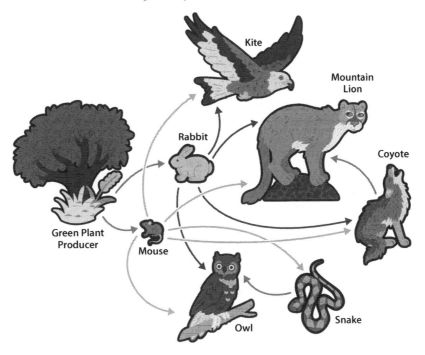

Figure 4.24. Food Web

Biomes are collections of plant and animal communities that exist within specific climates. They are similar to ecosystems, but they do not include abiotic components and can exist within and across continents. For example, the Amazon rainforest is a specific ecosystem, while tropical rainforests in general are considered a biome that includes a set of similar communities across the world. Together, all the living and nonliving parts of the earth are known as the **biosphere**.

Terrestrial biomes are usually defined by distinctive patterns in temperature and rainfall, and aquatic biomes are defined by the type of water and organisms found there. Examples of biomes include:

▶ **desert**: a biome with extreme temperatures and very low rainfall with specialized vegetation and small mammals

▶ **tropical rainforest**: a hot and wet biome with an extremely high diversity of species

▶ **temperate grassland**: a biome with moderate precipitation and distinct seasons with grasses and shrubs dominating

> **HELPFUL HINT**
>
> Deciduous trees lose their leaves in the winter. Evergreen trees keep their leaves year-round.

▸ **temperate broadleaf forest**: a biome with moderate precipitation and temperatures with deciduous trees dominating

▸ **tundra**: a biome with extremely low temperatures and short growing seasons with little or no tree growth

▸ **coral reef**: a marine (saltwater) system with high levels of diversity

▸ **lake**: an enclosed body of fresh water

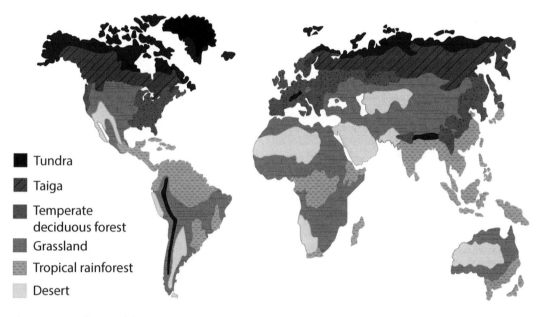

■ Tundra
▨ Taiga
■ Temperate deciduous forest
▦ Grassland
▨ Tropical rainforest
▨ Desert

Figure 4.25. The World's Biomes

If the delicate balance of an ecosystem is disrupted, the system may not function properly. For example, if all the secondary consumers disappear, the population of primary consumers would increase, causing the primary consumers to overeat the producers and eventually starve. Species called **keystone species** are especially important in a particular community, and removing them decreases the overall diversity of the ecosystem.

CONSIDER THIS

What would happen if all of the decomposers disappeared from an ecosystem?

SAMPLE QUESTIONS

21) **Which organism is a primary consumer?**

    A.   mushroom

    B.   corn

    C.   cow

    D.   lion

Answers:

A. Incorrect. Mushrooms are fungi, which are decomposers.

B. Incorrect. Corn is a plant, which is a producer.

C. Correct. Cows eat plants but do not eat other animals; therefore, cows are primary consumers.

D. Incorrect. Lions eat other consumers, which make lions a secondary or tertiary consumer.

22) **Which of the following terrestrial biomes is tropical, dominated by grasses, and has poor soil?**

A. taiga

B. estuary

C. chaparral

D. savanna

Answers:

A. Incorrect. Taiga is dominated by trees and found in extreme northern areas.

B. Incorrect. Estuaries are aquatic biomes located where rivers meet the oceans.

C. Incorrect. The chaparral is a type of shrubland biome.

D. Correct. The savanna is tropical grassland with nutrient-poor soil.

Physical Science

PROPERTIES OF MATTER

The basic unit of all **matter** is the **atom**. Atoms are composed of three subatomic particles: protons, electrons, and neutrons. **Protons** have a positive charge and are found in the nucleus, or center, of the atom. **Neutrons**, which have no charge, are also located in the nucleus. Negatively charged **electrons** orbit the nucleus. If an atom has the same number of protons and electrons, it will have no net charge. Charged atoms are called ions. Atoms that have more protons than electrons are positively charged and are called cations. Negatively charged atoms have more electrons than protons and are called anions.

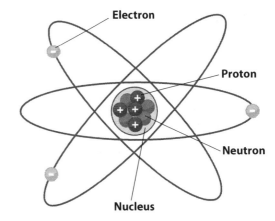

Figure 4.26. Atomic Structure

The mass of an atom is determined by adding the number of protons, neutrons, and electrons. However, electrons have very little mass, so the **atomic mass** is determined by adding just the mass of protons and neutrons.

HELPFUL HINT

The parts of an atom can be remembered using **PEN**: protons, electrons, neutrons.

Elements, such as hydrogen and oxygen, are substances in their simplest form that retain their unique characteristics. Each element has a distinct **atomic number** based on the number of protons in the nucleus. For example, hydrogen has one proton, and oxygen has six. An element is defined by the number of protons it has, but variations of an element that have different numbers of neutrons are called **isotopes**. Some isotopes are unstable and emit radiation as they decay. These are called radioactive isotopes or radioisotopes. Others do not decay over time and are called stable isotopes. A table of chemical elements arranged by atomic number is called **the periodic table**.

Figure 4.27. Periodic Table

When two or more atoms join together they form a **molecule**. For example, O_3 (ozone) contains three oxygen atoms bound together, and H_2O (water) contains two hydrogen atoms and one oxygen. Water is a **compound** because it is made by combining two or more different elements. Atoms can be joined together by different types of bonds by sharing or exchanging valence electrons, which are electrons that can participate in chemical reactions with other elements. In a **covalent bond**, the atoms share one or more valence electrons. In an **ionic bond**, one or more electrons are transferred from one element to another to create two ions with opposite charges that are attracted to each other and bind together.

All matter exists in one of four **states**: solid, liquid, gas, or plasma. **Solid** matter has densely packed molecules and does not change volume or shape. **Liquids** have more loosely packed molecules and can change shape but not volume. **Gas** molecules are widely dispersed and can change both shape and volume. **Plasma** is similar to gas but contains freely moving charged particles (although its overall charge is neutral).

Changes in temperature and pressure can cause matter to change states. Generally, adding energy (in the form of heat) changes a substance to a higher-energy state (e.g., solid to liquid). Transitions from a high- to lower-energy state (e.g., liquid to solid) release energy. Each of these changes has a specific name:

- solid to liquid: melting
- liquid to solid: freezing
- liquid to gas: evaporation
- gas to liquid: condensation
- solid to gas: sublimation
- gas to solid: deposition

Matter changing state is an example of a **physical change**, which is a change that does not alter the chemical composition of a substance. The state of matter changes, but the underlying chemical nature of the substance itself does not change. Other examples of physical changes include cutting, heating, or changing the shape of a substance.

When substances are combined without a chemical reaction to bond them, the resulting substance is called a **mixture**. In a mixture, the components can be unevenly distributed, such as in trail mix or soil. Alternatively, the components can be uniformly distributed, as in salt water. When the distribution is uniform, the mixture is called a **solution**. The substance being dissolved is the **solute**, and the substance it is being dissolved in is the **solvent**. Physical changes can be used to separate mixtures. For example, heating salt water until the water evaporates will separate a salt water solution, leaving the salt behind.

In contrast to a physical change, a **chemical change** occurs when bonds between atoms are made or broken, resulting in a new substance or substances. Chemical changes are also called **chemical reactions**. Chemical reactions are either **exothermic**, meaning energy (heat) is released, or **endothermic**, meaning energy is required for the reaction to take place.

Chemical reactions are represented by written mathematical equations. The **reactants**, the substances that are changing in the chemical reaction, are represented on the left side of the equation. The **products**, the new substances formed during the chemical reaction, are represented on the right side of the equation. The law of conservation of mass says that the amount of each element cannot change during a chemical reaction, so the same amount of each element must be represented on each side of the equation (i.e., the reactants and products must have the same amount

> **HELPFUL HINT**
>
> In both physical and chemical changes, matter is always conserved, meaning it can never be created or destroyed.

of each element). This is called a **balanced equation**. For example, the production of water from two molecules of hydrogen gas and one molecule of oxygen gas can be written as:

$$2H_2 + O_2 \rightarrow 2H_2O$$

The substances on the left side of the equations are called the reactants. The + sign means "reacts with," and the arrow means "produces." The substances on the right side of the equations are called the products. The number in front of the substances tells how many molecules of the substance are used, although the number is only written if it is more than one.

Common reactions include:

▶ **oxidation**: a chemical change in which a substance loses electrons, as when iron rusts when exposed to oxygen, forming iron oxide

▶ **combustion**: a chemical reaction that produces heat, carbon dioxide, and water, usually by burning a fuel

▶ **synthesis**: a chemical reaction in which two substances combine to form a single substance

▶ **decomposition**: a chemical reaction in which a single substance is broken down into two or more substances

▶ **neutralization**: a chemical reaction that occurs when an acid and a base react to produce a salt and water

Matter is classified by its **properties**, or characteristics. These properties include mass, weight, density, solubility, conductivity, and pH. **Mass** refers to the amount of matter in an object. Although the terms are often used interchangeably, mass is distinct from **weight**, which is the force of the gravitational pull on an object. Unlike weight, mass stays the same no matter where an object is located. When two objects of the same mass are on Earth and on the moon, the object on the moon will weigh less because the force of gravity on the moon is less than it is on Earth.

Density is the mass of the object divided by its volume, or the amount of space the object occupies. A denser object contains the same amount of mass in a smaller space than a less dense object. This is why a dense object, such as a bowling ball, feels heavier than a less dense object, like a soccer ball. The density of an object determines whether it will sink or float in a fluid. For example, the bowling ball will sink because it is denser than water, while the soccer ball will float.

Solubility refers to the amount of a solute that will dissolve in a solvent. **Conductivity** describes how well a material conducts heat or electricity. Silver, copper, aluminum, and iron are good conductors, while rubber, glass, and wood are poor conductors. Poor conductors are also called **insulators**.

Finally, the **pH scale** is used to describe the acidity of a substance. **Acids** are compounds that contribute a hydrogen ion (H+) when in solution, and **bases** are compounds that contribute a hydroxide ion (OH–) in solution. The pH scale goes from 1 to 14, with 7 considered neutral. Acids (such as lemon juice) have a pH lower than 7; bases (such as soap) have a pH greater than 7. Water is neutral with a pH of 7.

Figure 4.28. The pH Scale

SAMPLE QUESTIONS

23) **An atom has 5 electrons and 12 protons. What is the total charge of the atom?**

    A.   −17

    B.   −7

    C.   +7

    D.   +17

Answers:

    A.   Incorrect. An atom with a charge of −17e would have seventeen more electrons than protons.

    B.   Incorrect. An atom with a charge of −7e would have seven more electrons than protons.

    C.   **Correct.** This atom has a total charge of −5e + 12e = +7e.

D.   Incorrect. An atom with a charge of +17 would have seventeen more protons than electrons.

24)   **Which type of chemical reaction takes place when kerosene reacts with oxygen to light a lamp?**

A.   oxidation

B.   neutralization

C.   combustion

D.   convection

Answers:

A.   Incorrect. Oxidation is a chemical change in which a substance loses electrons, as when iron is exposed to oxygen and rusts.

B.   Incorrect. Neutralization is a chemical reaction that occurs when an acid and a base react to form a salt and water.

C.   **Correct.** Combustion is a chemical reaction that produces carbon dioxide and water. Burning lamp oil (fuel) is combustion.

D.   Incorrect. Convection is the transfer of heat caused by heat rising and cold sinking.

25)   **The state of matter at which particles are most loosely packed is**

A.   liquid.

B.   gas.

C.   solid.

D.   plasma.

Answers:

A.   Incorrect. Particles in a liquid are more tightly packed than particles in a gas, but there is more space among particles in a liquid than among them in a solid.

B.   **Correct.** Gas is the state of matter in which atomic particles are most loosely packed, and the greatest amount of space exists among atoms.

C.   Incorrect. Particles are most tightly packed in a solid.

D.   Incorrect. The nuclei within a plasma are electrically charged, and electrons move about freely.

FORCE AND MOTION

The motion of objects can be measured using a number of different variables, including speed, displacement, velocity, and acceleration. These variables are either **vector** (magnitude and direction) or **scalar** (magnitude only) measurements.

Speed is a scalar measure that describes how quickly something moves using the following equation:

$$\text{speed} = \frac{\text{distance}}{\text{time}}$$

Displacement is a vector measure of the shortest distance between the initial and final locations of a moving point as calculated using the equation:

$$\text{displacement} = \frac{1}{2}(v + v^0)t$$

where v is the velocity, v^0 is the initial velocity, and t is the elapsed time.

Velocity is a vector quantity that describes the rate at which an object changes position according to the following equation:

$$\text{velocity} = \frac{\text{displacement}}{\text{time}}$$

An object that travels a certain distance and then returns to its starting point has a velocity of zero because its final position did not change. Its speed, however, can be found by dividing the total distance it traveled by the time it took to make the trip.

Acceleration is also a vector quantity and describes how quickly an object changes velocity. It is found using the following equation:

$$\text{acceleration} = \frac{\text{change in velocity}}{\text{time}}$$

A push or pull that causes an object to move or change direction is called a **force**. Forces can arise from a number of different sources. **Gravity** is the attraction of one mass to another mass. For example, the earth's gravitational field pulls objects toward it, and the sun's gravitational field keeps planets in motion around it. Electrically charged objects create a field that causes other charged objects in that field to move. Other forces include **tension**, which is found in ropes pulling or holding up an object; **friction**, which is created by two objects moving against each other; and the **normal force**, which occurs when an object is resting on another object.

> **HELPFUL HINT**
>
> The normal force balances out gravity in resting objects. When a book rests on a table, gravity pulls down on it and the normal force pushes up, canceling each other out and holding the book still.

An object that is at rest or moving with a constant speed has a net force of zero, meaning all the forces acting on it cancel each other out. Such an object is said to be at **equilibrium**. Isaac Newton proposed three **laws of motion** that govern forces:

▶ **Newton's first law**: An object at rest stays at rest and an object in motion stays in motion unless acted on by a force.

▶ **Newton's second law**: Force is equal to the mass of an object multiplied by its acceleration ($F = ma$).

▶ **Newton's third law**: For every action there is an equal and opposite reaction.

The laws of motion have made it possible to build **simple machines**, which take advantage of those laws to make work easier to perform. Simple machines include the inclined plane, wheel and axle, pulley, screw, wedge, and lever.

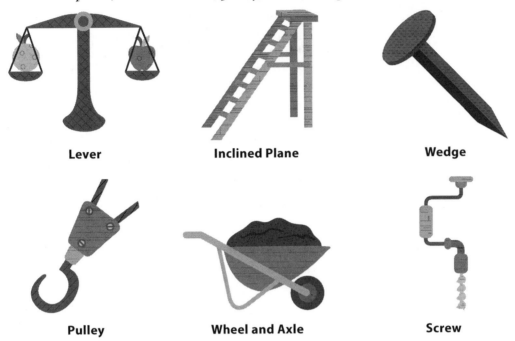

| Lever | Inclined Plane | Wedge |

| Pulley | Wheel and Axle | Screw |

Figure 4.29. Simple Machines

SAMPLE QUESTIONS

26) **The rate at which velocity changes is**

    A.   power.

    B.   force.

    C.   displacement.

    D.   acceleration.

Answers:

    A.   Incorrect. Power is a measure of the rate at which work is done.

    B.   Incorrect. A force is a push or pull that changes an object's velocity.

    C.   Incorrect. Displacement is the distance between an object's start and end positions.

    D.   **Correct.** Acceleration is the rate at which velocity changes.

27) **A box sliding down a ramp experiences all of the following forces EXCEPT**

    A.   tension.

    B.   friction.

    C.   gravitational.

    D.   normal.

Answers:

A. **Correct.** Tension is the force that results from objects being pulled or hung.

B. Incorrect. The box experiences friction as it slides against the ramp.

C. Incorrect. Gravity is the force pulling the box down the ramp.

D. Incorrect. The normal force is the upward force of the ramp on the box.

ENERGY AND MATTER

Energy is the capacity of an object to do work, or, in other words, to cause some sort of movement or change. There are two kinds of energy: kinetic and potential. Objects in motion have **kinetic energy**, and objects that have the potential to be in motion due to their position have **potential energy**. Potential energy is defined in relation to a specific point. For example, a book held ten feet off the ground has more potential energy than a book held five feet off the ground, because it has the potential to fall farther (i.e., to do more work).

Kinetic energy can be turned into potential energy and vice versa. In the example above, dropping one of the books turns its potential energy into kinetic energy. Conversely, picking up a book and placing it on a table turns kinetic energy into potential energy. In another example, a pendulum—an object with mass hanging from a fixed point—

> **HELPFUL HINT**
>
> Like matter, energy is always conserved. It can be changed from one form to another, but never created or destroyed.

is able to swing indefinitely after an initial input of mechanical energy to start the motion by repeatedly converting potential energy to kinetic energy and back again.

There are several types of potential energy. The energy stored in a book placed on a table is **gravitational potential energy**; it is derived from the pull of the earth's gravity on the book. **Electric potential energy** is derived from the interaction between positive and negative charges. Because opposite charges attract each other, and like charges repel, energy can be stored when opposite charges are moved apart or when like charges are pushed together. Similarly, compressing a spring stores **elastic potential energy**, which is then converted to kinetic energy when the compressed spring is released. Energy is also stored in chemical bonds as **chemical potential energy**.

Temperature is the name given to the kinetic energy of all the atoms or molecules in a substance. While it might look like a substance is perfectly still, in fact, its atoms are constantly spinning and vibrating. The more energy the atoms have, the higher the substance's temperature. **Heat** is the movement of energy from one substance to another. Energy will spontaneously move from high energy (high temperature) substances to low energy (low temperature) substances.

This energy can be transferred by radiation, conduction, or convection. **Radiation** does not need a medium; the sun radiates energy to Earth through the vacuum of space. **Conduction** occurs when two substances are in contact with each other. When a pan is placed on a hot stove, the heat energy is conducted from the stove to the pan and then to the food in the pan. **Convection** transfers energy through circular movement of air or liquids. For example, a convection oven transfers heat through the circular movement caused by hot air rising and cold air sinking.

SAMPLE QUESTIONS

28) **Which type of potential energy is stored in a compressed spring?**

    A.   chemical potential energy

    B.   electric potential energy

    C.   gravitational potential energy

    D.   elastic potential energy

Answers:

    A.   Incorrect. Gasoline stored in a car's gas tank is an example of chemical potential energy.

    B.   Incorrect. A battery is an example of electric potential energy.

    C.   Incorrect. A book sitting on a table is an example of gravitational potential energy.

    D.   Correct. A compressed spring is an example of elastic potential energy.

29) **Which process allows the transfer of heat to occur from the contact between two substances?**

    A.   conduction

    B.   convection

    C.   radiation

    D.   sublimation

Answers:

    A.   Correct. Conduction is the transfer of heat from the contact of a solid or liquid to another solid or liquid.

    B.   Incorrect. Convection is the transfer of heat from particle to particle within a fluid or gas during circular motion.

    C.   Incorrect. Radiation occurs as energy transfer in the form of a wave when a very hot object, such as the sun, emits a certain wavelength.

    D.   Incorrect. Sublimation occurs when a solid changes state directly to a gas without reaching a liquid state first.

WAVES

Energy can also be transferred through **waves**, which are repeating pulses of energy. Waves that travel through a medium, like ripples on a pond or compressions in a Slinky, are called **mechanical waves**. Mechanical waves travel faster through denser mediums; for example, sound waves move faster through water than air. Waves that vibrate up and down (like the ripples on the pond) are **transverse waves**, and those that travel through compression (like the Slinky) are **longitudinal waves**.

Energy waves are described by properties such as amplitude, wavelength, frequency, period, speed, and phase. **Amplitude** is a measure of the wave's displacement from its rest position. **Wavelength** is the distance between two points on back-to-back wave cycles. **Frequency** describes the number of times per second the wave cycles. The time between wave crests is the **period** and the speed is how fast the wave is moving. The **phase** of a wave is the position on a wave cycle at a given point in time.

Longitudinal Wave

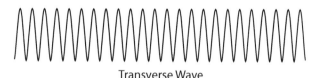

Transverse Wave

Figure 4.30. Types of Waves

Sound is a special type of longitudinal wave created by vibrations. Ears are able to interpret these waves as particular sounds. The frequency, or rate, of the vibration determines the sound's **pitch**. **Loudness** depends on the amplitude, or height, of a sound wave.

The **Doppler effect** is the difference in perceived pitch caused by the motion of the object creating the wave. For example, as an ambulance approaches, the siren's pitch appears to increase to the observer and then to decrease as the ambulance moves away. This occurs because sound waves are compressed as the ambulance approaches an observer and spread out as the ambulance moves away from the observer.

Electromagnetic waves are composed of oscillating electric and magnetic fields and thus do not require a medium to travel through. The electromagnetic spectrum classifies the types of electromagnetic waves based on their frequency. These include radio waves, microwaves, X-rays, and visible light.

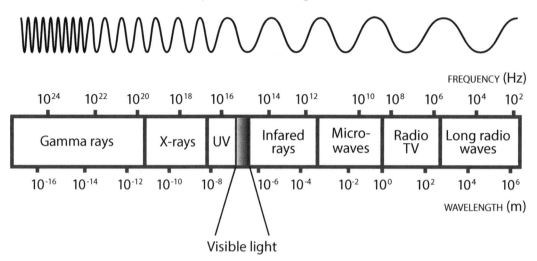

Figure 4.31. The Electromagnetic Spectrum

The study of light is called **optics**. Because visible light is a wave, it displays properties similar to other waves. It will **reflect**, or bounce off surfaces, which can be observed by shining a flashlight on a mirror. Light will also **refract**, or bend, when it travels between substances. This effect can be seen by holding a pencil upright in water and observing the apparent bend in the pencil.

CONSIDER THIS

What are some other ways to demonstrate refraction?

Curved pieces of glass called **lenses** can be used to bend light in a way that affects how an image is perceived. Some microscopes, for example, use specific types of lenses to make objects appear larger. Eyeglasses also use lenses to correct poor vision.

The frequency of a wave in the visible light spectrum is responsible for its **color**, with red/orange colors having a lower frequency than blue/violet colors. White light is a blend of all the frequencies of visible light. Passing white light through a prism will bend each frequency at a slightly different angle, separating the colors and creating a **rainbow**. Sunlight passing through raindrops can undergo this effect, creating rainbows in the sky.

HELPFUL HINT

The order of the colors in the spectrum of visible light can be remembered using **ROY G. BIV**: red, orange, yellow, green, blue, indigo, violet.

SAMPLE QUESTION

30)   **Which measurement describes the distance between crests in a wave?**

   A.   amplitude
   B.   wavelength
   C.   frequency
   D.   period

Answers:

   A.   Incorrect. The amplitude is the distance from the wave's midline to its crest or trough.

   B.   Correct. Wavelength is the length of each cycle of the wave, which can be found by measuring between crests.

   C.   Incorrect. Frequency is the number of cycles a wave passes through during a time period.

   D.   Incorrect. Period is the time it takes for a wave to complete one cycle.

ELECTRICITY AND MAGNETISM

Electric charge is created by a difference in the balance of protons and electrons, which causes an object to have a positive or negative charge. Charged objects create an electric field that spreads outward from the object. Other charged objects in that field will experience a force: objects that have opposite charges will be **attracted** to each other, and objects with the same charge will be **repelled**, or pushed away, from each other.

Because protons cannot leave the nucleus, charge is created by the movement of electrons. Static electricity, or **electrostatic** charge, occurs when a surface has a buildup of charges. For example, when people rub a balloon on their head, the friction causes electrons to move from their hair to the balloon. This creates a negative charge on the balloon and positive charge on the hair; the resulting attraction causes the hair to move toward the balloon.

Electricity is the movement of electrons through a conductor, and an electric circuit is a closed loop through which electricity moves. Circuits include a **voltage** source, which powers the movement of electrons, known as **current**. Sources of voltage include

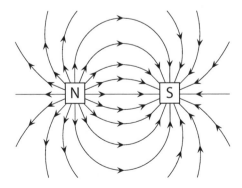

Figure 4.32. Magnetic Field Lines

batteries, **generators**, and wall outlets (which are in turn powered by electric power stations). Other items, such as lights, computers, or microwaves, can then be connected to the circuit to be powered by its electricity.

Magnets are created by the alignment of spinning electrons within a substance. This alignment occurs naturally in some substances, including iron, nickel, and cobalt, all of which can be used to produce **permanent magnets**. The alignment of electrons creates a **magnetic field** which, like an electric or gravitational field, can act on other objects. Magnetic fields have north and south **poles** that have properties similar to electric charges: opposite poles attract, and same poles repel each other. However, unlike electric charge, which must be either positive or negative, a magnetic field always has two poles. If a magnet is cut in half, the result is two magnets that each have a north and south pole. Magnetic fields are depicted visually using **magnetic field lines**, which show the direction of the field at different points.

Electricity and magnetism are closely related. A moving magnet creates an electric field, and a moving charged particle will create a magnetic field. A specific kind of **temporary magnet** known as an electromagnet can be made by coiling a wire around a metal object and running electricity through it. A magnetic field will be created when the wire contains a current but will disappear when the flow of electricity is stopped.

SAMPLE QUESTION

31) Two negative charges are held at a distance of 1 m from each other. When the charges are released, they will

A. remain at rest.

B. move closer together.

C. move farther apart.

D. move together in the same direction.

Answers:

A. Incorrect. The two charges are both negative and so will interact, causing them to move.

B. Incorrect. The charges are both negative, so they will repel, not attract, each other.

C. Correct. The two charges are both negative, so they will repel each other and move apart.

D. Incorrect. The two charges would move in the same direction only if they were being acted on by an outside force.

Science and Technology

MEDICAL TECHNOLOGY

Scientists have made great strides in developing **medical technology** to diagnose, prevent, and treat many medical conditions. Diagnostic equipment, which is used to identify medical conditions, uses technology such as **magnetic resonance imaging (MRI)**, **X-rays**, and **electrocardiography (EKG)**, all of which are used to observe organs and internal structures. Recent developments have also made it possible for doctors to identify some specific genetic disorders by testing a patient's DNA.

Many new or improved treatment options are also available to patients. **Defibrillators**, which reestablish heart rhythms, have become more common and portable. Patients also have reliable options for surgical interventions to treat heart disease, back pain, and damaged joints. Treatments for cancer, including chemotherapy (anticancer drugs) and radiation therapy, continue to improve.

New **medicines** are being discovered to treat diseases in better ways than ever before. These include **pharmaceuticals** that target conditions like heart disease, mental illness, and seizures as well as bacterial and viral infections. Researchers are also developing new **vaccines** to prevent common infections such as the flu and shingles and emerging diseases like the Ebola and Zika viruses.

Technology has also changed humans' relationship with food and nutrition. Processes like pasteurization and refrigeration reduce the risk of food-borne illnesses and allow food to be kept fresh longer. Similarly, water treatment facilities prevent the spread of previously common water-borne bacterial and parasitic infections. Scientists also occasionally revise the **food pyramid**, which is designed to help people understand which types of food, and how much of each, make up a healthy diet.

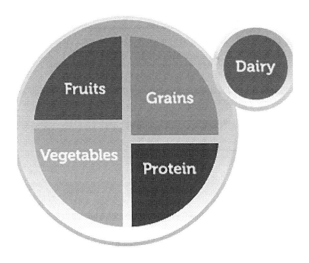

Figure 4.33. USDA Food Recommendations

SAMPLE QUESTION

32) Which medical technology can be used to detect cancerous tumors?

A. MRI

B. defibrillator

C. EKG

D. patient monitor

Answers:

A. **Correct.** MRI stands for magnetic resonance imaging and is used to observe organs and internal structures.

B. Incorrect. A defibrillator is used to reestablish heart rhythms.

C. Incorrect. An EKG, or electrocardiogram, is used to observe the rhythms of the heart.

D. Incorrect. A patient monitor measures and records vital signs.

TECHNOLOGY AND THE ENVIRONMENT

Fossil fuels, such as oil, natural gas, and coal, are nonrenewable resources, meaning that Earth contains a finite amount of those substances. These carbon-based fuels were produced over millions of years by the decomposition and compression of organisms that lived long ago. When burned, fossil fuels emit pollutants that damage the environment. Some of these pollutants include **greenhouse gases** such as carbon dioxide and methane, which, when emitted into the atmosphere, trap heat and contribute to **global warming**.

As **nonrenewable resources** become depleted, scientists are making advancements in using **renewable resources** as replacements. Such possible sources of energy include nuclear energy, hydropower, **wind energy**, solar energy, **biomass**, and geothermal power. These all have less of an impact on the environment than fossil fuels, but many need to be more thoroughly researched and developed before they can supply the energy the world needs.

Nuclear power is created by releasing the energy stored in large atoms by breaking them into smaller atoms. Nuclear power does not release gases into the atmosphere like burning fossil fuels does, but nuclear power produces dangerous radioactive waste that has the potential to cause other environmental problems.

Damming rivers allows **hydropower** to convert the energy in moving water into mechanical energy, which can then be transformed into electricity. Dams do not release harmful emissions like fossil fuels do, but they can be disruptive to natural environments and waterways.

Energy from the **wind** is harnessed using turbines (also called windmills), transforming mechanical energy into electricity. Wind turbines are becoming more common in areas where windy conditions are common, including plains regions and coastlines. **Solar energy** transforms energy from the sun into electricity using solar panels. These panels can be laid out in giant arrays called solar farms in order to provide energy to a large area, but they can also be installed on individual homes or buildings.

CONSIDER THIS

What would be the pros and cons of using wind, solar, nuclear, and hydropower in your area?

Biofuels are biological matter that can be burned to produce heat, steam, or electricity. While biofuels such as ethanol are renewable, they can create many of the same environmental concerns as fossil fuels. Finally, **geothermal energy** converts heat from below Earth's surface into steam. This type of energy has been used since ancient times to heat water and homes and has recently been harnessed to produce electricity.

While commercial agriculture is able to provide food for an extraordinary number of people, many agricultural practices can be damaging to the environment. For example, fertilizers and pesticides may run off fields and pollute nearby lands and waterways. The large swaths of land required for farming can also damage the diversity and stability of ecosystems. Recently, **genetically modified organisms (GMOs)**, which contain genes from other organisms inserted into their DNA, have come under scrutiny. While some believe that these GMOs, which include corn, soybean, and potatoes, can create a safer, more plentiful food supply, others question whether the new plants will have detrimental effects on natural environments.

Scientists urge people to protect the environment and Earth's natural resources through **conservation**. One main aspect of conservation is the attempt to limit the number of natural resources that are used to manufacture and dispose of consumer products. **Recycling** or reusing common materials like glass, steel, and paper, reduces the amount of resources needed to produce new products. Recycling also reduces the amount of waste put into landfills.

Another important means of conservation is setting aside dedicated tracts of land for protection. National, state, and local parks are important ways to preserve species and ecosystem diversity. Similarly, many **endangered species**—those that are at risk for extinction—are protected by national governments and international agreements.

> **CONSIDER THIS**
>
> How can students conserve resources and reduce waste in schools?

SAMPLE QUESTION

33) **Which is a nonrenewable natural resource?**

   A. water

   B. wind

   C. coal

   D. sun

Answers:

   A. Incorrect. Water is a renewable resource.

   B. Incorrect. Wind is a renewable resource.

   C. Correct. Coal is a nonrenewable resource that comes from the remains of plants that lived in swamps millions of years ago.

   D. Incorrect. Solar power is a renewable resource.

Science Skills and Processes

SCIENTIFIC INQUIRY

Investigation, or **inquiry-based** science, provides the strongest foundation for scientific thinking. Inquiry-based science is guided by the scientific method, which provides a framework for observing, measuring, and drawing conclusions about the world.

The first step in the scientific method is **observation**. From observations, scientists develop questions and research the currently available information about a particular topic. This research helps them formulate a reasonable and testable explanation for their observations, a statement known as a **hypothesis**. Scientists then design and conduct an **experiment** in which they collect data that will demonstrate whether their hypothesis is false or not. It is important to note that a hypothesis can never be proven true—it can be confirmed as false, or enough data can be collected to *infer* that it is true. In order for data to support a hypothesis, it must be consistent and reproducible.

When scientists have repeatedly tested a hypothesis, and that hypothesis has become widely accepted, it becomes known as a **theory**. Theories provide a widely accepted explanation for a natural phenomenon. The theory of evolution, for example, states that natural selection is the mechanism that led to the current diversity of species found on Earth. A scientific **law** is a description of a natural phenomenon. However, unlike a theory, it does not explain how something happens. For example, Newton's law of universal gravitation states that the gravitational force between two objects depends on their distance and mass.

Science, while grounded in observation and data, is not perfect, and scientific knowledge is always growing and changing. Scientists must be able to react to new observations and adjust their hypotheses as needed to address new evidence. By constantly observing, asking questions, and rigorously testing hypotheses, scientists are able to slowly build on the collective pool of scientific knowledge.

SAMPLE QUESTIONS

34) Which step should students take before making a hypothesis in a scientific experiment?

    A.   interpret data

    B.   make a graph

C. research

D. do the experiment

Answers:

A. Incorrect. Interpreting data comes after an experiment; the hypothesis comes before.

B. Incorrect. Displaying data comes after an experiment; the hypothesis comes before.

C. **Correct.** Students (and scientists) need to conduct research before making a reasonable and testable hypothesis.

D. Incorrect. The hypothesis comes before an experiment and guides the experimental process.

35) **Evolution is an example of which of the following?**

A. theory

B. law

C. hypothesis

D. fact

Answers:

A. **Correct.** Evolution is a scientific theory, which is a set of explanatory ideas substantiated by evidence through repeated experiments and observations.

B. Incorrect. A scientific law is a statement of a phenomenon; evolution is an explanation of a phenomenon so that it is considered a theory.

C. Incorrect. The theory of evolution emerged from many different hypotheses being proved correct over time.

D. Incorrect. Evidence for the theory of evolution is backed up by facts.

EXPERIMENTAL DESIGN

Scientists use a rigorous set of rules to design experiments. The protocols of **experimental design** are meant to ensure that scientists are actually testing what they set out to test. A well-designed experiment will measure the impact of a single factor on a system, thus allowing the experimenter to draw conclusions about that factor.

Every experiment includes variables, which are the factors or treatments that may affect the outcome of the experiment. **Independent variables** are controlled by the experimenter. They are usually the factors that the experimenter has hypothesized will have an effect on the system. Often, a design will include a treatment group and a **control group,** which does not receive the treatment. The **dependent variables** are factors that are influenced by the independent variable.

For example, in an experiment investigating which type of fertilizer has the greatest effect on plant growth, the independent variable is the type of fertilizer used. The scientist is controlling, or manipulating, the type of fertilizer. The dependent variable is plant growth because the amount of plant growth depends on the type of fertilizer. The type of plant, the amount of water, and the amount of sunlight the plants receive are controls because those variables of the experiment are kept the same for each plant.

When designing an experiment, scientists must identify possible sources of **experimental error**. These can be **confounding variables**, which are factors that act much like the independent variable and thus can make it appear that the independent variable has a greater effect than it actually does. The design may also include unknown variables that are not controlled by the scientists. Finally, scientists must be aware of human error, particularly in collecting data and making observations, and of possible equipment errors.

During the experiment, scientists collect data, which must then be analyzed and presented appropriately. This can mean running a statistical analysis on the data (e.g., finding the mean) or putting the data in graph form. An analysis allows scientists to see trends in the data and determine if those trends are statistically significant. From the data and its analysis, scientists can draw a **conclusion** about the experiment.

Scientists often use **models** in their research. These models are a simplified representation of a system. For example, a mathematical equation that describes fluctuations in a population might be used to test how a certain variable is likely to affect that population. Or scientists might use a greenhouse to model a particular ecosystem so they can more closely control the variables in the environment.

SAMPLE QUESTION

36) Which of the following is the variable in a scientific investigation that is manipulated by the researcher in order to test the hypothesis?

A. control

B. experimental

C. dependent

D. hypothetical

Answers:

A. Incorrect. Controlled variables are variables that remain constant throughout the entire experiment.

B. Correct. Experimental variables, also known as independent variables, are the variables that are changed by the scientist.

C. Incorrect. Dependent variables are controls that change as a result of the manipulation of the independent variable.

D. Incorrect. There is no definition for a hypothetical variable.

EQUIPMENT AND SAFETY PROCEDURES

When choosing and setting up a lab, teachers need to remember that they are liable for any accidents or hazardous incidents that occur under their supervision. For an elementary classroom, **standard laboratory equipment** includes flat top tables with stools so students can view experiments from several angles. Safety gear, microscopes, beakers, **measurement tools**, test tubes, eyedroppers, weights, magnets, and timers should be some of the available equipment. Measurement tools for length include metric rulers and tape measures. Beakers and graduated cylinders are used to measure volume. Balance scales measure mass.

Standard safety equipment like goggles, aprons, protective gloves, and a fire extinguisher must be available. In addition to using standard safety equipment, students should be instructed on appropriate **apparel**. For example, long hair should be tied back and loose clothing and jewelry should be secured. Closed-toe shoes should be worn.

Student **behavior** guidelines are important, but they take on even more significance when students are working in potentially dangerous situations. Adults should model safety practices, such as wearing goggles. Parents and students should be required to sign a document that outlines safety procedures. Students should be warned about potential dangers as they arise in each experiment. Students must be diligently supervised, and those who do not comply with safety standards should be removed from the lab. At the end of an experiment, students must know how to properly clean up equipment and dispose of waste.

Emergency procedures should include proactively monitoring students and equipment and wearing safety gear. Plans for emergency first aid for electric shock, poisoning, burns, fire, evacuations, spills, and animal bites should be established.

SAMPLE QUESTION

37) **Which tool measures the volume of an object?**

- A. thermometer
- B. graduated cylinder
- C. balance
- D. barometer

Answers:

- A. Incorrect. A thermometer measures temperature.
- **B. Correct.** A graduated cylinder measures volume.
- C. Incorrect. A balance measures mass.
- D. Incorrect. A barometer measures atmospheric pressure.

Terms

acceleration: how quickly an object changes velocity

acid: a compound that is able to contribute a hydrogen ion and has a pH lower than 7

alto– **cloud**: a cloud located in the middle level of the sky

amphibians: a class of cold-blooded vertebrate animals that have gills when they hatch but develop lungs in adulthood

amplitude: a measure of a wave's displacement from its rest position

anatomy: the study of the structure of living organisms

Animalia: the kingdom that contains multicellular organisms that can move around and must consume other organisms for energy

anther: part of the male reproductive organ of a flowering plant where pollen is stored

antibodies: special proteins that bind to foreign substances in the body and neutralize them

antigens: substances that the body recognizes as foreign

artery: a blood vessel that carries blood away from the heart

asexual: does not require the union of sex cells to reproduce

asteroid: a large rocky body, smaller than a planet, that orbits the sun

asthenosphere: the hot, semisolid part of the mantle under the lithosphere

atmosphere: the mass of gases that surround Earth

atom: the smallest particle of a chemical element that retains the properties of the element

atomic mass: the mass of an atom calculated by adding the number of protons and neutrons

atomic number: the number of protons in the nucleus of an atom

attraction: a force that draws objects closer

B cells: (also called B lymphocytes) produce special proteins called antibodies that bind to foreign substances, called antigens, and neutralize them

balanced equation: a chemical equation where the same amount of each element is represented on both sides (the reactants and the products have equal amounts of each element)

base: a compound that is able to contribute a hydroxide ion and has a pH greater than 7

biofuel: biological matter that can be burned to produce heat, steam, or electricity

biomass: plant-based fuel, usually burned, for generating heat, steam, or electricity

biomes: large geographic areas that provide the environmental conditions in which certain organisms live

birds: endothermic vertebrate animals that have wings, feathers, scaly legs, beaks, and no teeth, and bear their young in a hard-shelled egg

black holes: a massive star that has collapsed and has a gravitational force so strong that light cannot escape

calyx: all of the sepals of a flower together

capillaries: the smallest blood vessels in the body where gas exchange occurs

carbohydrates: the sugars that act as a source of energy for all living things

carpel: the ovary of a flowering plant where the ova are produced

cell: the smallest living part of an organism

cell division: the separation of a cell into two cells with identical genes

cell membrane: the outer covering of a cell

cell wall: hard outer structure of a plant cell

cellular metabolism: (also called cellular respiration) how cells produce energy

cerebellum: part of the brain located at the back and bottom that controls motor movements

cerebrum: the biggest part of the brain, the wrinkly gray part at the front and top, that controls different body functions like thinking, vision, hearing, touch, and smell

cervix: the passage that connects the uterus to the vagina

chemical change: making or breaking chemical bonds between atoms in a chemical reaction

chlorophyll: a chemical in the leaves of plants that uses energy from sunlight to convert water and carbon dioxide into sugars

chromosome: dense strands of DNA that contain the genetic code of an organism

cinder cone volcano: a small, steep volcano formed by ash with a single lava vent and a crater on top

cirrus cloud: a thin, wispy cloud that appears high in the sky

classification: sorting according to characteristics

climate: an area's weather conditions over time

climate zone: a large area that experiences similar average temperature and precipitation

cloud: billions of tiny water droplets floating in the air together

color: frequency of a light wave

combustion: a chemical reaction that produces carbon dioxide and water, usually from the burning of fuels

comet: a small object made of ice and dust that orbits the sun

communities: interdependent organisms living together in a habitat

competition: occurs when two organisms need to use the same resources

composite volcano: a cone-shaped volcano with steep sides made of lava, ash, and rock

compound: a combination of two or more elements

conclusions: inferences based on data collected in an experiment

condensation: the process by which water vapor in the air turns into liquid water when it comes into contact with a cold surface

conduction: the transfer of heat through physical contact

conductivity: a property that determines how well a material conducts electricity and heat

conifers: non-flowering plants that produce seeds protected by woody cones

conservation: protecting the environment and natural resources

continent: one of seven large land masses on Earth's surface

continental drift: slow movement of Earth's tectonic plates

control group: the parts of an experiment that stay the same

convection: transfer of heat that occurs in a circular motion caused by heat rising and cold sinking

convergent plate boundary: when two tectonic plates crash into one another

coral reef: a marine (saltwater) system with high levels of diversity

core: the layer at the center of the earth

corolla: all of the petals of a flower together

cotyledon: plant embryo inside a seed

covalent bond: a chemical bond in which electrons are shared

crust: thin and broken outermost surface layer of the earth

cumulus cloud: tall, puffy clouds that are often dark at the bottom and whiter toward the top

current: the movement of electrons through a circuit

currents: movements of ocean water caused by differences in salt content or temperature and winds

decomposer: organism that breaks down dead matter

decomposition: a chemical reaction in which a single substance is broken down into two or more substances

density: a property of matter that can be determined by dividing mass by volume

dependent variable: part of an experiment that responds to, or depends on, the independent variable

deposition: the laying down of sediment in a new location

desert: a biome with extreme temperatures and very low rainfall with specialized vegetation and small mammals

dicot: a seed with two cotyledons

displacement: a measure of the shortest distance between the initial and final locations of a moving point

divergent plate boundary: a boundary between two tectonic plates that are moving away from one another

DNA: deoxyribonucleic acid (carries genetic information)

dominant: genetic traits that are expressed as characteristics of an organism

Doppler effect: the change in wavelength when waves are compressed as an object approaches an observer and spread out as the object moves away from the observer

drainage basin: a given area of land from which all rainfall flows into a single body of water

earthquake: violent shaking of the ground caused by tectonic plates crashing into or scraping against each other

eclipse: when Earth, the moon, and the sun align so that light from one object is blocked

ecological succession: the process by which ecosystems change and develop over time

ecology: study of organisms' interactions with each other and the environment

ecosystem: a community of organisms and their interaction with each other and the environment

ectotherm: a cold-blooded organism

electric charge: a difference in the balance of protons and electrons that creates a positively or negatively charged object

electricity: energy of moving electrons

electromagnetic waves: waves composed of oscillating electric and magnetic fields

electron: subatomic particle with a negative charge found outside the nucleus of an atom

elements: substances made of one type of atom

endosperm: part of a seed that provides nourishment for the plant embryo

endotherm: a warm-blooded organism

endothermic: a chemical reaction that requires energy

energy: the capacity of an object to do work

enzyme: a special type of protein that can cause or speed up a specific chemical reaction

equilibrium: a state of balance

erosion: the movement of sediments from one place to another

eukaryotic cells: cells that contain a nucleus and are found in multicellular organisms

evaporation: the process of changing from a liquid to a gas

evolution: the progressive changes of living things throughout Earth's history

exothermic: a chemical reaction in which energy (heat) is released

experimental design: an experiment that includes an objective, standard protocols, a control group, and independent and dependent variables

experimental error: mistakes made during an experiment caused by limitations of the equipment or external influences

fallopian tubes: tubes that transfer eggs from the ovaries to the uterus in the female reproductive system

fertilization: joining of the male and female reproductive cells

filament: a long stalk-like structure that supports a plant's anther

food web: producers, consumers, predators, and decomposers that live interdependently in an ecosystem

force: any push or pull on an object

fossil: preserved remains or traces of ancient life

fossil fuels: nonrenewable fuels made from organisms that lived millions of years ago

frequency: the number of times per second a wave cycles

friction: the force of one object resisting another

fruit: provides protection and nourishment for the seeds of flowering plants

function: the activity of a part of an organism

fungi: a group of unicellular and multicellular organisms that have cell walls and reproduction strategies that differ from those in the other kingdoms of life

galaxy: a large system of stars, gas, and dust held together by gravity

gas: matter with widely dispersed molecules that can change both shape and volume

gene: genetic code that determines the characteristics of an organism

generator: a device that transforms mechanical energy into electrical energy

genetic: hereditary

genetic disorder: a hereditary abnormality that creates a health condition

genus: the level of taxonomic classification that ranks above species

geology: the study of Earth

geothermal energy: converting heat from below Earth's surface to make steam

germination: when a seed begins to grow

gestation: the development of an embryo in the uterus

glacier: a large mass of slowly moving ice and snow

gravity: the attraction of one mass to another mass

greenhouse gases: gases that trap heat in the atmosphere

groundwater: water that is stored underground in rock layers called aquifers

gymnosperm: a non-flowering plant that produces seeds

heart: the organ that pumps blood throughout the body

heat: movement of energy from one substance to another

helper T cells: coordinate production of antibodies by B cells and removal of infected cells by T cells

homeostasis: regulation and stabilization of internal conditions

hormones: chemicals that regulate bodily processes

hurricane: a large, violent storm with winds 74 mph or greater

hydrology: the study of water

hydropower: transforms the energy of moving water into mechanical energy and then electricity

hydrosphere: the water found on and below Earth's surface and in the atmosphere

hypothesis: an educated guess

iceberg: a large chunk of ice that has broken off from a continental glacier and is floating in the ocean

igneous rock: formed from magma brought to Earth's surface as a result of tectonic processes

independent variables: part of an experiment that is manipulated to test the effect on the dependent variable

inheritance: a feature passed down from one generation to the next

insulators: materials that do not conduct heat or electricity well

invertebrate: an organism that does not have a backbone

ionic bond: a chemical bond that involves the attraction between two ions with unlike charges

isotope: a variation of an element with a different number of neutrons in its nucleus

keystone species: a species whose removal decreases the overall diversity of the ecosystem

killer T cells: destroy infected body cells after they are identified and removed by T cells

kinetic energy: the energy of motion

kingdom: the highest level of taxonomic classification

lake: inland body of fresh water

laws: descriptions of scientific phenomena

leaves: the part of a plant where photosynthesis takes place

lens: curved piece of glass that can be used to bend light

life cycle: the stages of life of an organism

lipids: organic molecule used for energy storage and other cellular functions

liquid: matter with more loosely packed molecules that can change shape but not volume

lithosphere: the outer layer of the earth that includes the crust and upper layer of the mantle

loudness: the amplitude of a sound wave

lunar eclipse: when Earth lines up between the moon and sun; the moon moves into Earth's shadow and appears dark in color

magma: melted rock

magnetic field lines: show the direction of a magnetic field at different points

magnets: materials that create a magnetic field

mammals: a class of warm-blooded vertebrate animals that have hair, give birth to live young (with a few exceptions), and produce milk

mantle: the layer of Earth below the crust

mass: the amount of matter in an object

matter: any substance that takes up space and has mass

measurement tools: equipment used to collect data

medical technology: research and development for improving patient care

medicine: pharmaceuticals used to treat or prevent medical conditions

medulla: (also called the brain stem) the part of the brain where it connects to the spinal cord and controls automatic body functions like breathing and heartbeat

meiosis: formation of reproductive cells

memory cells: these cells remember antigens that have been removed so the immune system can respond more quickly if they enter the body again

metamorphic rock: forms when extreme temperature and pressure cause the structure of preexisting rocks to change

meteorology: the study of the atmosphere and weather

mineral: a naturally occurring, solid, inorganic substance with a crystalline structure

mitochondria: cell organelle that produces energy in the form of ATP

mitosis: process of cell division

mixture: two or more substances combined without a chemical reaction to bond them

models: representations of the real world

molecule: two or more atoms bonded together

monera: unicellular organisms that have no nucleus

monocot: a seed with only one cotyledon

moon: a large body that orbits a planet

mutation: a change in genetic information that may be passed on to future generations

natural selection: Darwin's theory that living things that adapt to their environment have a higher survival rate and produce more offspring

nervous system: processes external stimuli and sends signals throughout the body

neurons: cells that make up the peripheral nervous system and transmit information through electrical signals

neutralization: a chemical reaction that occurs when an acid and a base react to form a salt and water

neutron: subatomic particle with no charge found within the nucleus of an atom

Newton's first law of motion: an object at rest stays at rest, and an object in motion stays in motion, unless a force acts on it

Newton's second law of motion: force equals mass multiplied by acceleration; $F = ma$

Newton's third law of motion: for every action, there is an equal and opposite reaction

nimbus cloud: one that has a lot of water vapor in it and will most likely lead to precipitation

nonrenewable resources: resources that take millions of years to replenish

nuclear power: energy stored in large atoms that is released when such atoms are broken into smaller atoms

nucleic acid: linear biomolecules composed of nucleotide bases that store the genetic code of an organism

nucleus: the center of a cell that contains DNA

ocean: large body of salt water

optics: the study of light

organ: a body part that serves an important function in a system

organ systems: groups of organs that work together to perform one or more functions

organelle: part of a cell that is specialized to perform a specific function

organism: a living thing

ova: (also called eggs) the female reproductive cells of a plant

ovaries: organs which produce female gametes (eggs)

oxidation: a chemical change in which a substance loses electrons

ozone layer: part of the stratosphere that captures harmful radiation from the sun

paleontology: the study of the history of life through fossils

parasitism: a relationship between two organisms when one organism benefits to the detriment of the other

penis: organ of the male reproductive system through which sperm and urine pass out of the body

period: the time between wave crests

periodic table: a table of chemical elements listed in order by atomic number

petals: special brightly colored leaves that form flowers

pH scale: a standard measure of acidity or alkalinity where 7 is neutral

phase: the position on a wave cycle at a given point in time

phloem: a special tissue that transports sugar and other nutrients throughout a plant

photosynthesis: the process by which plants use energy from sunlight to make food (glucose) from carbon dioxide and water

physical change: change in a substance that does not change the composition of the substance

physiology: the study of the functions of living organisms

pistil: the female reproductive organ of a flowering plant

pitch: the frequency of vibrations

planet: a large body in space that orbits a star

plants: a kingdom of organisms that make food using photosynthesis

plasma: a state of matter similar to a gas that contains freely moving charged particles, although its charge remains neutral

polar ice: large sheets of ice covering the North and South Poles

poles: the ends of a magnet

pollen: male reproductive cells of a plant

population: a group of organisms of the same species

potential energy: the amount of energy of an object due to its position

precipitation: any form of water that falls from the sky

predators: animals that kill other animals for food

prey: an organism that is hunted and killed for food

primary consumer: animal that consumes plant matter (herbivore)

primary succession: the development and changes that occur during colonization of a new habitat

producer: an organism that produces energy directly from the sun

product: new substance formed during a chemical reaction

prokaryotic cells: cells that do not have a nucleus and are found in single-celled organisms like bacteria

property: a characteristic**prostate**: a muscular gland approximately the size of a walnut that is located between the male bladder and penis and produces a fluid that nourishes and protects sperm

proteins: chains of linked amino acids that perform a variety of biological functions

protist: unicellular organisms with a nucleus

protons: subatomic particle with a positive electric charge found within the nucleus of an atom

Punnett square: a special chart that shows all of the possible genetic combinations from parents with given genotypes

radiation: transfer of heat without a medium

reactant: a substance that is changing in a chemical reaction

recessive: genetic traits that are not expressed as characteristics of an organism

reflect: change the direction of a light wave by bouncing the wave off a surface

refract: bend a light wave as the wave travels through different media

renewable resources: resources that replenish quickly

reproduction: the process of making a copy

reptiles: a class of cold-blooded vertebrates that have scales and lay eggs on land

repulsion: a force that pushes objects away

ribosome: cell organelle that produces proteins

river: body of water that flows across the land as a result of rainfall, usually toward a lake, sea, or ocean

rock: a naturally occurring organic or inorganic solid that is composed of one or more minerals

rock record: a biological history of Earth recorded in rocks

roots: the part of a plant that absorbs water and nutrients from the soil

scalar: a measure of magnitude only

sea: smaller body of salt water

secondary consumer: animal that consumes herbivores (carnivore)

secondary succession: changes to previously colonized habitats that have been disrupted

sedimentary rock: formed from the compaction of rock fragments that results from weathering and erosion

seed: plant embryo

sepals: special leaves that support the petals of a flower

sexual: requires the union of gametes (sex cells) to reproduce

shield volcano: a dome-shaped volcano with gently sloping sides made mostly of fluid lava flows

solar eclipse: when the moon lines up between the earth and sun, blocking the sunlight

solar energy: converts energy from the sun into electricity

solar system: a system that includes a star or stars, along with planets, moons, asteroids, meteoroids, and comets, that is held together by gravity

solid: matter with densely packed molecules that does not change volume or shape

solubility: the amount of a solute that will dissolve in a solvent

solute: a substance being dissolved

solution: a mixture that is evenly distributed and thoroughly dissolved

solvent: a substance in which another material is being dissolved

sound: a longitudinal wave created by vibrations

species: the most specific level of taxonomic classification, in which organisms with similar genetics can breed

speed: distance divided by time

spores: a single-celled reproductive body produced by some plants

stamen: male reproductive organ of a flowering plant where pollen is produced

stars: large masses of gas

stem: the main stalk of a plant that carries the nutrients and water from the roots to other parts of the plant

stigma: a female reproductive organ of a flowering plant where pollen is received

stratus cloud: a flat, wispy cloud found in the lower level of the sky

stream: smaller body of water that flows across the land as a result of rainfall, usually toward a river

style: an extended stalk that supports the stigma of a flowering plant

sun: the star in Earth's solar system

synthesis: a chemical reaction in which two substances combine to form a single substance

system: a collection of interconnected parts that make up a complex whole with defined boundaries

T cells: (also called T lymphocytes) remove body cells that have been infected by foreign invaders like bacteria or viruses

tectonic plates: large plates that form the outer surface of the earth's crust and float on deeper liquid layers

temperate broadleaf forest: a biome with moderate precipitation and temperatures with deciduous trees dominating

temperate grassland: a biome with moderate precipitation and distinct seasons with grasses and shrubs dominating

temperature: a measure of the kinetic energy of all the atoms or molecules in a substance, observed as how hot or cold the object is

tertiary consumer: carnivore that eats other carnivores

testes: organs which produce male gametes (sperm)

theory: principle explained by science

tides: the movement of large bodies of water caused by the gravitational pull of the moon and the sun

tissue: groups of cells that have a similar function

tornado: fast-moving, rotational winds that occur when unstable warm and cold air masses collide

traits: characteristics

transform plate boundary: when two tectonic plates slide against each other in opposite directions

tropical rainforest: a hot and wet biome with an extremely high diversity of species

tundra: a biome with extremely low temperatures and short growing seasons with little or no tree growth

urethra: pass through which sperm passes

uterus: organ in which embryos develop

vacuole: cell organelle that stores water and other molecules

vas deferens: tube that carries sperm from the testes

vector: a measure of both magnitude and direction

vein: a blood vessel that carries blood to the heart from other parts of the body

velocity: the rate at which an object changes position; change of distance divided by change of time

vertebrate: an organism that has a backbone

volcanoes: vents in Earth's crust that allow molten rock to reach the surface

water cycle: the circulation of water throughout Earth's surface, atmosphere, and hydrosphere

watershed: a given area of land from which all rainfall flows into a single body of water

wave: movement of energy through water

wave: a pulse of energy

wavelength: the distance between two points on back-to-back wave cycles

weather: daily atmospheric conditions

weathering: the mechanical and/or chemical process by which rocks break down

weight: the force of the gravitational pull on an object

wind energy: energy from the wind is transformed into mechanical energy and then electricity

xylem: the special tissue that plants use to transport water and minerals

Part II: Practice

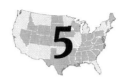

Reading and Language Arts Practice

1

A teacher asks, "What word am I trying to say, /p/ /i/ /n/?" and instructs students to say the word. Which strategy is the teacher using to build phoneme awareness?

A.   phoneme blending

B.   phoneme deletion

C.   phoneme segmentation

D.   phoneme substitution

2

Which letter or word part forms the rime in the word *cake*?

A.   c

B.   e

C.   cak

D.   ake

3

An English-language learner who attempts to write simple sentences but uses a very limited vocabulary is functioning at which of the following language proficiency levels?

A.   L1

B.   L2

C.   L3

D.   L4

4

How many phonemes are in the word *chick*?

A.   2

B.   3

C.   4

D.   5

5

The *cl* in the word *clap* is an example of

A.   a syllable.

B.   an onset.

C.   a phoneme.

D.   a rime.

6

A student is able to orally substitute the initial consonant /g/ for /b/ in the word *boat* to make the word *goat*. What concept is the student demonstrating?

A.   phonemic awareness

B.   letter-sound correspondence

C.   phonological awareness

D.   manipulation of onsets and rimes

7

Which of the following letters is most likely to be introduced first in progressive phonics instruction?

A.   a

B.   g

C.   y

D.   m

8

Which of the following best describes reading rate?

A.   using appropriate vocal cues when reading aloud

B.   decoding words correctly when reading aloud

C.   having a significant inventory of known sight words

D.   reading smoothly and steadily when reading aloud

9

Which part of the word *dream* is a phoneme?

A.   *ea*

B.   *dr*

C.   *eam*

D.   *re*

10

What is the purpose of sight word instruction?

A.   to help students learn letter-sound correspondences to improve accuracy

B.   to help students manipulate sounds in words to improve auditory skills

C.   to help students recognize words automatically to improve fluency

D.   to help students use word parts to improve reading comprehension

Questions 11 – 16 refer to the following text excerpt from *Black Beauty* by Anna Sewell.

The name of the coachman was John Manly; he had a wife and one little child, and they lived in the coachman's cottage, very near the stables.

The next morning he took me into the yard and gave me a good grooming, and just as I was going into my box, with my coat soft and bright, the squire came in to look at me, and seemed pleased. "John," he said, "I meant to have tried the new horse this morning, but I have other business. You may as well take him around after breakfast; go by the common and the Highwood, and back by the watermill and the river; that will show his paces."

"I will, sir," said John. After breakfast he came and fitted me with a bridle. He was very particular in letting out and taking in the straps, to fit my head comfortably; then he brought a saddle, but it was not broad enough for my back; he saw it in a minute and went for another, which fitted nicely. He rode me first slowly, then a trot, then a canter, and when we were on the common he gave me a light touch with his whip, and we had a splendid gallop.

11

Which inference can the reader make based on the text?

A.   John Manly does not like his job.

B.   John Manly has respect for horses.

C.   John Manly is a coachman with a family.

D.   John Manly has bought a new horse.

12

Which point of view is used by the author?

A.   first-person

B.   second-person

C.   third-person objective

D.   third-person omniscient

13

Which is the best summary of the excerpt?

A.   John Manly is a coachman who lives with his wife and a child in a cottage near a set of stables. He works in the stables grooming horses for the squire.

B.   After he has breakfast, John Manly has a splendid gallop by the watermill and along the river with a new horse from the stables.

C.   The horse is new to the stables, but the squire does not have time to check his paces, so he asks John Manly to do it, but John has to have breakfast first.

D.   The coachman, John Manly, grooms the horse and fits him comfortably with a bridle and saddle. Then, he takes the horse for a ride to test the horse's paces for the squire.

14

Who are the main characters in this excerpt?

A.   John Manly, the squire, and the horse

B.   John Manly and the horse

C.   John Manly and the squire

D.   John Manly and his family

15

How can the reader best use the context of the excerpt to understand the meaning of the word *paces*?

A.   The reader can find the definition of the word in the paragraph that follows.

B.   The reader can figure out the word's meaning by analyzing its root and affix.

C.   The reader can use the connotation of the word to determine its meaning.

D.   The reader can analyze the setting for a hint to the meaning of the word.

16

What is the tone of the excerpt?

A.   negative and foreboding

B.   cheerful and positive

C.   sad and depressing

D.   elated and ecstatic

Questions 17 – 19 refer to the following text and picture excerpt from *Frederick Francois Chopin: The Story of the Boy Who Made Beautiful Melodies.*

During his boyhood Chopin played much in public, journeying to some of the great cities of Europe, among them Vienna, Berlin, and Munich.

Therefore, when he played in Paris it was as an artist. Here, as at home, he charmed everyone by the beauty of his music and the loveliness of his touch.

He possessed the true piano hand. It was somewhat narrow. The fingers were long and tapering. It seemed at once strong and vigorous, yet delicate and sensitive.

Figure 5.1. The True Piano Hand

17

This excerpt is an example of which type of text?

A. literary

B. informal

C. discipline-specific

D. informational

18

How does the picture of the "true piano hand" help a reader comprehend the excerpt?

A. It helps the reader better understand the tone of the text.

B. It helps the reader feel the beauty of Chopin's music.

C. It helps the reader better understand the word *tapering*.

D. It helps the reader recognize the hands of an artist.

19

Which text feature would best help the reader comprehend where Chopin played?

A. a chart

B. a map

C. a graph

D. a sidebar

20

Which is the root word of *loveliness*?

A. love

B. lovely

C. lov

D. loveli

Questions 21 – 25 refer to the following text excerpt from "King Midas and the Golden Touch" as told by Jean Lang.

The gods had indeed bestowed upon Gordias, the low-born peasant, a surprising gift, but he showed his gratitude by dedicating his wagon to the deity of the oracle and tying it up in its place with the wiliest knot that his simple wisdom knew, pulled as tight as his brawny arms and strong rough hands could pull. Nor could anyone untie the famous Gordian knot, and therefore become, as the oracle promised, lord of all Asia, until centuries had passed, and Alexander the Great came to Phrygia and sliced through the knot with his all-conquering sword.

In time Midas, the son of Gordias, came to inherit the throne and crown of Phrygia. Like many another not born and bred to the purple, his honours sat heavily upon him. From the day that his father's wain had entered the city amidst the acclamations of the people, he had learned the value of power, and therefore, from his boyhood onward, power, always more power, was what he coveted. Also his peasant father had taught him that gold could buy power, and so Midas ever longed for more gold, that could buy him a place in the world that no descendant of a long race of kings should be able to contest. And from Olympus the gods looked down and smiled, and vowed that Midas should have the chance of realising his heart's desire.

21

Which genre does this text excerpt represent?

A. myth

B. fairy tale

C. narrative poem

D. drama

22

What can the reader infer about Midas from reading the excerpt?

A. He is physically strong.

B. He is generous.

C. He is insecure.

D. He is angry.

23

Which stage of plot development best describes the excerpt?

A. rising action

B. exposition

C. climax

D. resolution

24

How best can a reader use the excerpt's context to decipher the meaning of the word *coveted*?

A. The reader can use the excerpt's register to determine the word's meaning.

B. The reader can use structural analysis to determine the word's meaning.

C. The reader can use the sentence's syntax to determine the word's meaning.

D. The reader can use the word's connotation to determine the word's meaning.

25

The phrase *born and bred to the purple* is an example of which of the following literary elements?

A.   hyperbole

B.   personification

C.   simile

D.   idiom

26

Which genre features animals and includes an explicit moral lesson?

A.   myth

B.   fable

C.   legend

D.   fairy tale

27

Which best describes the theme of a story?

A.   the way the story is organized

B.   the lesson the author wants to teach

C.   the basic idea the author wants to convey

D.   the point of view of the story

28

How do the two sentences below differ?

The park naturalist visited the class to talk about the migration of Monarch butterflies.

The naturalist visited the class to talk about the migration of Monarch butterflies from the park.

A.   The word *park* acts as an adjective in the first sentence and is part of an adjective phrase in the second sentence.

B.   The word *park* is the subject of the first sentence, and the word *naturalist* is the subject of the second sentence.

C.   The word *park* is the subject of the first sentence and the predicate in the second sentence.

D.   The word *park* acts as an adjective in the first sentence and is part of an adverb phrase in the second.

29

The sentence below is an example of what sentence type?

Despite the fact that the larger dog was ten times its size, the tiny dog continued to bark with ferocity.

A.   simple sentence

B.   compound sentence

C.   complex sentence

D.   compound-complex sentence

30

Which of the answer choice statements about the sentence below is true?

The trail is for advanced hikers because of it's steep incline.

A.   The sentence is written correctly.

B.   There should be a comma before *because*.

C.   The word *it's* should be possessive.

D.   The verb should be past tense.

31

What error has been made in the sentence below?

Lucy thought the first movie was better then the second one.

A.   The verbs are past tense.

B.   *Then* indicates time, not comparison.

C.   *One* is a dangling modifier.

D.   The subject is misplaced.

32

Which of the following strategies is most beneficial for students who are at the beginning stage of writing a story?

A.   revising the story's first paragraph

B.   organizing ideas in a story element chart

C.   drafting the exposition of the story

D.   sharing the story with a classmate

Questions 33 – 36 refer to the poem below, "The Moon," from *A Child's Garden of Verses* by Robert Louis Stevenson.

The moon has a face like the clock in the hall;
She shines on thieves on the garden wall;
On streets and fields and harbor quays,
And birdies asleep in the forks of the trees.

The squalling cat and the squeaking mouse,
The howling dog by the door of the house,
The bat that lies in bed at noon,
All love to be out by the light of the moon.

But all of the things that belong to the day
Cuddle to sleep to be out of her way;
And flowers and children close their eyes
Till up in the morning the sun shall rise.

33

Which type of figurative language is used to describe the moon's face?

A.   metaphor

B.   assonance

C.   alliteration

D.   simile

34

How does the reader know that the word *quays* is pronounced using /ē/ as opposed to /ā/?

A.   from the poet's use of simile

B.   from the poet's use of rhyme scheme

C.   from the poet's use of personification

D.   from the poet's use of point of view

35

Which of the poet's word choices are examples of onomatopoeia?

A.   *squalling, squeaking, howling*

B.   *garden, streets, fields*

C.   *asleep, bed, cuddle*

D.   *shines, light, sun*

36

What type of writing does the poem represent?

A.   expository

B.   narrative

C.   descriptive

D.   persuasive

37

Review the following sentence; then review the revision.

> *Original Sentence*:
>
> The scientist looked at the rocks to learn interesting things about the past.
>
> *Revision*:
>
> The geologist examined the rocks to discover evidence of historical events.

The revised sentence reflects an improvement in which of the following elements of writing?

A.   conventions

B.   organization

C.   sentence fluency

D.   word choice

38

Which best states the purpose of the drafting stage of the writing process?

A.   revising the story's first paragraph

B.   organizing ideas in a story element chart

C.   drafting the exposition of the story

D.   sharing the story with a classmate

39

Which is the primary reason elementary students learn how to paraphrase and cite information from outside sources?

A.   to learn the names of authors

B.   to identify secondary sources

C.   to avoid plagiarism

D.   to condense writing

40

Which is the best writing style for a research paper?

A. expository

B. descriptive

C. narrative

D. persuasive

41

Which is an example of a secondary source?

A. a handwritten letter by a former president

B. a photograph from the turn of the century

C. an audio recording of a jazz composition

D. a book that discusses a historical time period

42

Which of the following can be classified as narrative writing?

A. an opinion piece on a political candidate

B. an essay on the causes and effects of erosion

C. a poem that evokes the feeling of a spring thunderstorm

D. a funny story about an adventure at the zoo

43

Which of the following is considered an unreliable research source?

A. a self-published report

B. an edited book of essays

C. a newspaper article

D. a university study

44

Which best states the purpose of the rewriting stage of the writing process?

A. presenting outcomes

B. organizing ideas

C. correcting errors

D. recording thoughts

45

What is the primary purpose of expository writing?

A.   to entertain

B.   to explain

C.   to convince

D.   to describe

46

Which of the following is NOT a positive nonverbal clue in active listening?

A.   smiling at the speaker

B.   leaning forward slightly

C.   looking down at the floor

D.   sitting up straight

47

A student is giving a speech on school start times. The following quote is included in his presentation:

> "Elementary school should start at 9:00 a.m. instead of 7:30 a.m. because children do their best thinking when they get enough sleep and have time to eat a healthy breakfast."

Which of the following is the best paraphrase of the speaker's message?

A.   Later school start times are better for learning because children get more rest and eat properly.

B.   School should start at 9:00 a.m. instead of 7:30 a.m. because children do their best thinking when they get enough sleep and have time to eat a healthy breakfast.

C.   Elementary school should start earlier than it does now.

D.   Many students are too tired during the school day to concentrate on learning.

48

Which behaviors best demonstrate focusing on a speaker during active listening?

A.   moving around and eye contact

B.   sitting up straight and interjecting questions

C.   frowning and crossed arms

D.   eye contact and leaning forward

49

Which of the following is Mr. Kahn modeling for students?

Every morning, Mr. Kahn posts a morning message for students that contains errors in Standard English. Students read the message, identify the errors, and make suggestions for corrections.

A. paraphrasing

B. editing

C. decoding

D. inferring

50

What is finger spelling?

A. making crayon rubbings of sandpaper letters

B. using the hands to sign letters

C. counting letters in words using the fingers

D. writing letters in trays of colored sand

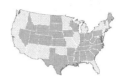

Answer Key

1)

A. **Correct.** The strategy of phoneme blending requires students to combine phonemes to make a word.

B. Incorrect. The strategy of phoneme deletion requires students to remove phonemes in words to make new words.

C. Incorrect. The strategy of phoneme segmentation requires students to separate the phonemes in a word.

D. Incorrect. The strategy of phoneme substitution requires students to replace phonemes in words to make new words.

2)

A. Incorrect. The beginning consonant forms the onset of the word *cake*.

B. Incorrect. The *e* is silent in the word *cake* and makes the *a* long.

C. Incorrect. Dropping the *e* changes the word *cake* into a nonsense word.

D. **Correct.** The rime in *cake* is formed by all of the letters that follow the beginning consonant.

3)

A. Incorrect. An English-language learner at the L1 level is not yet attempting to write simple sentences.

B. **Correct.** An English-language learner at the L2 stage is at the very beginning stages of reading and writing and has a very limited vocabulary.

C. Incorrect. An English-language learner at the L3 stage demonstrates an expanded vocabulary and an ability to speak in more complex sentences.

D. Incorrect. An English-language learner at the L4 stage can function at the same level as his or her English-speaking peers.

4)

A. Incorrect. The word *chick* is made up of three phonemes, or units of sound. They are the consonant diagraph /ch/, the short vowel /ĭ/, and the consonant diagraph /ck/.

B. Correct. The word *chick* is made up of three phonemes, or units of sound: /ch/, /ĭ/, and /ck/.

C. Incorrect. The word *chick* is made up of three phonemes, or units of sound. Both /ch/ and /ck/ are letter combinations that work together to produce one sound.

D. Incorrect. The word *chick* is made up of five letters but only three phonemes, or units of sound. They are the consonant diagraph /ch/, the short vowel /ĭ/, and the consonant diagraph /ck/.

5)

A. Incorrect. The word *clap* is one syllable, and it contains both an onset and a rime.

B. Correct. The onset of a syllable is the beginning consonant or consonant blend.

C. Incorrect. The consonant blend *cl* contains two phonemes, /c/ and /l/.

D. Incorrect. The rime of a syllable includes the vowel and remaining consonants, in this case *ap*.

6)

A. Correct. Phonemic awareness is an understanding of how phonemes can be orally manipulated to change the meanings of words.

B. Incorrect. When a student connects oral sounds to written letters, he or she is demonstrating an understanding of phonics.

C. Incorrect. Phonemic awareness is only one part of phonological awareness, which also includes creating rhyming words and breaking one-syllable words into onsets and rimes.

D. Incorrect. When students are able to orally manipulate onsets and rimes, they are demonstrating one aspect of phonological awareness.

7)

A. Incorrect. The letter *a* is a vowel with both a short and long sound, which makes it less likely to be introduced during phonics instruction before the less complex consonant *m*.

B. Incorrect. While the letter *g* does contain its hard sound in its name, it also has a soft sound, so it's a more complex letter than *m*, and thus, less likely to be introduced first.

8)

C. Incorrect. The letter *y* does not contain its sound in its name and can change sounds depending on how it is placed in a word, so it is not likely to be introduced before the letter *m*.

D. Correct. The letter *m* is most likely to be introduced first because it contains its sound in its name and only forms one sound in words.

8)

A. Incorrect. Using appropriate vocal expressions when reading aloud demonstrates prosody.

B. Incorrect. Decoding words correctly when reading aloud demonstrates a reader's accuracy.

C. Incorrect. Having a significant inventory of known sight words relates to reading accuracy.

D. Correct. Reading smoothly and steadily when reading aloud is an example of reading rate.

9)

A. Correct. The diphthong *ea* produces one small unit of sound, /ē/, that cannot be reduced into a smaller unit.

B. Incorrect. The consonant blend *dr* can be separated into two smaller units of sound, /d/ and /r/, so it is not a phoneme. It is the onset of the word *dream*.

C. Incorrect. The word part *eam* contains two small units of sound, /ē/ and /m/. It is the rime of the word *dream*.

D. Incorrect. The word part *re* includes two sounds, /r/ and /ĕ/, and does not represent an appropriate way of breaking the word *dream* into parts.

10)

A. Incorrect. Phonics instruction is designed to help students learn letter-sound correspondences so they can decode accurately while reading.

B. Incorrect. Phonemic awareness instruction is designed to help students understand how language is formed by the manipulation of small units of sound.

C. Correct. Sight word instruction is designed to help students recognize high-frequency words automatically, without decoding, so they can read with fluency.

D. Incorrect. Word analysis instruction is designed to help students break words into meaningful parts in order to decipher their meanings in text.

11)

A. Incorrect. Nothing about John Manly's words or actions leads the reader to infer that he does not like his job.

B. **Correct.** The way that John Manly takes care to make the horse comfortable before riding leads the reader to infer that he has respect for horses.

C.   Incorrect. This is information that is directly stated in the text; therefore, it does not need to be inferred.

D.   Incorrect. The text leads the reader to understand that John Manly is an employee at a horse farm, not the owner of the horse.

12)

A. **Correct.** First-person point of view is written from the direct experience of one character—in this case, the horse—as indicated by the pronouns *I* and *my*.

B.   Incorrect. Second-person point of view is written from the perspective of an external *you*, whether that be the reader or unknown other.

C.   Incorrect. Third-person objective point of view is written from the perspective of a detached narrator.

D.   Incorrect. Third-person omniscient point of view is written from the perspective of an all-knowing, detached narrator.

13)

A.   Incorrect. This is not an adequate summary of the excerpt because all it does is provide details about one of the main characters. It does not address the relationship between John Manly and the narrator.

B.   Incorrect. This summary leaves out many important details a reader needs to know, such as who John Manly is and why he is riding the new horse.

C.   Incorrect. This is a confusing summary because it contains irrelevant details and makes it seem as though the squire is one of the main characters instead of focusing on how John Manly interacts with the horse.

D. **Correct.** This is the best summary because it provides a brief explanation of the excerpt's main idea and key details. It only includes the most necessary information a reader needs to comprehend the story section.

14)

A.   Incorrect. The squire is a minor character in this excerpt. His presence simply moves the story along.

B. **Correct.** The excerpt is mainly about the interaction between John Manly and the horse. The focus is on the words and actions of both.

C.   Incorrect. The squire is a minor character in the excerpt, while John Manly is a main character.

D.   Incorrect. John Manly is one of the main characters, but his family does not play a role in the excerpt. They are mentioned only as a detail of John Manly's life.

15)

    A.   **Correct.** The author provides a definition of the word *paces* in the next paragraph when he lists them as trot, canter, and gallop.

    B.   Incorrect. In this instance, the Latin root could be deceptive and thus would not be helpful for determining the meaning of this word. *Pace* means *peace* in Latin; the English word *paces* comes from the Latin *passus* (to step or stretch).

    C.   Incorrect. The denotation of *paces* is used in this excerpt, so there is no connotation attached.

    D.   Incorrect. The setting does offer a limited hint as to the meaning of the word *paces*, in that it suggests that a large area is required, but the definition that the author provides within the third paragraph is clearer and more accessible.

16)

    A.   Incorrect. The horse describes a pleasant afternoon and does not suggest any negative events to come.

    B.   **Correct.** The horse describes an ordinary scene, expressing enjoyment at his grooming and ride with the attentive John Manly.

    C.   Incorrect. The horse expresses pleasure, not sadness.

    D.   Incorrect. The passage is positive, but not overwhelmingly euphoric.

17)

    A.   Incorrect. This excerpt is an example of informational text, or nonfiction text that provides information on a topic. Literary text is the fictional text of novels, stories, and poetry.

    B.   Incorrect. This excerpt uses academic language, or the language of school, as opposed to the informal language of conversation.

    C.   Incorrect. The informational text in this excerpt is accessible to the general public; thus it is not written with terms known specifically to music experts, or discipline specific.

    D.   **Correct.** This text provides information about the composer Chopin in academic language that is accessible to the general public.

18)

    A.   Incorrect. The author's word choice, rather than the picture, determines the tone of the excerpt.

B.   Incorrect. The picture does not help the reader feel the beauty of Chopin's music. This would be accomplished with an audio excerpt or more descriptive text.

C.   Correct. The picture of the "true piano hand" allows the reader to see that the fingers become thinner at the tips, which is a clue to the meaning of the word *tapering*.

D.   Incorrect. The picture shows a "true piano hand," not a "true artist's hand." Although Chopin is described as an artist, there are many different types of artists who require different types of hands, depending on their expertise.

19)

A.   Incorrect. A chart listing the places Chopin played would just restate the text. It would not add to the reader's understanding.

B.   Correct. A map would enable the reader to visualize the locations where Chopin played in relation to each other, thus giving the reader a clearer view of Chopin's area of impact.

C.   Incorrect. A graph is not useful in this instance because there are no numbers to compare.

D.   Incorrect. Places are best visualized on maps or in photographs, so a sidebar with additional text information would not be particularly helpful in this instance.

20)

A.   Correct. *Love* is the smallest unit of the word *loveliness* to contain meaning; therefore, it is the root word. Some root words like *love* can stand on their own and are sometimes referred to as base words.

B.   Incorrect. *Lovely* contains both the root word *love* and the suffix *-ly* (meaning "the essence of something").

C.   Incorrect. *Lov* is a combination of letters with no meaning; thus, it cannot be a root word.

D.   Incorrect. *Loveli* is the simply word *lovely* with the *y* changed to an *i* before the second suffix (-*ness*, meaning "the state or condition of") is added.

21)

A.   Correct. Myths typically include gods and goddesses with abilities that surpass those of humans. Myths describe an earlier version of the world and often attempt to explain how the world came to be as it is.

B.   Incorrect. Fairy tales are make-believe stories that include magic but not gods and goddesses. Fairy tales often include royal characters and standard beginnings and endings such as "once upon a time" and "they lived happily ever after."

C. Incorrect. Narrative poems are stories told with a poetic structure instead of in prose.

D. Incorrect. A drama includes stage directions and parts, or dialogue, for different characters; the story is acted out instead of read like a book.

22)

A. Incorrect. The excerpt describes Midas' father as physically strong, but it does not indicate that Midas is as well.

B. Incorrect. Midas' thoughts and actions in the excerpt do not suggest generosity. Instead, they reveal his insecurity at not descending from a long line of royalty.

C. Correct. The excerpt suggests that Midas' yearning for power comes from concern that he is judged negatively by those with a long lineage of royalty; therefore, the reader can conclude that Midas is insecure about his standing as king.

D. Incorrect. Midas' thoughts and actions in the excerpt do not suggest anger. Instead, they reveal his insecurity at not being from a long line of royalty.

23)

A. Incorrect. This excerpt includes background information about the character of Midas, but no action, so it has not yet developed beyond the exposition phase of the story.

B. Correct. This excerpt is introducing background information about the character of Midas, which is a characteristic of the exposition of a story.

C. Incorrect. This excerpt has not yet developed beyond the exposition phase of the story, so the climax has not yet been revealed.

D. Incorrect. So far, there is no action in the story, only background information about the character of Midas. Therefore, this excerpt comes from the story's exposition.

24)

A. Incorrect. The excerpt does have a particular register that includes vocabulary and usage from the Edwardian era, but in this instance, the register does not aid the reader in determining the meaning of the word *coveted*.

B. Incorrect. Structural analysis is not the optimal choice for determining the meaning of the word *coveted* because it is not a word that has an obvious or common Greek or Latin root.

C. Correct. The repetition of the word *power* and the use of the words *always* and *more* in an additional phrase emphasize the idea that Midas desires power; thus, the syntax of the sentence, or the way it is constructed, provides significant clues to the meaning of *coveted*.

D. Incorrect. While *coveted* tends to have a negative connotation, this connotation would not be understood apart from the meaning of the word, so in this instance, connotation is not the best choice for helping a reader to comprehend the word's meaning.

25)

A. Incorrect. The expression *born and bred to the purple* does not use the over-exaggeration characteristic of hyperbole.

B. Incorrect. Personification is the attribution of human characteristics to a nonhuman thing or abstract idea; the expression *born and bred to the purple* does not feature personification.

C. Incorrect. A simile is a comparison using *like* or *as*. The expression *born and bred to the purple* does not make such a comparison.

D. **Correct.** The expression *born and bred to the purple* is an idiom, or an expression that means more than the sum of its parts. An idiom is commonly understood and used by a specific population; its connotations may not be understood beyond that population, even by people who speak the same language. Here, the expression connotes *royalty*.

26)

A. Incorrect. Myths feature gods and goddesses and explain the origins of places, things, circumstances, etc.

B. **Correct.** Fables feature animals and include explicit moral lessons for readers.

C. Incorrect. Legends are unverified stories from long ago featuring heroes and heroines who overcome overwhelming obstacles.

D. Incorrect. Fairy tales are imaginary, dream-like stories that feature royalty and magical creatures.

27)

A. Incorrect. The way a story is organized may help convey the theme, but it is not the underlying idea that runs through the story.

B. Incorrect. The moral of a story is the lesson the author wants to teach, not the underlying idea that weaves in and out of the text from start to finish.

C. **Correct.** The theme runs throughout a story from start to finish and is the underlying idea that an author wants to convey.

D. Incorrect. Point of view describes the perspective from which a story is told, not the underlying idea that runs through it from start to finish.

28)

    A.   **Correct.** The word *park* acts as an adjective describing the noun *naturalist* in the first sentence and is part of an adjective phrase *from the park*, which modifies the noun *migration* in the second sentence.

    B.   Incorrect. The word *naturalist* is the subject of both sentences. The word *park* acts as an adjective to describe the subject in the first sentence.

    C.   Incorrect. The word *park* is an adjective that describes the subject in the first sentence and part of an adjective phrase that describes the noun *migration* in the second sentence. The predicate of the second sentence includes the word *park* along with all of the other words following the subject (i.e., "visited the class to talk about the migration of Monarch butterflies from the park").

    D.   Incorrect. While the word *park* does act as an adjective to describe the noun *naturalist* in the first sentence, "from the park" is an adjective phrase that modifies the noun *migration*, not the verb *visited*.

29)

    A.   Incorrect. A simple sentence is constructed of only one independent clause.

    B.   Incorrect. A compound sentence is constructed of two or more independent clauses.

    C.   **Correct.** The sentence is an example of a complex sentence with one dependent clause and one independent clause.

    D.   Incorrect. A compound-complex sentence has two or more independent clauses and one or more dependent clauses.

30)

    A.   Incorrect. The use of the contraction *it's* is incorrect. The possessive *its*, without an apostrophe, should be used instead.

    B.   Incorrect. No comma is needed before *because* because the dependent clause follows the independent clause.

    C.   **Correct.** The word *it's* is a contraction meaning *it is*. The possessive form of *its* is written without an apostrophe.

    D.   Incorrect. The use of a present tense verb is correct because the steepness of the trail is a general truth.

31)

    A.   Incorrect. The verb tenses are consistent and explain Lucy's thoughts after the movies have been viewed.

    B.   **Correct.** The word *than*, which is a conjunction used to make comparisons, should be used instead of *then*, which is an adverb that means *at that time*.

    C.   Incorrect. The word *one* refers back to a countable noun, in this instance, *movie*. It is not a dangling modifier, which is a word, phrase, or clause that modifies a subject misplaced in or missing from the sentence.

D. Incorrect. The subject of the sentence is *Lucy*, and it is correctly placed at the beginning of the sentence.

32)

A. Incorrect. Revising part of a story without an organizational framework is less beneficial.

B. Correct. It is most beneficial for students to use graphic organizers to shape their ideas before writing.

C. Incorrect. Drafting the beginning of a story without an organizational framework is less beneficial.

D. Incorrect. Sharing an original story with a classmate should come at the end of the writing process, when the writing has gone through all stages and is ready for an audience.

33)

A. Incorrect. A metaphor is a direct comparison made without the words *like* or *as*.

B. Incorrect. Assonance is the use of similar vowel sounds in a line of poetry.

C. Incorrect. Alliteration is the repetition of closely positioned words that begin with the same sound.

D. Correct. A simile is a comparison made using the words *like* or *as*.

34)

A. Incorrect. It is the poet's choice of rhyme scheme that leads the reader to the correct pronunciation of *quays*, not a comparison using *like* or *as*.

B. Correct. The poet uses an *aabb* rhyme scheme throughout the poem, which lets the reader know that the word *quays* should be pronounced to rhyme with *trees*.

C. Incorrect. It is the poet's choice of rhyme scheme that leads the reader to the correct pronunciation of *quays*, not the attribution of a human quality.

D. Incorrect. It is the poet's choice of rhyme scheme that leads the reader to the correct pronunciation of *quays*, not the point of view used to relate the poem.

35)

A. Correct. Onomatopoeia is the use of words that imitate or resemble sounds.

B. Incorrect. These words describe the poem's setting.

C. Incorrect. These words contribute to the calming tone of the poem.

D. Incorrect. These are sensory words that emphasize illumination.

36)

A. Incorrect. Expository writing is used to explain or inform a reader about a topic in a formal style.

B. Incorrect. Narrative writing is used to relate a highly structured fictional story or personal memoir.

C. **Correct.** Descriptive writing produces sensory imagery and vivid impressions and is often used in poetry.

D. Incorrect. Persuasive writing is used to convince a reader of an opinion or point of view.

37)

A. Incorrect. The conventions remain the same.

B. Incorrect. The sentences share similar organization.

C. Incorrect. Both sentences read naturally.

D. **Correct.** The revised sentence replaces vague and non-descriptive words with more specific words that provide the reader with a clearer idea of the author's message.

38)

A. Incorrect. Revising part of a story without an organizational framework is less beneficial.

B. **Correct.** It is most beneficial for students to use graphic organizers to shape their ideas before writing.

C. Incorrect. Drafting the beginning of a story without an organizational framework is less beneficial.

D. Incorrect. Sharing an original story with a classmate should come at the end of the writing process, when the writing has gone through all stages and is ready for an audience.

39)

A. Incorrect. Learning the names of authors is secondary to avoiding plagiarism, which is a serious issue in the field of research.

B. Incorrect. Categorizing source material relies more on content knowledge than paraphrasing and citing information. It is also secondary to avoiding plagiarism, which is a serious issue in the field of research.

C. **Correct.** Learning the importance of avoiding plagiarism is a critical component of writing instruction for school and career success.

D. Incorrect. Learning how to condense writing for maximum impact relies more on content knowledge than paraphrasing and citing information.

40)

A. **Correct.** Expository writing is most appropriate for the formal and objective presentation of information required in a research paper.

B. Incorrect. A research paper needs to be written with a formal structure and an objective, straightforward tone, so writing that emphasizes imagery is not the best style choice.

C. Incorrect. Narrative writing is used to tell a personal or fictional story that entertains a reader, so it is not the best style choice for a research paper.

D. Incorrect. Persuasive writing is used to convince the reader of an opinion or point of view, but a research paper needs to be written with an objective tone.

41)

A. Incorrect. A handwritten letter by an established historical figure is an example of a primary source because it is significant original, first-hand material.

B. Incorrect. A photograph is an example of a primary source because it is original, first-hand material.

C. Incorrect. An audio recording is an example of a primary source because it is original, first-hand material.

D. **Correct.** A book that discusses a historical time period is an example of a secondary source because it's written by an author who synthesizes and analyzes primary sources to form conclusions.

42)

A. Incorrect. An opinion piece is an example of persuasive writing that aims to influence the reader to agree with what is stated and act accordingly.

B. Incorrect. A cause-and-effect essay is an example of expository writing that explains and provides information.

C. Incorrect. A poem that evokes feeling through imagery is an example of descriptive writing.

D. **Correct.** A personal story with a plot arc is an example of narrative writing.

43)

A. **Correct.** Self-published materials are considered unreliable sources because expertise has not been established.

B. Incorrect. An edited book of essays is considered a reliable research source because expertise is authenticated by the editor selecting the essays.

C. Incorrect. A newspaper article is considered a reliable research source because expertise is authenticated by the publisher.

D.   Incorrect. A university study is considered a reliable research source because expertise is authenticated by the reputation of the institution.

44)

A.   Incorrect. Presenting outcomes is the purpose of the final stage of the writing process.

B.   Incorrect. Organizing ideas is the purpose of the first stage of the writing process.

C.   Correct. Correcting errors is the purpose of the rewriting stage of the writing process.

D.   Incorrect. Recording thoughts is the purpose of the drafting stage of the writing process.

45)

A.   Incorrect. The primary purpose of narrative writing is to entertain.

B.   Correct. The primary purpose of expository writing is to explain.

C.   Incorrect. The primary purpose of persuasive writing is to convince.

D.   Incorrect. The primary purpose of descriptive writing is to describe.

46)

A.   Incorrect. Smiling at the speaker demonstrates active listening because one's focus is on the speaker.

B.   Incorrect. Leaning forward slightly demonstrates active listening because one's focus is on hearing the speaker's words.

C.   Correct. Looking down at the floor does not demonstrate active listening because one's focus is not on the speaker.

D.   Incorrect. Sitting up straight demonstrates active listening because it indicates alertness and concentration.

47)

A.   Correct. This sentence paraphrases the original sentence most accurately because it restates the speaker's main idea and reasoning in a revised and concise way.

B.   Incorrect. This sentence is practically identical to the original statement, so it is not a proper example of paraphrasing.

C.   Incorrect. This sentence restates the speaker's main idea, but it excludes his reasoning, so it is not a good example of paraphrasing.

D.   Incorrect. This sentence alters the speaker's message because it excludes the speaker's main idea, which is that school start times should be later.

48)

A.   Incorrect. Moving around demonstrates a lack of focus and is distracting to a speaker.

B.   Incorrect. Interjecting questions does not demonstrate active listening because it interrupts the speaker.

C.   Incorrect. Frowning and crossed arms do not demonstrate active listening because they are nonverbal cues that convey judgment.

D.   Correct. Eye contact and leaning forward demonstrate that the listener is actively focusing on the speaker's message.

49)

A.   Incorrect. Students are not restating the message in their own words; they are learning editing skills.

B.   Correct. Mr. Kahn is modeling the editing process and reinforcing concepts related to the conventions of Standard English.

C.   Incorrect. This lesson is designed for students who have advanced beyond the decoding stage of reading instruction.

D.   Incorrect. Mr. Kahn is modeling the editing process, not the comprehension skill of inferencing.

50)

A.   Incorrect. Making crayon rubbings helps students internalize letter shapes, but it is not finger spelling.

B.   Correct. Finger spelling is a form of sign language that uses the hands to represent letters.

C.   Incorrect. Using the fingers to count the number of letters in words develops the concept of print, but it is not finger spelling.

D.   Incorrect. Writing letters in trays of sand helps students practice forming letters, but it is not finger spelling.

Mathematics Practice

1

Which equation demonstrates the associative property of addition?

A. $2 + (1 + 5) = (2 + 1) + 5$

B. $2(1 \times 5) = (2 \times 1)5$

C. $1 \times 3 = 3 \times 1$

D. $2(7 + 4) = 2 \times 7 + 2 \times 4$

2

Using the information in the table, which equation demonstrates the linear relationship between x and y?

x	y
3	3
7	15
10	24

A. $y = 6x - 6$

B. $y = 5x - 6$

C. $y = 4x - 6$

D. $y = 3x - 6$

3

Using the table, which equation demonstrates the linear relationship between x and y?

x	y
3	−18
7	−34
10	−46

A. $y = -6x - 6$

B. $y = -5x - 6$

C. $y = -4x - 6$

D. $y = -3x - 6$

4

Students board a bus at 7:45 a.m. and arrive at school at 8:20 a.m. How long are the students on the bus?

A. 30 minutes

B. 35 minutes

C. 45 minutes

D. 60 minutes

5

Which expression has only prime factors of 3, 5, and 11?

A. 66×108

B. 15×99

C. 42×29

D. 28×350

6

Robbie has a bag of treats that contains 5 pieces of gum, 7 pieces of taffy, and 8 pieces of chocolate. If Robbie reaches into the bag and randomly pulls out a treat, what is the probability that Robbie will get a piece of taffy?

A. 1

B. $\frac{1}{7}$

C. $\frac{5}{8}$

D. $\frac{7}{20}$

7

Which figure is a concave polygon?

A.

B.

C.

D.

8

Micah invites 23 friends to his house and is having pizza for dinner. Each pizza feeds approximately 4 people. Micah does not want a lot of leftovers. How many pizzas should he order?

A. 4

B. 5

C. 6

D. 7

9

Kim and Chris are writing a book together. Kim writes twice as many pages as Chris. Altogether, there are 240 pages in the book. Which equation shows how many pages Chris writes?

A. $2 + 2p = 240$

B. $p + 2p = 240$

C. $2p - p = 240$

D. $p - 2p = 240$

10

An ice chest contains 24 sodas, some regular and some diet. The ratio of diet soda to regular soda is 1:3. How many regular sodas are there in the ice chest?

A. 1

B. 3

C. 18

D. 24

11

Which inequality is equivalent to $10 \leq k - 5$?

A. $k \leq 15$

B. $k \geq 15$

C. $k \geq 5$

D. $k \geq 10$

12

What is $\frac{5}{8}$ as a percent?

A. 0.625%

B. 1.6%

C. 16%

D. 62.5%

13

Simplify $(5^2 - 2)^2 + 3^3$.

A. 25

B. 30

C. 556

D. 538

14

Which statement describes the images?

 $\frac{1}{5}$

 $\frac{2}{5}$

 $\frac{3}{5}$

 $\frac{4}{5}$

A. When the numerator stays the same and the denominator increases, the fraction increases.

B. When the numerator increases and the denominator stays the same, the fraction increases.

C. When the numerator and the denominator increase, the fraction decreases.

D. When the numerator stays the same and the denominator decreases, the fraction decreases.

15

Danny collects coins. The table shows how many of each type of coin Danny collects for 4 days. Which statement is true?

Danny's Coin Collection				
Coin	Day 1	Day 2	Day 3	Day 4
Pennies	1	4	5	1
Nickels	4	3	2	5
Dimes	3	2	2	3
Quarters	0	5	4	1

A. The mean number of nickels is greater than the mean number of quarters.

B. The mean number of quarters is greater than the mean number of pennies.

C. The range of dimes is greater than the range of quarters.

D. The median number of pennies is 5.

16

Solve for x.

$x = 6(3^0)$

A. 0

B. 18

C. 180

D. 6

17

A table is 150 centimeters long. How many millimeters long is the table?

A. 1.5 mm

B. 15 mm

C. 150 mm

D. 1500 mm

18

Students are asked if they prefer vanilla, chocolate, or strawberry ice cream. The results are tallied on the table below.

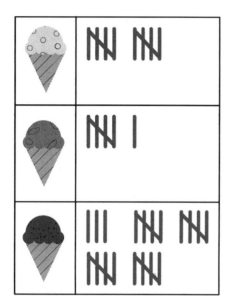

The students display the information from the table in a bar graph. Which student completes the bar graph correctly?

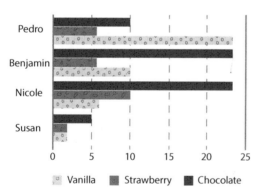

A.   Pedro

B.   Benjamin

C.   Nicole

D.   Susan

19

If the pattern continues, what is the next number?

{2, 5, 14, 41, 122, …}

A.   244

B.   264

C.   422

D.   365

20

What is the value of $3x + 7x$ if $x = 8$?

A.   10

B.   21

C.   31

D.   80

21

What is the value of the digit 4 in the number 654,123?

A.   one thousand

B.   four thousand

C.   ten thousand

D.   forty thousand

22

Which equation is described by the data in the table?

x	y
1	3
2	0
3	−5

A. $y = 4 - x^2$

B. $x^2 + y = 4$

C. $x^2 + y = 2^2$

D.   all of the above

23

The formula for distance is $d = r \times t$. How long will it take a plane to fly 4000 miles from Chicago to London if the plane flies at a constant rate of 500 mph?

A. 20 hours

B. 8 hours

C. 45 hours

D. 3.5 hours

24

Justin has a summer lawn care business. Justin earns $400 per week by taking care of 10 lawns. Justin pays $35/week in business-related expenses. The money Justin saves after x weeks is represented by the expression $x(400 - 35)$. If y represents Justin's total earnings, which expression shows how many dollars Justin earns in a summer?

A. $y = 365x$

B. $35x = 400y$

C. $x + y = 365$

D. $x = 365y$

25

Which expression can be solved using the following steps?

1. Subtract 5 from m.

2. Multiply the result by 2.

3. Cube the result.

A. $[2(m - 5)]^3$

B. $2m^3 - 5$

C. $2m - 5^3$

D. $2(m - 5)^3$

26

Which property is demonstrated by the equivalent expressions?

$7(3 + 5) = 7 \times 3 + 7 \times 5$

A. distributive

B. associative

C. commutative

D. multiplicative

27

Using the function table, what is the value of $f(20)$?

x	$f(x)$
5	12
10	22
15	32
20	
25	52

A. 20

B. 25

C. 42

D. 50

28

Which number has a prime factorization of 3 odd numbers and 1 even number?

A. 9

B. 21

C. 45

D. 90

29

How much longer is line segment MN than line segment KL?

A. 15 mm
B. 20 mm
C. 2 mm
D. 55 mm

30

Which conclusion can be drawn from the graph?

A. More than twice as many students score an "A" in science than score an "F" in science.

B. The majority of the students score a "C" in math.

C. The number of students who score a "B" in reading is equal to the number of students who score a "B" in math.

D. Next year's students do not need very much science instruction because students already know science.

31

In the fall, 425 students pass the math benchmark. In the spring, 680 students pass the same benchmark. What is the percentage increase in passing scores from fall to spring?

A.   40%

B.   55%

C.   60%

D.   80%

32

Noah and Jennifer have a total of $10.00 to spend on lunch. If each buys his or her own order of french fries and a soda, how many orders of chicken strips can they share?

Menu	
Item	**Price**
Hamburger	$4.00
Chicken Strips	$4.00
Onion Rings	$3.00
French Fries	$2.00
Soda	$1.00
Shake	$1.00

A.   0

B.   1

C.   2

D.   3

33

Lynn has 4 grades in science class. Each grade is worth 100 points. Lynn has an 85% average. If Lynn makes 100% on each of the first 3 grades, what does she earn on her 4th grade?

A.   40%

B.   55%

C.   85%

D.   100%

34

Which expression is equivalent to dividing 300 by 12?

A. $2(150 - 6)$

B. $(300 \div 4) \div 6$

C. $(120 \div 6) + (180 \div 6)$

D. $(120 \div 12) + (180 \div 12)$

35

Aprille has $50 to buy the items on her list. Assuming there is no sales tax, about how much change will Aprille receive after buying all the items on her list?

Aprille's List	
Item	**Price**
Hammer	$13.24
Screwdriver	$11.99
Nails	$4.27
Wrench	$5.60

A. $10

B. $15

C. $35

D. $50

36

Which number has the greatest value?

A. 9299 ones

B. 903 tens

C. 93 hundreds

D. 9 thousands

9,030

9,300

37

Which number has the least value?

A. 0.305

B. 0.035

C. 0.35

D. 0.30

38

What is the perimeter of the shape?

A. 2 mm

B. 4 mm

C. 10 mm

D. 20 mm

39

What is the area of the shape?

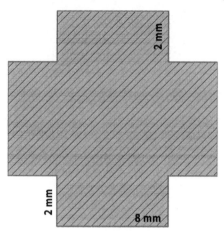

A. 64 mm²

B. 16 mm²

C. 128 mm²

D. 6 mm²

40

Which three-dimensional solid has 2 triangular faces and 3 rectangular faces?

A. pyramid

B. cube

C. rectangular prism

D. triangular prism

41

What are the coefficients and the degrees of the terms in the polynomial?

$4x^3 + 5x^2 + 1$

A. coefficients {4, 5}, degrees {3, 2}

B. coefficients {1, 4, 5}, degrees {3, 2}

C. coefficients {3, 2}, degrees {4, 5}

D. coefficients {3, 2}, degrees {1, 4, 5}

42

In which quadrant is the point (−3, −4) located?

A.   I

B.   II

C.   III

D.   IV

43

Which terms can be used to describe the polygon?

A.   irregular and convex

B.   irregular and concave

C.   regular and convex

D.   regular and concave

less than 180
greater than 180

44

How many times larger is the digit 3 in the first number compared to the second number?

Number One: 846,3̲07

Number Two: 209,023

A.   2

B.   4

C.   10

D.   100

3 00
3

45

A fruit stand sells apples, bananas, and oranges at a ratio of 3:2:1. If the fruit stand sells 20 bananas, how many total pieces of fruit does the fruit stand sell?

A.   10

B.   30

C.   40

D.   60

3 : 2 :
3 : 20 : 1

46

Which type of number is shown below?

3.65555555…

A.   natural number

B.   whole number

C.   integer

D.   rational number

47

Out of 1560 students at Ward Middle School, 15% want to take French. Which equation can determine how many students want to take French?

A. $x = 1560 \div 15$

B. $x = 15 \div 1560$

C. $x = 1560 \times 0.15$

D. $x = 1560 \div 100$ ✗

1560 = 15

48

What is the 6̲th term of the sequence if the pattern is to find the difference between the 2 preceding numbers and then multiply by −3?

{3, 0, −9, −36, 81̲ , ? }

A.   −81

B.   −135

C.   135

D.   81

- 27
- 45

49

Kim drives 75 mph for t hours. If t = time and d = distance, the equation $d = 75t$ describes Kim's drive. Which statement is true?

A. The dependent variable is t because time depends on the distance Kim travels.

B. The independent variable is t because the time is being multiplied by the independent rate of 75.

C. The dependent variable is d because the distance depends on the number of hours Kim drives.

D. The dependent and independent variables cannot be determined in the equation.

$75\,mph$ $d = 75t$

50

Which graph shows the solution to $y = 2x + 1$?

A.

B.

C.

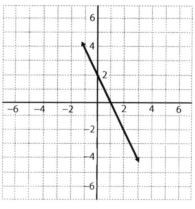

D.

$y = mx + b$

$x \quad , \quad y$
$0 \quad , \quad 1$
$1 \quad , \quad 3$
$2 \quad , \quad 5$

$y = 2(0) + 1$
$1 = 1$ $3 = 3$

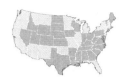

Answer Key

1)

A. **Correct.** $2 + (1 + 5) = (2 + 1) + 5$ is the correct answer. When using the associative property, the answer will remain the same in an addition problem regardless of where the parentheses are placed.

B. Incorrect. $2(1 \times 5) = (2 \times 1)5$ is not the correct answer. This equation demonstrates the associative property of multiplication.

C. Incorrect. $1 \times 3 = 3 \times 1$ is not the correct answer. This equation demonstrates the commutative property of multiplication where the answer in a multiplication problem will remain the same regardless of the order of the numbers.

D. Incorrect. $2(7 + 4) = 2 \times 7 + 2 \times 4$ is not the correct answer. This equation demonstrates the distributive property, which says that multiplication can be distributed over addition.

2)

A. Incorrect. $y = 6x - 6$ is not the correct answer. Solve for y by replacing x with 3.

$y = 6(3) - 6$

$y = 18 - 6$

$y = 12$

The table says that when $x = 3$, $y = 3$, not 12.

B. Incorrect. $y = 5x - 6$ is not the correct answer. Solve for y by replacing x with 3.

$y = 5(3) - 6$

$y = 15 - 6$

$y = 9$

The table says that when $x = 3$, $y = 3$, not 9.

C. Incorrect. $y = 4x - 6$ is not the correct answer. Solve for y by replacing x with 3.

$y = 4(3) - 6$

$y = 12 - 6$

$y = 6$

The table says that when $x = 3$, $y = 3$, not 6.

D. **Correct.** $y = 3x - 6$ is the correct answer. Solve for y by replacing x with 3.

$y = 3(3) - 6$

$y = 9 - 6$

$y = 3$

This is the correct answer because the table says that when $x = 3$, $y = 3$.

3)

A. Incorrect. $y = -6x - 6$ is not the correct answer. Solve for y by replacing x with 3.

$y = -6(3) - 6$

$y = -18 - 6$

$y = -24$

The table says that when $x = 3$, $y = -18$, not -24.

B. Incorrect. $y = -5x - 6$ is not the correct answer. Solve for y by replacing x with 3.

$y = -5(3) - 6$

$y = -15 - 6$

$y = -21$

The table says that when $x = 3$, $y = -18$, not -21.

C. **Correct.** $y = -4x - 6$ is the correct answer. Solve for y by replacing x with 3.

$y = -4(3) - 6$

$y = -12 - 6$

$y = -18$

The table says that when $x = 3$, $y = -18$.

D. Incorrect. $y = -3x - 6$ is not the correct answer. Solve for y by replacing x with 3.

$y = -3(3) - 6$

$y = -9 - 6$

$y = -15$

The table says that when $x = 3$, $y = -18$, not -15.

4)

A. Incorrect. 30 minutes is not correct. There are 15 minutes between 7:45 a.m. and 8:00 a.m. and 20 minutes from 8:00 a.m. until 8:20 a.m.; 15 minutes + 20 minutes = 35 minutes, not 30 minutes.

B. **Correct.** 35 minutes is the correct answer. There are 15 minutes between 7:45 a.m. and 8:00 a.m. and 20 minutes from 8:00 a.m. until 8:20 a.m.; 15 minutes + 20 minutes = 35 minutes.

C.   Incorrect. 45 minutes is not correct. There are 15 minutes between 7:45 a.m. and 8:00 a.m. and 20 minutes from 8:00 a.m. until 8:20 a.m.; 15 minutes + 20 minutes = 35 minutes, not 45 minutes.

D.   Incorrect. 60 minutes is not correct. There are 15 minutes between 7:45 a.m. and 8:00 a.m. and 20 minutes from 8:00 a.m. until 8:20 a.m.; 15 minutes + 20 minutes = 35 minutes, not 60 minutes.

5)

A.   Incorrect. 66 × 108 is not the correct answer. Both numbers are even, so 2 is a factor of both numbers.

B.   **Correct.** 15 × 99 is the correct answer. The factor trees show the factors for 15 and 99.

This answer choice has 3, 5, and 11 as the only prime factors.

C.   Incorrect. 42 × 29 is not the correct answer. Forty-two is an even number, so 2 is a factor.

D.   Incorrect. 28 × 350 is not the correct answer. Both numbers are even, so 2 is a factor of both numbers.

6)

A.   Incorrect. 1 is not the correct answer. $7 \div 20 \neq 1$.

B.   Incorrect. $\frac{1}{7}$ is not the correct answer. $7 \div 20 \neq \frac{1}{7}$.

C.   Incorrect. $\frac{5}{8}$ is not the correct answer. $7 \div 20 \neq \frac{5}{8}$.

D.   **Correct.** 7/20 is the correct answer. Probability is the number of favorable events divided by the number of possible events. In this case, Robbie pulls out 1 treat from a bag that contains 7 pieces of taffy; therefore 7 is the number of favorable events. There are 20 total treats in the bag because $5 + 7 + 8 = 20$. $7 \div 20 = \frac{7}{20}$.

7)

A.   Incorrect. A concave polygon must have an interior angle that measures greater than 180 degrees. A rectangle has four 90-degree angles.

B.   Incorrect. A concave polygon must have an interior angle that measures greater than 180 degrees. The figure depicted is actually a convex polygon.

C.   Incorrect. A concave polygon must have an interior angle that measures greater than 180 degrees. In contrast, the hexagon is a convex polygon.

D. **Correct.** The interior angle on the left side of the figure is greater than 180 degrees.

8)

A. Incorrect. 4 is not the correct answer. 23 people ÷ 4 pizzas = 5.75 people/pizza. This would not be enough because each pizza feeds 4 people.

B. Incorrect. 5 is not the correct answer. 23 people ÷ 5 pizzas = 4.6 people/pizza. This would not be enough because each pizza feeds 4 people.

C. **Correct.** 6 is the correct answer. 23 people ÷ 6 pizzas = 3.8 people/pizza. There would be some pizza left, but this is the closest Micah will be able to get to 4 people/pizza.

D. Incorrect. 7 is not the correct answer. 23 people ÷ 7 pizzas = 3.3 people/pizza. Micah would have too much pizza left.

9)

A. Incorrect. $2 + 2p = 240$ is not the correct answer. If p is the number of pages Chris writes, the equation shows only the pages written by Kim ($2p$) and credits Chris with writing only 2 pages.

B. **Correct.** $p + 2p = 240$ is the correct answer. If p is the number of pages Chris writes, the equation shows that Kim writes $2p$, or twice as many pages as Chris writes. If the number of pages Chris writes is added to the number of pages Kim writes, the total is 240 pages.

C. Incorrect. $2p - p = 240$ is not the correct answer. Adding, not subtracting, will find the total number of pages.

D. Incorrect. $p - 2p = 240$ is not the correct answer. Adding, not subtracting, will find the total number of pages.

10)

A. Incorrect. 1 is not the correct answer; it represents the number of diet sodas for every 3 regular sodas.

B. Incorrect. 3 is not the correct answer; it represents the number of regular sodas for every 1 diet soda.

C. **Correct.** 18 is the correct answer. One way to find the answer is to draw a picture.

Put 24 cans into groups of 4. One out of every 4 cans is diet (light gray) so there is 1 light gray can for every 3 dark gray cans. That leaves 18 dark gray cans (regular soda).

Another way to solve the problem is to use ratios. There is 1 diet soda for every 3 regular sodas, for a total of 4 sodas. Diet = 1, regular = 3, total = 4.

$$\frac{\text{Regular}}{\text{Total}} = \frac{3}{4} = \frac{x}{24}$$

Cross-multiply $4x = 72$ and $x = 18$.

D. Incorrect. 24 is not the correct answer; it simply represents the total number of sodas.

11)

A. Incorrect. $k \leq 15$ is not the correct answer. Use the steps to solve the inequality.

$10 \leq k - 5$

$5 + 10 \leq k - 5 + 5$ Add 5 to both sides to isolate the variable.

$15 \leq k$

15 is less than or equal to k. Notice that the answer choice is written as k is less than or equal to 15 ($k \leq 15$), which is backward.

B. Correct. $k \geq 15$ is the correct answer. The sign is flipped from what is shown in the problem, but k is equal to or greater than 15.

C. Incorrect. $k \geq 5$ is not the correct answer. Add 5 rather than subtract 5 from both sides of the inequality to isolate the variable.

D. Incorrect. $k \geq 10$ is not the correct answer. Isolate the variable to solve the problem.

12)

A. Incorrect. 0.625% is not the correct answer. This answer results from correctly dividing the numerator by the denominator but forgetting to multiply the answer by 100.

B. Incorrect. 1.6% is not the correct answer. This answer results from confusing the numerator (top number) and the denominator (bottom number) and forgetting to multiply by 100.

C. Incorrect. 16% is not the correct answer. To change a fraction to a percent, divide the numerator by the denominator and then multiply by 100. This answer results from dividing the denominator by the numerator.

D. Correct. 62.5% is the correct answer; $5 \div 8 = 0.625$ and $0.625 \times 100 = 62.5\%$.

13)

A. Incorrect. 25 is not the correct answer. Remember that 5^2 is equal to 5×5.

B. Incorrect. 30 is not the correct answer. To solve the expression, use the order of operations. Step One: Solve the exponent in parentheses. Step Two: Subtract the numbers in parentheses. Step Three: Solve the exponents. Step Four: Add the numbers.

C. Correct. 556 is the correct answer. $(5^2 - 2)^2 + 3^3$

$(25 - 2)^2 + 3^3$

$(23)^2 + 3^3$

$529 + 27 = 556$

D. Incorrect. 538 is not the correct answer. The answer resulted from the mistake of multiplying 3×3 rather than solving 3^3. Remember $3^3 = 3 \times 3 \times 3$.

14)

A. Incorrect. (A) is not correct because the images show the numerator increasing, not the denominator. If the denominator increases and the numerator remains constant ($\frac{1}{5}, \frac{1}{6}, \frac{1}{7}, \frac{1}{8}$), the fraction decreases.

B. **Correct.** The images show the numerator increasing while the denominator stays the same; meanwhile, the fraction is increasing.

C. Incorrect. When both the numerator and denominator increase, there are inconsistencies in the comparative size of the fraction.

D. Incorrect. If the numerator stays the same and the denominator decreases, the fraction will increase.

15)

A. **Correct.** To calculate the mean, add all the numbers in a set and divide by how many numbers are in the set. The mean number of nickels is $4 + 3 + 2 + 2 = 11$ divided by 4 (because there are 4 numbers in the set) $= 2.75$ nickels. The mean number of quarters is $0 + 5 + 4 + 1 = 10$ divided by $4 = 2.5$ quarters. $2.75 > 2.5$.

B. Incorrect. The mean of the pennies is $1 + 4 + 5 + 1 = 11$ divided by $4 = 2.75$. The mean number of quarters is $0 + 5 + 4 + 1 = 10$ divided by $4 = 2.5$. The mean number of pennies is greater than the mean number of quarters.

C. Incorrect. The range is the difference between the highest number and the lowest number in the set. For the dimes, the highest number is 3 and the lowest number is 2, so $3 - 2 = 1$. For the quarters, the highest number is 5 and the lowest number is 0. $5 - 0 = 5$. $1 < 5$.

D. Incorrect. The median is a middle number in a set. The set of pennies in numerical order is {1, 1, 4, 5}. In this case, there are two numbers in the middle; therefore, averaging the one and the four will find the median. The median of the set of pennies is 2.5.

16)

A. Incorrect. 0 is not the correct answer. The answer results from multiplying 3×0. Remember that $3^0 = 1$, not 0.

B. Incorrect. 18 is not the correct answer. The first step in the equation is to solve the exponent.

C. Incorrect. 180 is not the correct answer. The problem is not solved by multiplying 6×30.

D. **Correct.** 6 is the correct answer. Any number with a 0 exponent equals 1. Therefore, $6(3^0) = 6(1) = 6$.

17)

A. Incorrect. 1.5 mm is not the correct answer. One centimeter = 10 millimeters. The answer results from moving the decimal point two places and in the wrong direction.

B. Incorrect. 15 mm is incorrect. The answer results from moving the decimal point one place in the wrong direction.

C. Incorrect. 150 mm is not the correct answer. Millimeters are not equal to centimeters.

D. **Correct.** 1500 mm is the correct answer. 1 centimeter = 10 millimeters and $150 \times 10 = 1500$.

18)

A. Incorrect. Pedro's graph is incorrect. He confuses the number of students who prefer vanilla with the number of students who prefer chocolate.

B. **Correct.** Benjamin completed the graph correctly. His bar graph indicates that 10 students prefer vanilla, 6 students prefer strawberry, and 23 students prefer chocolate ice cream.

C. Incorrect. Nicole did not complete the graph correctly. She confuses the number of students who like vanilla with the number of students who like strawberry.

D. Incorrect. Susan's graph is not correct. She did not accurately count the tallies before making her bar graph.

19)

A. Incorrect. 244 is not the correct answer. The answer results from multiplying the last number in the set by 2. Numbers in the set do not follow the pattern of multiplying by 2 because $2 \times 2 \neq 5$.

B. Incorrect. 264 is not the correct answer. Numbers in the set are not following a sequence that would match the answer.

C. Incorrect. 422 is not the correct answer. Numbers in the set are not following a sequence that would match the answer.

D. **Correct.** 365 is the correct answer. The pattern follows the equation $3n - 1 = x$. n = the last number in the set, and x = the next number in the set. Another pattern is adding by exponents of 3. Remember $3 \times 3 \times 3 \times 3 \times 3 = 3^5 = 243$. The pattern is $2 + 3^1 = 5$, $5 + 3^2 + 14$, $14 + 3^3 = 41$, $41 + 3^4 = 122$, $122 + 3^5 = 365$.

20)

A.   Incorrect. 10 is not the correct answer because $3(8) + 7(8) = 24 + 56 \neq 10$.

B.   Incorrect. 21 is not the correct answer because $3(8) + 7(8) = 24 + 56 \neq 21$.

C.   Incorrect. 31 is not the correct answer because $3(8) + 7(8) = 24 + 56 \neq 31$.

D.   Correct. 80 is the correct answer. $3(8) + 7(8) = 24 + 56 = 80$. Or, put another way, $3x + 7x = 10x$ and $(10)(8) = 80$.

21)

A.   Incorrect. While 4 is in the thousands place, a 4 in that position is equal to 4000.

B.   Correct. 4000 is the correct answer because
$654,123 = 600,000 + 50,000 + 4000 + 100 + 20 + 3$.

C.   Incorrect. 10,000 is incorrect because 5 is in the ten-thousands place.

D.   Incorrect. 40,000 is incorrect because 4 is in the thousands place, not the ten-thousands place.

22)

A.   Incorrect. $y = 4 - x^2$ is a correct answer, but it is not the only correct answer. Substitute 1 for x and 3 for y.

$3 = 4 - 1^2$

$3 = 4 - 1$

$3 = 3$

B.   Incorrect. $x^2 + y = 4$ is a correct answer, but it is not the only correct answer. Substitute 1 for x and 3 for y.

$1^2 + 3 = 4$

$1 + 3 = 4$

$4 = 4$

C.   Incorrect. $x^2 + y = 2^2$ is a correct answer, but it is not the only correct answer. Substitute 1 for x and 3 for y.

$1^2 + 3 = 2^2$

$1 + 3 = 4$

$4 = 4$

D.   Correct. All of the above are correct. For each equation, replacing the variables with the numbers in the function table makes a true statement.

23)

A.   Incorrect. Multiplying the rate by the distance does not find the time, so 20 hours cannot be the correct answer.

B.   Correct. 8 hours is the correct answer. Time is distance divided by rate; $4000 \text{ mi}/500 \text{ mph} = 8$ hours.

C. Incorrect. 45 hours is not the correct answer. Adding the rate and the distance is not a way to find the time.

D. Incorrect. 3.5 hours is not the correct answer. Subtracting the rate from the distance is a not a way to find the time.

24)

A. **Correct.** $y = 365x$ is the correct answer. The total savings is equal to the number of weeks Justin works times $365/week profit.

B. Incorrect. $35x = 400y$ is incorrect because the equation says that 400 times the total savings is equal to the business expenses times the number of weeks worked.

C. Incorrect. The weekly profit is not found by adding the number of weeks worked to the total savings.

D. Incorrect. The total number of weeks worked is not equal to the $365/week profit multiplied by the total savings.

25)

A. **Correct.** $[2(m - 5)]^3$ is the correct answer. Using order of operations, the expression is solved using the steps.

B. Incorrect. $2m^3 - 5$ is not the correct answer. In this expression, 5 is subtracted from $2m^3$.

C. Incorrect. $2m - 5^3$ is not the correct answer. In this expression, only 5 is cubed.

D. Incorrect. $2(m - 5)^3$ is not the correct answer. In this expression, only the expression in the parentheses is cubed.

26)

A. **Correct.** The equivalent expressions demonstrate the distributive property, which says that multiplication distributes over addition: $a(b + c) = ab + ac$.

B. Incorrect. The associative property states that multiplication or addition problems can be regrouped: $(ab)c = a(bc)$ or $(a + b) + c = a + (b + c)$.

C. Incorrect. The commutative property states that order does not matter when multiplying or adding: $ab = ba$ or $a + b = b + a$.

D. Incorrect. The multiplicative property states that both sides of the equation remain the same if they are multiplied by the same number; on the other hand, the distributive property says that multiplication distributes over addition.

27)

A. Incorrect. 20 is not the correct answer. The relationship between x and $f(x)$ is $\neq$.

    B.   Incorrect. 25 is not the correct answer. The relationship between x and $f(x)$ is $\neq +5$.

    C.   **Correct.** 42 is the correct answer. The relationship between x and $f(x)$ is $2x + 2$.

    D.   Incorrect. 50 is not the correct answer. The relationship between x and $f(x)$ is $\neq 2x + 10$.

28)

    A.   Incorrect. 9 is incorrect because the prime factorization of 9 is 3×3: there are no even factors.

    B.   Incorrect. 21 is incorrect because the prime factorization of 21 is 3×7: there are no even numbers.

    C.   Incorrect. 45 is incorrect because the prime factorization of 45 is $3 \times 3 \times 5$: there are no even numbers.

    D.   **Correct.** 90 is correct because the prime factorization of 90 is $2 \times 3 \times 3 \times 5$. Ninety, as the only even number of the answer choices, has an even number (2) as a factor.

29)

    A.   Incorrect. 15 mm is the length of line segment $\overline{KL}$.

    B.   **Correct.** Line segment $\overline{MN}$ begins at 35 mm and ends at 70 mm, so $70 - 35 = 35$ mm. Line segment $\overline{MN}$ is 35 mm. The length of line segment $\overline{KL}$ is 15 mm. To find out how much longer $\overline{MN}$ is than $\overline{KL}$, subtract, 35 mm $- 15$ mm $= 20$ mm.

    C.   Incorrect. 20 mm $= 2$ cm, not 2 mm.

    D.   Incorrect. 55 mm is not the correct answer. 70 mm is where $\overline{MN}$ ends, 15 mm is the length of $\overline{KL}$, and $70 - 15 = 55$; however the distance between L and M is ignored.

30)

    A.   **Correct.** Twenty-five students score an "F" in science, and 70 students score an "A" in science; $2(25) < 70$.

    B.   Incorrect. There are 170 students total with math grades. A majority would be more than half (85). Only 35 students score a "C" in math.

    C.   Incorrect. Forty students score a "B" in reading and 35 students score a "B" in math.

    D.   Incorrect. The graph does not include information about next year's students.

31)

A.   Incorrect. 40% is incorrect: $680 - 425 = 255$, $255 \div 425 = .60$, and $.60 \times 100 \neq 40\%$.

B.   Incorrect. 55% is incorrect: $680 - 425 = 255$, $255 \div 425 = .60$, and $.60 \times 100 \neq 55\%$.

C.   Correct. 60% is the correct answer. To calculate the percentage increase, find the difference between the ending number and the beginning number ($680 - 425 = 255$). Divide the difference by the beginning number ($255 \div 425 = .60$), and then multiply the decimal by 100 to change to a percentage ($.60 \times 100 = 60\%$).

D.   Incorrect. 80% is incorrect: $680 - 425 = 255$, $255 \div 425 = .60$, and $.60 \times 100 \neq 80\%$.

32)

A.   Incorrect. 0 is not the correct answer because $4.00 can buy 1 order of chicken strips.

B.   Correct. 1 is the correct answer. To find out how many orders of chicken strips Jennifer and Noah can buy, use the equation:

$\$10 - 2(\$2.00 + \$1.00) = x$

$\$10 - 2(\$3.00) = x$

$\$10 - \$6.00 = \$4.00$

Four dollars is enough money to buy 1 order of chicken strips to share.

C.   Incorrect. 2 is incorrect because $4.00 is insufficient to buy 2 orders of chicken strips.

D.   Incorrect. 3 is incorrect because $4.00 is not enough money to buy 3 orders of chicken strips.

33)

A.   Correct. 40% is the correct answer. To calculate the average, add all of the scores and divide by the total number of scores. Use the variable "x" in place of the missing score. $(100 + 100 + 100 + x) \div 4 = 85$

Isolate the variable. $(300 + x) \div 4 = 85$

Multiply both sides by 4. $(300 + x) = 340$

Subtract 300 from both sides. $x = 40$

B.   Incorrect. If Lynn had scored 55%, her average would be 88.75% because $355 \div 4 = 88.75\%$.

C.   Incorrect. If Lynn had scored 85%, her average would be 96.25% because $385 \div 4 = 96.25\%$.

D.   Incorrect. If Lynn had scored 100%, her average would be 100% because $400 \div 4 = 100\%$.

34)

A.   Incorrect. $2(150 - 6)$ is not the correct answer.

$2(150 - 6) \neq 300 \div 12$

$2(144) \neq 25$

$288 \neq 25$

B.   Incorrect. $(300 \div 4) \div 6$ is not the correct answer.

$(300 \div 4) \div 6 \neq 300 \div 12$

$75 \div 6 \neq 25$

$12.5 \neq 25$

C.   Incorrect. $(120 \div 6) + (180 \div 6)$ is not the correct answer.

$(120 \div 6) + (180 \div 6) \neq 300 \div 12$

$20 + 30 \neq 300 \div 12$

$50 \neq 25$

D.   Correct. $(120 \div 12) + (180 \div 12)$ is the correct answer.

$(120 \div 12) + (180 \div 12) = 300 \div 12$

$(10) + (15) = 25$

$25 = 25$

35)

A.   Incorrect. $10 is insufficient change.

B.   Correct. To estimate the amount of the change, round the price of each item to the nearest dollar amount and subtract from the total:

$\$50 - (\$13 + \$12 + \$4 + \$6)$

$\$50 - \$35 = \$15$

The correct answer is $15.

C.   Incorrect. $35 is not the correct answer. Adding the price of each item will equal approximately $35. To find out the amount of change, subtract $35 from $50.

D.   Incorrect. $50 is not the correct answer; it is the amount before any purchases are made.

36)

A.   Incorrect. 9299 ones is not the correct answer because 9299 ones = 9299.

B.   Incorrect. 903 tens is not the correct answer because 903 tens = 9030.

C.   Correct. 93 hundreds is the correct answer because 93 hundreds = 9300, and 9300 is greater than the other answer choices.

D.   Incorrect. 9 thousands is not the correct answer because 9 thousands = 9000.

37)

A. Incorrect. 0.305 is not the correct answer because $0.305 = \frac{305}{1000}$.

B. **Correct.** 0.035 is the correct answer because $0.035 = \frac{35}{1000}$; notice the 0 in the tenths place.

C. Incorrect. 0.35 is not the correct answer because $0.35 = \frac{350}{1000}$.

D. Incorrect. 0.3 is not the correct answer because $0.3 = \frac{300}{1000}$.

38)

A. Incorrect. One side is 2 mm long, but the shape has 10 sides.

B. Incorrect. Each of the 10 sides of this shape must be added to find the perimeter, not just the labeled sides.

C. Incorrect. There are 5 points to a star, but each point has 2 sides. While 5×2 mm = 10 mm, the lengths of all 10 sides must be added to get the perimeter.

D. **Correct.** 20 mm is the correct answer. There are 10 sides and each side is 2 mm in length. To find the perimeter, add the length of each side to find the total. P= $2 + 2 + 2 + 2 + 2 + 2 + 2 + 2 + 2 + 2 = 20$ mm.

39)

A. Incorrect. 64 mm^2 is not the correct answer; it is the area of the four small rectangles that protrude on each side.

B. Incorrect. 16 mm^2 is not the correct answer; it is the area of one of the small rectangles that protrude on each side.

C. **Correct.** 128 mm^2 is the correct answer. Find the area of the square as if it did not have cut-outs; each side would be 12 mm long. 12 mm $\times$ 12 mm = 144 mm^2. Next, subtract the area of the cut-outs from the total area of the square. The area of each cut-out is 2 mm $\times$ 2 mm = 4 mm^2. There are cut-outs in each of the 4 corners; therefore, multiply by 4; $4 \times 4 = 16$. Subtract the total area of the four cut-outs from the total area of the square without the cut-outs; $144 - 16 = 128$ mm^2.

D. Incorrect. 6 mm^2 is not the correct answer. Subtracting $8 - 2$ will not find the area of the shape.

40)

A. Incorrect. There are no rectangular faces on a pyramid.

B. Incorrect. There are no triangular faces on a cube.

C. Incorrect. There are no triangular faces on a rectangular prism.

D. **Correct.** A triangular prism has 2 triangular faces and 3 rectangular faces.

41)

A. **Correct.** Coefficients {4, 5}, degrees {3, 2} is the correct answer. The coefficients are the numbers before the exponent in a polynomial. The degrees are the exponents in a polynomial.

B. Incorrect. Coefficients {1, 4, 5}, degrees {3, 2} is not the correct answer. The number 1 is a constant in this polynomial; it is neither a coefficient nor a degree.

C. Incorrect. Coefficients {3, 2}, degrees {4, 5} is not the correct answer. The degrees and coefficients are switched.

D. Incorrect. Coefficients {3, 2}, degrees {1, 4, 5} is not the correct answer. The degrees and coefficients are switched, and 1 is neither a coefficient nor a degree.

42)

A. Incorrect. Points in quadrant I have a positive x and a positive y coordinate.

B. Incorrect. Points in quadrant II have a negative x and a positive y coordinate.

C. **Correct.** Points in quadrant III have a negative x and a negative y coordinate.

D. Incorrect. Points in quadrant IV have a positive x and a negative y coordinate.

43)

A. **Correct.** The polygon is irregular and convex. A polygon is irregular if the sides and angles are not the same. In the trapezoid, the side on top is shorter than the bottom; therefore the trapezoid is irregular. Convex polygons have interior angles that are less than 180 degrees, which is true for this trapezoid.

B. Incorrect. This polygon is irregular, but it is not concave. Concave polygons have interior angles that are greater than 180 degrees. All interior angles in the trapezoid are less than 180 degrees.

C. Incorrect. The polygon is convex, but it is not regular. The trapezoid is not a regular polygon because all sides are not the same length.

D. Incorrect. The polygon is neither regular nor concave. Furthermore, all regular polygons are convex.

44)

A. Incorrect. The 3 has a difference of 2 place values and 2 place values are equal to 100.

B. Incorrect. The number 846,307 is about four times 209,023, but that is not what the question is asking. For this problem, only consider the digit in each number.

C. Incorrect. If there is 1 place value difference between the digits, this would be the correct answer, but there are 2 place value differences between the digits.

D. **Correct.** 100 is the correct answer. In number one, the digit 3 represents 300. In number two, the digit 3 represents 3. $300 \div 3 = 100$.

45)

A. Incorrect. Ten oranges were sold; this number does not account for apples or bananas.

B. Incorrect. Thirty apples were sold; this number does not account for oranges or bananas.

C. Incorrect. Altogether, 40 oranges and apples were sold, but bananas are not accounted for here.

D. **Correct.** 60 is the correct answer:

1. Assign variables: $x = $ apples; $y = $ oranges

2. Write the ratios as fractions.
   apples/bananas $= \frac{3}{2} = \frac{x}{20}$.
   oranges/bananas $= \frac{1}{2} = \frac{y}{20}$.

3. Cross-multiply to solve.
   $60 = 2x, x = 30$ apples
   $2y = 20, y = 10$ oranges

4. To find the total, add the number of apples, oranges, and bananas together. $30 + 20 + 10 = 60$ pieces of fruit.

46)

A. Incorrect. Natural numbers are used when counting. This number contains a repeating decimal.

B. Incorrect. Whole numbers are the set of natural numbers including zero.

C. Incorrect. Integers are positive or negative whole numbers and do not include repeating decimals.

D. **Correct.** This is a rational number. Rational numbers include fractions and repeating decimals.

47)

A. Incorrect. $x = 1560 \div 15$ is not the correct answer. The total is never divided by the percent.

B. Incorrect. $x = 15 \div 1560$ is not the correct answer. The percentage is never divided by the total.

C. **Correct.** $x = 1560 \times 0.15$ is the correct answer. To find a percentage, use a proportion: $15\%/100\% = x/1560$. Cross-multiply: $100x = 1560 \times 15$. Isolate the variable by dividing both sides of the equation by 100: $x = 1560 \times 15/100$. 15/100, expressed as a decimal, is 0.15.

D. Incorrect. $x = 1560 \div 100$ is not the correct answer. This is part of the solution; do not forget to multiply by the percentage.

48)

A. Incorrect. −81 is incorrect; it is the 5th term in the sequence. The question asks for the 6th term.

B. **Correct.** −135 is the correct answer. The difference between −9 and −36 is 27. 27 × −3 = −81. This is the 5th term in the set. To find the 6th term, find the difference between −81 and −36 (45). 45 × −3 = −135.

C. Incorrect. 135 is incorrect; it is the opposite of the 6th term in the sequence.

D. Incorrect. 81 is incorrect; it is the opposite of the 5th term.

49)

A. Incorrect. t is not the dependent variable because the hours driven do not depend on the distance that is driven.

B. Incorrect. The rate of 75 mph is a constant and is neither a dependent nor an independent variable.

C. **Correct.** The distance that Kim travels depends on the number of hours Kim drives.

D. Incorrect. Distance is the dependent variable and can be calculated using the constant and the independent variable.

50)

A. **Correct.** Graph A is correct. To solve this problem, use a table to find some coordinates:

x	y
0	1
1	3
2	5

When plotting the coordinates on the graph, graph A is the only graph that has (0,1), (1,3), and (2,5) as points on the line.

B. Incorrect. Graph B is not correct. The point (0,−2) is on the line. Substituting into the equation $y = 2x + 1$, if $x = 0$, then $y = 2(0) + 1$ and $y = 1$, so this cannot be the correct answer.

C. Incorrect. Graph C is not correct. The line contains (0,1), but not (1,3) or (2,5).

D. Incorrect. Graph D is not the correct answer. The point (0,2) is on the line. Substituting into the equation $y = 2x + 1$, if $x = 0$, then $y = 1$, and this cannot be the correct answer.

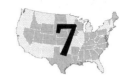

Social Studies Practice

1

Which of the following events contributed to the United States' entry into World War II?

A.   Germany's unrestricted submarine warfare

B.   the attack on Pearl Harbor

C.   the Battle of Britain

D.   the Battle of the Bulge

2

Which of the following factors might contribute to inflation?

A.   high interest rates and a low amount of printed currency

B.   high unemployment rates

C.   a decrease in supply and a low amount of printed currency

D.   a decrease in supply and a large amount of printed currency

3

Luther and Barbara wanted to start a business in the engineering field. They were trying to decide between hiring one staff member and using the leftover money to purchase new inventory, or hiring two staff members to increase their marketing reach. These choices would be an example of

A.   needs.

B.   scarcity.

C.   opportunity cost.

D.   supply and demand.

4

Which of the following continents is located in both the Eastern and Western Hemispheres?

A.   Europe

B.   Africa

C.   North America

D.   A and B

5

Which of the following events is recognized as the beginning of the American Civil War?

A.   the Battle of Palmito Ranch

B.   the Battle of Fort Sumter

C.   the Missouri Compromise

D.   the Battle of Yorktown

6

Which of the following most contributed to the fall of the ancient Egyptians?

A.   the death of Cleopatra

B.   Alexander the Great conquering their land

C.   severe droughts

D.   Canaanite settlers entering Egypt

7

Which of the following is most likely a lasting influence ancient Romans had on modern society?

A.   the development of direct democracy

B.   the usage of columns in architecture

C.   the development of republican democracy

D.   literacy

8

Which of the following is NOT a true statement about the ancient Greek civilization?

A.   Men and women lived in different parts of a house.

B.   They built aqueducts to carry water to public toilets.

C.   Greek cities had an agora.

D.   Socrates was a famous Greek philosopher.

9

Which of the following terms describes the economic principle of allowing industry to grow without any government intervention?

A.   interdependence

B.   free-market economy

C.   communism

D.   monopoly

10

Which of the following does NOT describe gender roles?

A.   Gender roles feature behaviors considered appropriate for each sex by society, which generally acknowledges only male and female.

B.   There is a consensus that gender roles are socially constructed.

C.   Gender roles center on the ideas of masculinity and femininity.

D.   Prevailing gender roles have been challenged.

11

Which of the following would be the most useful for studying population patterns within the state of Texas over a period of time?

A.   a bar graph detailing population numbers over a period of 30 years

B.   a map with the number of people living in different parts of Texas in the year 2000

C.   a photograph showing how many people were at a state fair

D.   a bar graph detailing population percentages compared with other states

12

Which of the following presidents was responsible for the New Deal?

A.   Herbert Hoover

B.   Rutherford Hayes

C.   Franklin D. Roosevelt

D.   Jimmy Carter

13

Which of the following is NOT a responsibility of the executive branch?

A.   approving laws

B.   making laws

C.   implementing laws

D.   enforcing laws

14

Which of the following describes a significant effect of the depletion of the ozone layer?

A. people get darker skin

B. more UV rays enter the earth

C. increased skin cancer rates, build-up of greenhouse gases, and increased UV levels

D. increased build-up of greenhouse gases

15

Which of the following constitutional amendments is NOT considered part of the Bill of Rights?

A. the right to bear arms

B. the right to address witnesses arranged by the government when on trial

C. the right to equal protection under the law

D. freedom of speech

16

Antitrust law strengthens market forces to prevent monopolies. Which of the following terms best describes the implementation of antitrust law?

A. social regulation

B. economic regulation

C. health regulation

D. social security

17

Which of the following is an example of human geography?

A. studying climate

B. studying the spread of Christianity across the world

C. studying the effect of land features on animals and plants

D. studying continental movement over a period of time

18

Which of the following is a positive effect of urbanization?

A. increased tenement housing

B. sanitary conditions

C. political machines

D. increased employment opportunities

19

Asking citizens to be civil minded and independent and making the people as a whole sovereign is characteristic of

A. republicanism.

B. government.

C. economics.

D. communism.

20

A map of France shows a small box around Nice. Nice is portrayed in greater detail in a box at the bottom. Which of the following terms describes this box?

A. legend

B. inset

C. compass

D. insert

21

Which of the following did NOT contribute to the outbreak of the American Revolution?

A. the Boston Tea Party, in which colonists threw 298 chests of tea into the sea

B. Britain banning further westward expansion with the Proclamation of 1763

C. General Thomas Gage ordering troops to capture Thomas Jefferson and Samuel Adams

D. Charles Townshend taxing glass, oil, lead, and paint

22

Which of the following is an event that successfully ended the Cold War?

A. the August coup

B. the fall of the Berlin Wall

C. the Cuban missile crisis

D. the success of the Sputnik program

23

Which of the following established the concept of judicial review?

A. the John Peter Zenger trial

B. *Marbury v. Madison*

C. the Dred Scott case

D. the Scopes Monkey trial

24

Which of the following is an example of the separation of powers?

A.   No members of Congress can serve in another branch of government.

B.   The president cannot vote on legislation.

C.   checks and balances

D.   all of the above

25

Which of the following is a significant contribution of ancient China?

A.   Mahjong

B.   toothbrushes

C.   gunpowder

D.   the animal zodiac

26

Which of the following best exemplifies a global marketplace?

A.   A US freelancer goes on vacation in Paris and does remote work for a US client.

B.   A business in the United States orders parts from Taiwan, India, and Mexico then assembles the final product in Germany.

C.   A commercial website purchases inventory from China.

D.   Appliances share a standardized electrical system.

27

Which of the following periods contributed to advancements of mathematics in ancient Greece?

A.   the Classical period (500 – 336 BC)

B.   the Early Bronze Age (2900 – 2000 BC)

C.   the Hellenistic period (336 – 146 BC)

D.   the Archaic period (750 – 500 BC)

28

Which of the following is a responsibility of a citizen of the United States?

A.   to treat others with kindness

B.   to join after-school clubs

C.   to suffer the consequences of breaking a law

D.   to start a business

29

Fred wants to write a paper on Benjamin Franklin and his influence on science. He wants to include Franklin's theories about electricity. Which of the following resources should he use?

A. a chart depicting what devices used electricity after the invention of the lightbulb

B. an essay about the effects of lightning

C. a newspaper report on Franklin's many inventions

D. a draft scientific report Franklin wrote on electricity

30

Which of the following lands was acquired during the Louisiana Purchase?

A. the land roughly bordered by the Rocky Mountains, the Mississippi River, and the Rio Grande River

B. the land roughly bordered by the Rocky Mountains, the Mississippi River, and the northern border of modern-day Texas

C. the land between the Rocky Mountains and the Mississippi River, and modern-day Georgia

D. the land roughly bordered by the Rocky Mountains and the Mississippi River, and including modern-day New Mexico

31

Which of the following major events in US history led to a decline in immigration?

A. the Immigration Act of 1965

B. the Immigration Act of 1924 and the Great Depression

C. World War I, the Great Depression, and the Immigration Act of 1924

D. the Great Depression only

32

Which of the following was NOT a consequence of the scarcity of oil that led to the energy crisis in the 1970s?

A. The president urged US citizens to heat only one room in their homes in the winter.

B. The automotive industry suffered as Japan created more fuel-efficient vehicles.

C. Political leaders asked gas stations to close for one day a week.

D. Oil prices were high for most of the decade.

33

Which of the following is not a responsibility of the president of the United States?

A. setting foreign policy

B. writing legislations

C. delivering the State of the Union address

D. pardoning felons

34

A sign on the freeway indicates that you are 150 miles from the city of Pittsburgh. This shows your

A. absolute location.

B. physical geography.

C. geographic feature.

D. relative location.

35

Why did Congress pass the Neutrality Acts?

A. only to prevent the United States from loaning any money to nations at war

B. to help the United States have the best chance of winning a foreign war

C. to prevent the United States from engaging in civil war

D. to prevent direct and indirect US involvement in foreign conflict

36

Which of the following emerged during World War I?

A. penicillin

B. aircraft carriers

C. radar

D. nuclear power

37

Which of the following was a method people used to prevent risk of discovery when helping slaves escape through the Underground Railroad?

A. Escape routes were usually indirect in order to confuse pursuers.

B. Escape routes were usually direct to get slaves to freedom more quickly.

C. Children stayed with their mothers.

D. Information about routes was passed along by small notes.

38

Which of the following historical figures was a major architect of the US Constitution?

A.   Thomas Jefferson

B.   George Washington

C.   James Madison

D.   Patrick Henry

39

Which of the following protects freedom of religion in the United States?

A.   separation of powers

B.   the First Amendment

C.   power of eminent domain

D.   popular sovereignty

40

Which of the following amendments prevents the government from quartering troops in private homes?

A.   the Seventh Amendment

B.   the Fourth Amendment

C.   the Third Amendment

D.   the Ninth Amendment

41

A project in which students research and explore significant contributions made by their community is an example of

A.   questioning only

B.   collaboration

C.   data interpretation only

D.   inquiry-based learning

42

A student completes a research project on significant events of the American Revolution. Which of the following is an appropriate method to determine the credibility of the resources he or she has used to conduct research?

A.   checking the author and date of research

B.   reviewing website design and writing style

C.   assuming all online resources are not credible

D.   reviewing website design and domain name

43

Which of the following were part of the New England colonies?

A.   New York, Connecticut, and Massachusetts

B.   Connecticut, Massachusetts, and New Hampshire

C.   New Hampshire, Massachusetts, and New Jersey

D.   New York, New Jersey, Pennsylvania, and Delaware

44

Which of the following are considered geographical features on a map?

A.   plains, plateaus, valleys, and mountains

B.   continents, plateaus, cardinal directions, and mountains

C.   bodies of water, plains, plateaus, and countries

D.   plains, plateaus, areas depicting agricultural products, and mountains

45

Which of the following ideas from Thomas Hobbes influenced the US Constitution?

A.   Individual rights should take priority over collective rights.

B.   People should give up some of their rights and form a government to ensure order in society.

C.   Communism is the only way to govern people.

D.   People should create a utopia to avoid the evils of government.

46

Which of the following examples could be used to describe the theme of respect to elementary school students?

A.   defending one's beliefs even when they are unpopular

B.   paying a parking ticket

C.   returning a library book on time

D.   foregoing an opportunity to cut a line

47

Which of the following is considered a negative consequence of the Civil War?

A.   sharecropping in the South

B.   the South was forgiven for leaving the Union

C.   adding amendments to the Constitution to address equal protection for people under the law

D.   the Union helped the South rebuild roads and farms

48

Which of the following statements best describes Reconstruction in the US after the Civil War?

A.   Debates over legalizing slavery in the US were ongoing.

B.   During its military occupation of the South, the Union developed Black Codes to appease disaffected Southern aristocrats who had lost slaves.

C.   Northern troops occupied the South to ensure that laws were being followed and to help reunite the country after the Civil War.

D.   President Lincoln led Reconstruction efforts.

49

The framers instituted a system of checks and balances because they were concerned about

A.   one branch of government gaining too much power.

B.   mob rule.

C.   the military taking over the government.

D.   the states overpowering the national government.

50

Which of the following is true about the Trail of Tears?

A.   The Trail of Tears drove Native Americans to Indian Territory (later, Oklahoma) because white settlers no longer required their assistance in agricultural production.

B.   Removal treaties were enacted fairly and peacefully.

C.   The Indian Removal Act of 1831 began the forced relocation of Native Americans that year.

D.   The Cherokee Nation was forced to give up land east of the Mississippi River during Andrew Jackson's presidency.

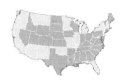

Answer Key

1)

A. Incorrect. Unrestricted submarine warfare occurred in 1917, during World War I.

B. Correct. On December 7, 1941, Japan bombed Pearl Harbor, hoping to prevent the US from interfering with its intent to invade Southeast Asia and other territories such as Guam and Hong Kong.

C. Incorrect. The 1940 Battle of Britain was the first major battle of World War II; the US was still technically a neutral party (although it was effectively supporting Britain through the Lend-Lease Act).

D. Incorrect. The Battle of the Bulge took place after the United States entered World War II.

2)

A. Incorrect. High interest rates and a low amount of printed currency usually contribute to deflation.

B. Incorrect. High unemployment rates do not lead to price increases.

C. Incorrect. A decrease in supply and a low amount of printed currency usually contribute to deflation.

D. Correct. Inflation occurs when prices increase. Both of these factors contribute to inflation.

3)

A. Incorrect. This situation describes a choice, not a need, which is something a person absolutely requires.

B. Incorrect. Scarcity refers to situations when there is not enough supply to meet demand, which does not apply to this situation.

C. **Correct.** Opportunity cost refers to the cost of the loss of one option when it is rejected for another (in this case, if Luther and Barbara choose to hire one staff member, they lose the marketing potential another employee would make possible, whereas if they choose to hire two, they lose the leftover money).

D. Incorrect. Supply and demand refers to the number of goods and their demand, which isn't the case here.

4)

A. Incorrect. The Eastern and Western Hemispheres are divided by the Prime Meridian, which intersects the European countries of the United Kingdom, France, and Spain. Furthermore, Ireland and Portugal are located in the Western Hemisphere, so Europe is indeed in both hemispheres. However, there is a better answer choice.

B. Incorrect. The Eastern and Western Hemispheres are divided by the Prime Meridian, which intersects the African countries of Algeria, Mali, Burkina Faso, Togo, and Ghana. Furthermore, Morocco, Western Sahara, Mauritania, Senegal, the Gambia, Guinea, Guinea-Bissau, Sierra Leone, Liberia, Côte d'Ivoire, and Cape Verde are located in the Western Hemisphere, so Africa is indeed in both hemispheres. However, there is a better answer choice.

C. Incorrect. North America is located entirely in the Western Hemisphere, which is divided from the Eastern Hemisphere by the Prime Meridian and the 180th Meridian.

D. **Correct.** Both Europe and Africa are located in both the Eastern and Western Hemispheres.

5)

A. Incorrect. The Battle of Palmito Ranch, the final encounter between Union and Confederate forces, is considered the end of the Civil War.

B. **Correct.** On April 12, 1861, the Confederate army attacked the Union-controlled Fort Sumter in Charleston, South Carolina, triggering the US Civil War.

C. Incorrect. The Missouri Compromise, also known as the Compromise of 1820, contributed to divisions between the North and the South; however the war did not begin until 1861.

D. Incorrect. The Battle of Yorktown was the last battle of the American Revolution.

6)

A. **Correct.** After Cleopatra's death, ancient Egypt became part of the Roman Empire.

B. Incorrect. The Egyptians welcomed him, and the new administration was based on an Egyptian model.

C.   Incorrect. Severe droughts started in 2200 BCE.

D.   Incorrect. The Canaanite settlers accepted Egyptian governance.

7)

A.   Incorrect. Athenian democracy is the first known example of direct democracy; furthermore, the Romans did not practice this form of government.

B.   Incorrect. The Greeks developed columns; the Romans adopted them.

C.   **Correct.** Before it was an empire, Rome was a republic led by senators elected to the Senate.

D.   Incorrect. The earliest known written language is cuneiform, developed by the Sumerians.

8)

A.   Incorrect. In ancient Greece, women lived in the back and upstairs part of the house, away from men.

B.   **Correct.** The ancient Romans, not the ancient Greeks, built aqueducts and developed public toilets.

C.   Incorrect. An agora was a central marketplace where the ancient Greeks could meet and conduct business.

D.   Incorrect. Socrates was a Greek philosopher whose thinking was the foundation for later Greek and much modern Western philosophical thought.

9)

A.   Incorrect. Interdependence describes the circumstances in which economic actors rely on each other to meet their needs.

B.   **Correct.** In a free-market economy, the prices of goods and services are determined by sellers and consumers.

C.   Incorrect. Communism is an economic and social system in which resources are collectively owned.

D.   Incorrect. When one business dominates an entire industry, it holds a monopoly.

10)

A.   Incorrect. Gender roles are behavioral norms that influence human behavior.

B.   **Correct.** There is debate over the degree to which gender is defined by physical features, social and cultural expectations, or both.

C.   Incorrect. Femininity and masculinity are the main concepts of gender.

D.   Incorrect. Notions of gender roles, gender identity, and inequality continue to be debated in public discourse.

11)

    A.   **Correct.** A bar graph that features the population over a number of years would help researchers analyze population patterns.

    B.   Incorrect. While a population map may help, it only details one year; more information is needed to analyze population patterns.

    C.   Incorrect. This photograph does not indicate the population in the whole of Texas.

    D.   Incorrect. Researchers would use this to compare the population of Texas with that of other states.

12)

    A.   Incorrect. President Hoover was president during the Great Depression.

    B.   Incorrect. Rutherford Hayes served from 1877 to 1881.

    C.   **Correct.** Franklin D. Roosevelt supported laws that helped those unemployed and impoverished due to the Great Depression.

    D.   Incorrect. Jimmy Carter served from 1977 to 1981.

13)

    A.   Incorrect. The executive branch has the power to approve laws—the president signs or vetoes a bill once it has passed through Congress.

    B.   **Correct.** While the executive branch can approve them, only Congress can make laws.

    C.   Incorrect. The executive branch has the power to implement laws.

    D.   Incorrect. The executive branch has the power to enforce laws, and federal law enforcement agencies are part of the executive branch.

14)

    A.   Incorrect. This is not a significant effect.

    B.   Incorrect. More UV rays do enter the earth, but there are more significant effects of ozone layer depletion.

    C.   **Correct.** All of these are consequences of the depletion of the ozone layer.

    D.   Incorrect. An increase in build-up of greenhouse gases is not the only significant effect of ozone layer depletion.

15)

    A.   Incorrect. The Second Amendment guarantees the right to bear arms.

    B.   Incorrect. The Sixth Amendment states that the people have a right to confront witnesses arranged by the government.

    C.   **Correct.** The Bill of Rights is composed of the first ten amendments. The Fourteenth Amendment guarantees equal protection under the law.

D.   Incorrect. The First Amendment ensures freedom of speech, religion, and assembly; the right to petition the government; and freedom of the press.

16)

A.   Incorrect. Social regulations deal with how businesses behave, such as prohibiting harmful behaviors.

B.   Correct. Antitrust law breaks up monopolies to allow fair competition within the economy.

C.   Incorrect. Any health regulations would be classified as social regulation.

D.   Incorrect. Social security provides direct assistance to individuals; it does not affect the market in that sense.

17)

A.   Incorrect. Studying climate only addresses the earth's physical processes.

B.   Correct. Human geography studies the relationship between humans and the physical world; studying how Christianity spread worldwide would need to address this relationship.

C.   Incorrect. Studying the effect of land features on animals and plants does not address humans and so is physical geography.

D.   Incorrect. Studying the movement of continents is an example of physical geography.

18)

A.   Incorrect. Tenement housing created poor living conditions due to its unsanitary conditions.

B.   Incorrect. Diseases were common because of rapid population increases and poor living conditions.

C.   Incorrect. Corrupt politicians would provide services to immigrants only if people voted for them.

D.   Correct. Urbanization itself is the development of urban areas due to the arrival of job seekers; employment opportunities are themselves pull factors.

19)

A.   Correct. Republicanism also stresses natural rights as central values.

B.   Incorrect. There are many forms of government that do not necessarily welcome a civil-minded or independent populace.

C.   Incorrect. Economics is the study of the production and consumption of wealth.

D.   Incorrect. Communism stresses that all property is owned publicly by a classless society.

20)

A.   Incorrect. A legend explains the symbols on a map.

B.   Correct. An inset features details that are considered important on a map.

C.   Incorrect. A compass depicts the cardinal and intermediate directions on a map.

D.   Incorrect. As insert is not a cartographic feature.

21)

A.   Incorrect. Colonists were enraged that Britain adjusted the Tea Act to benefit the Crown.

B.   Incorrect. The Great Proclamation was at odds with colonial desire for expansion.

C.   Correct. While troops were ordered to capture Samuel Adams, they were not asked to capture Thomas Jefferson.

D.   Incorrect. The chancellor of the exchequer imposed these duties in 1767.

22)

A.   Correct. This 1991 event in which members of the Soviet government attempted to take control from Mikhail Gorbachev contributed to the dissolution of the USSR, effectively ending the Cold War.

B.   Incorrect. The fall of the Berlin Wall dissolved communism in Germany.

C.   Incorrect. The Cuban missile crisis was in 1962, at the height of the Cold War.

D.   Incorrect. This event happened at the height of the Cold War.

23)

A.   Incorrect. This colonial trial helped to establish freedom of the press in the United States.

B.   Correct. This case established judicial review.

C.   Incorrect. Dred Scott was a slave who sued for his freedom; the case did not establish judicial review.

D.   Incorrect. This trial revolved around the question of teaching evolution in schools.

24)

A.   Incorrect. Members of Congress can only serve in one branch of government during their term; however, all of the options presented are also applicable.

B.   Incorrect. The president can only sign or veto legislation; he or she cannot vote on it in Congress; the executive branch is separate from the legislative branch. However, this is not the best answer choice.

C.   Incorrect. Checks and balances show the importance of the separation of powers; no one part of the government controls decision making. However, there is a better answer choice here.

D.   Correct. All choices are different examples of the separation of powers.

25)

A.   Incorrect. Although this was an ancient Chinese invention, it was not a significant one.

B.   Incorrect. The toothbrush was invented by the ancient Egyptians.

C.   Correct. Gunpowder is one of the most important inventions of ancient China.

D.   Incorrect. Although the animal zodiac was an ancient Chinese invention, it is not as globally significant as gunpowder.

26)

A.   Incorrect. The freelancer is still a resident of the United States; despite the freelancer's location, he or she is exchanging services within the US market, not internationally.

B.   Correct. A global marketplace involves the exchange of goods and labor around the world.

C.   Incorrect. It is unclear where the commercial website is based, so it is unclear whether the purchase is international.

D.   Incorrect. This is an opinion, not necessarily a fact about the global marketplace (although it could facilitate global trade).

27)

A.   Incorrect. The Classical period is most known for its development of the principles of democracy.

B.   Incorrect. The Early Bronze Age is most known for its invention of bronze.

C.   Correct. This period in time saw advancements such as the Pythagorean Theorem and the calculation of the circumference of the earth.

D.   Incorrect. The Archaic period is most known for its development in pottery and sculpture.

28)

A.   Incorrect. While being kind is likely to help a citizen strengthen personal relationships, it is not his or her responsibility.

B.   Incorrect. Joining after-school clubs is voluntary.

C.   Correct. Citizens have a responsibility to understand laws and pay the consequences if they break them.

D.   Incorrect. Starting a business can help a citizen generate wealth, but it is voluntary.

29)

A.   Incorrect. This example does not address Franklin's thoughts on electricity.

B.   Incorrect. An essay about the effects of lightning does not address Franklin's thoughts on electricity unless he wrote it himself, and it is not clear from this example that he did.

C.   Incorrect. A newspaper report on Franklin's inventions is a secondary resource that only talks about Franklin's inventions, not his thoughts on electricity.

D.   Correct. This is a primary resource that delves into the thought process behind Franklin's theories on electricity.

30)

A.   Incorrect. The Louisiana Purchase did not include land as far south as the Rio Grande; this territory (mainly Texas) belonged to Spain.

B.   Correct. Napoleon sold this section of land in 1803 to finance his European wars.

C.   Incorrect. Georgia was not included in the Louisiana Purchase; it was one of the original colonies and first states.

D.   Incorrect. New Mexico was not part of the Louisiana Purchase; the Southwest was controlled by Spain at the time.

31)

A.   Incorrect. The Immigration Act of 1965 encouraged more immigration in order to attract skilled labor and reunite families.

B.   Correct. Both the Immigration Act of 1924 and the Great Depression discouraged immigration to the United States.

C.   Incorrect. World War I did not contribute to declining immigration.

D.   Incorrect. This was only one contributing factor to declining immigration; furthermore, it was a global event not isolated to the United States. There is a better answer choice.

32)

A.   Correct. The British prime minister recommended limiting heat usage in winter; the US president did not.

B.   Incorrect. The US automotive industry slowed down because it produced larger cars that required more fuel.

C.   Incorrect. In an effort to limit overwhelming lines at gas pumps and to conserve gasoline, political leaders asked that gas stations close for one day a week.

D.   Incorrect. Scarcity (in this case, oil scarcity) results in higher demand and thus higher prices.

33)

A.   Incorrect. The president has the Senate's consent to carry out foreign policy.

B.   Correct. The president is responsible for enforcing law, not creating it.

C.   Incorrect. The president periodically reports on the state of the nation, in what has become known as the annual State of the Union address.

D.   Incorrect. Presidents can pardon felons convicted of federal crimes.

34)

A.   Incorrect. Absolute location refers to a specific location based on geographic coordinates.

B.   Incorrect. Physical geography is the study of the earth's natural processes, not location.

C.   Incorrect. A geographical feature refers to a location's physical features.

D.   Correct. Relative location refers to the location of a place relative to another, in this case Pittsburgh.

35)

A.   Incorrect. This stipulation was only part of the Neutrality Acts.

B.   Incorrect. The Neutrality Acts were meant to prevent US involvement in foreign wars.

C.   Incorrect. The Neutrality Acts were meant to keep the United States out of foreign wars.

D.   Correct. The purpose of the Neutrality Acts was to prevent direct and indirect US interference in armed conflict overseas.

36)

A.   Incorrect. Penicillin was discovered and used during World War II.

B.   Correct. The first time an airplane flew from a ship was in 1912.

C.   Incorrect. Radar was developed and used during World War II.

D.   Incorrect. Nuclear power was developed, weaponized, and used during the Second World War.

37)

    A.   **Correct.** Routes were indirect to thwart pursuers chasing escapees and their allies.

    B.   Incorrect. Direct routes posed too great a risk; pursuers could more easily catch fugitives.

    C.   Incorrect. Sometimes children were separated because they were unable to keep up with their groups; furthermore, women were rarely able to escape the plantation unnoticed.

    D.   Incorrect. Information was transmitted verbally in an effort to maintain confidentiality.

38)

    A.   Incorrect. Jefferson drafted the Declaration of Independence.

    B.   Incorrect. Washington was the commander-in-chief of the Continental Army during the American Revolution and later became the first president of the United States.

    C.   **Correct.** Madison not only advocated the ratification of the Constitution; he had also helped to write the Federalist Papers.

    D.   Incorrect. Henry was an anti-Federalist who opposed the ratification of the Constitution.

39)

    A.   Incorrect. Separation of powers is meant to prevent any one branch— executive, legislative, or judicial—from dominating government.

    B.   **Correct.** The First Amendment protects freedom of religion as well as freedom of speech, assembly, the press, and the right of the people to petition the government.

    C.   Incorrect. Eminent domain refers to the government's ability to seize private property for public use in certain situations. According to the Fifth Amendment, private property cannot be taken for public use without proper compensation.

    D.   Incorrect. Popular sovereignty is the concept that government is a social contract, legitimized only by the consent of the people.

40)

    A.   Incorrect. The Seventh Amendment states that civil cases may be tried by a jury.

    B.   Incorrect. The Fourth Amendment protects citizens from searches and seizures without a warrant.

    C.   **Correct.** The Third Amendment forbids the government from quartering troops in homes, an abuse suffered by Americans under British rule.

D.   Incorrect. The Ninth Amendment states that citizens may enjoy rights other than those outlined in the Constitution and that the Constitution does not override those rights.

41)

A.   Incorrect. Questioning is only one aspect of inquiry-based learning. This project asks students to draw conclusions as well.

B.   Incorrect. The description of this project does not specify whether the students work in groups.

C.   Incorrect. This project involves data interpretation, but it requires other steps as well.

D.   Correct. In inquiry-based learning, students gather relevant sources and interpret them in order to develop their own conclusions.

42)

A.   Correct. Checking the author and date of research helps to determine if the information is credible and up-to-date.

B.   Incorrect. Website design and writing style may provide indications as to the credibility of a source, but they alone do not determine legitimacy.

C.   Incorrect. There are many credible online resources.

D.   Incorrect. A domain name can indicate the legitimacy of a source, but website design is not always indicative of a credible source.

43)

A.   Incorrect. New York was not part of the New England colonies.

B.   Correct. All three were part of the New England colonies.

C.   Incorrect. New Jersey was not part of the New England colonies.

D.   Incorrect. These were all part of the Middle Colonies.

44)

A.   Correct. Geographical features depict the physical aspects of a place on a map.

B.   Incorrect. Cardinal directions are not considered geographical features.

C.   Incorrect. Countries are considered political features.

D.   Incorrect. Agricultural products are not considered a geographical feature.

45)

A.   Incorrect. Hobbes believed in collective rights; otherwise, he believed individuals would only address their own needs, to the detriment of others.

B.   **Correct.** Hobbes advocated governments creating and ensuring social order.

C.   Incorrect. Hobbes believed that a monarchy was the best way to govern people.

D.   Incorrect. Hobbes believed that people were naturally negative and that a utopia would be impossible to construct.

46)

A.   Incorrect. Defying unpopularity exhibits courage, a theme of citizenship.

B.   Incorrect. Paying a parking ticket is a responsibility, an element of citizenship.

C.   Incorrect. It is responsible to return a library book on time; responsibility applies to citizenship.

D.   **Correct.** Respect, another aspect of citizenship, involves taking into consideration the feelings of others.

47)

A.   **Correct.** Sharecropping enabled landowners in the South to maintain control of former slaves.

B.   Incorrect. Forgiving the South for their actions helped to unite the nation as a whole.

C.   Incorrect. Equal protection as addressed in the Fourteenth Amendment was a positive outcome of the Civil War.

D.   Incorrect. Rebuilding the South benefitted the country as a whole.

48)

A.   Incorrect. Slavery was illegal according to the Thirteenth Amendment of the United States Constitution, of which ratification was a requirement for readmission into the Union.

B.   Incorrect. Southern governments developed Black Codes in an effort to continue oppression of freed black Americans.

C.   **Correct.** During Reconstruction, there were efforts to rebuild the devastated South, which was under Union military occupation following the Civil War.

D.   Incorrect. While Lincoln did make some plans for Reconstruction, he died before he had a chance to implement them.

49)

    A.   **Correct.** The purpose of checks and balances was to prevent tyranny in any branch of the government.

    B.   Incorrect. While there was some concern among the founders about the dangers of a pure democracy, checks and balances do not address the relationship between the government and the people.

    C.   Incorrect. Separation of powers kept the military in check. Also, with a civilian commander in chief, the military remains accountable to civilian authority.

    D.   Incorrect. Checks and balances do not refer to the relationship between the state and national governments.

50)

    A.   Incorrect. White settlers wanted to grow cotton on Native American land themselves; they never employed Native American workers.

    B.   Incorrect. President Jackson and the government frequently ignored the legal rights of Native Americans.

    C.   Incorrect. The Indian Removal Act was passed in 1831, but the forced migration of the Cherokee and other tribes did not occur that year.

    D.   **Correct.** This series of incidents happened in 1838 and 1839.

Science Practice

1

Which of these is a biome?

A. a desert

B. a cornfield

C. a herd of bison

D. a beehive

2

What is the name of the phenomenon when a star suddenly increases in brightness and then disappears from view?

A. aurora

B. galaxy

C. black hole

D. supernova

3

What term describes the resistance to motion caused by one object rubbing against another object?

A. inertia

B. friction

C. velocity

D. gravity

4

Which planet orbits closest to Earth?

A.   Mercury

B.   Venus

C.   Jupiter

D.   Saturn

5

Which tool is used to measure the mass of an object?

A.   a thermometer

B.   a graduated cylinder

C.   a balance

D.   an abacus

6

Which organism has cells that contain mitochondria?

A.   whale

B.   mushroom

C.   tulip

D.   all of the above

7

Which condition can be diagnosed by an electrocardiogram (EKG)?

A.   diabetes

B.   torn ligaments

C.   cancer

D.   tachycardia

8

Which action is an example of mechanical weathering?

A.   Calcium carbonate reacts with water to form a cave.

B.   An iron gate rusts.

C.   Tree roots grow under the foundation of a house and cause cracks.

D.   Bananas turn brown after they are peeled.

9

What are the negatively charged particles inside an atom?

A.   protons

B.   neutrons

C.   electrons

D.   ions

10

Organisms in the same class are also in the same_____.

A.   phylum

B.   order

C.   genus

D.   species

11

Which type of rock forms when lava cools and solidifies?

A.   igneous

B.   sedimentary

C.   metamorphic

D.   sandstone

12

Which unit measures pressure?

A.   kilometers

B.   grams

C.   grams per second

D.   pounds per square foot

13

Which organism regulates its body temperature externally?

A.   lobster

B.   dolphin

C.   whale

D.   pelican

14

Which organism is a decomposer?

A.   apple trees

B.   mushrooms

C.   goats

D.   lions

15

Which pH level is classified as a base?

A.   2

B.   4

C.   6

D.   8

16

Which body system is responsible for the release of growth hormones?

A.   digestive system

B.   endocrine system

C.   nervous system

D.   circulatory system

17

Which example illustrates a physical change?

A.   Water becomes ice.

B.   Batter is baked into a cake.

C.   An iron fence rusts.

D.   A firecracker explodes.

18

Which energy source is nonrenewable?

A.   water

B.   wind

C.   coal

D.   sunlight

19

How long does it take the earth to rotate on its axis?

A. one hour

B. one day

C. one month

D. one year

20

Which organism is a reptile?

A. crocodile

B. frog

C. salamander

D. salmon

21

By what process do producers make sugars and release oxygen?

A. digestion

B. chloroplast

C. decomposition

D. photosynthesis

22

Which type of wave is a longitudinal wave?

A. surface wave

B. light wave

C. sound wave

D. electromagnetic wave

23

Which example demonstrates refraction?

A. rainbow

B. echo

C. mirror

D. radio

24

Which factor is an abiotic part of an ecosystem?

A.   producers

B.   consumers

C.   water

D.   decomposers

25

What term describes a relationship between two organisms where one organism benefits to the detriment of the other organism?

A.   mutualism

B.   parasitism

C.   commensalism

D.   predation

26

Which organelle makes proteins?

A.   mitochondria

B.   cytoplasm

C.   vacuole

D.   ribosomes

27

Which statement is true?

A.   Earth is much closer to the sun than it is to other stars.

B.   The moon is closer to Venus than it is to Earth.

C.   At certain times of the year, Jupiter is closer to the sun than Earth is.

D.   Mercury is the closest planet to Earth.

28

Which metal attracts magnets?

A.   iron

B.   copper

C.   silver

D.   gold

29

Which example demonstrates electrostatic attraction?

A. Items in a car continue to move forward when the car stops suddenly.

B. Tides are affected by the moon.

C. The moon revolves around Earth.

D. Plastic wrap sticks to a person's hand.

30

In which part of a plant does photosynthesis take place?

A. the roots

B. the stem

C. the leaves

D. the flower

31

Which example has the least amount of kinetic energy?

A. a plane flying through the sky

B. a plane sitting on the runway

C. a ladybug flying toward a flower

D. a meteorite falling to Earth

32

Which of the following is caused by geothermal heat?

A. geysers

B. glaciers

C. tsunamis

D. tornadoes

33

Which term describes space weather?

A. supernova

B. black hole

C. volcanic lightning

D. solar flares

34

Which gas is found in large quantities in Earth's atmosphere?

A. carbon monoxide

B. bromine

C. nitrogen

D. fluorine

35

Which term describes an element?

A. atom

B. molecule

C. proton

D. ion

36

Which statement is true?

A. Mass and weight are the same thing.

B. Mass is affected by gravitational pull.

C. Weight is affected by the gravitational pull.

D. Mass is related to the surface area of an object.

37

When Earth moves between the moon and the sun, it is called a

A. solar eclipse.

B. lunar eclipse.

C. black hole.

D. supernova.

38

Which element is most common in the universe?

A. carbon

B. lithium

C. potassium

D. titanium

39

Which storm is least likely to form over ocean water?

A. hurricane

B. typhoon

C. cyclone

D. tornado

40

Which substance can be used to neutralize an acid spill?

A. sodium bicarbonate

B. citric acid

C. cat litter

D. water

41

Which gas is produced by burning fossil fuels?

A. helium

B. oxygen

C. nitrogen

D. carbon dioxide

42

A warm air mass moving into a cold air mass is called a

A. warm front.

B. cold front.

C. isobar.

D. tornado.

43

Which of the following is NOT a cause of extinction?

A. poor reproduction

B. climate change

C. habitat conservation

D. overexploitation by humans

44

Which term describes the top layer of the earth's surface?

A.   stratosphere

B.   lithosphere

C.   atmosphere

D.   biosphere

45

What term describes the speed and direction of a moving soccer ball?

A.   velocity

B.   momentum

C.   mass

D.   energy

46

Which substance is a good thermal conductor?

A.   plastic

B.   rubber

C.   porcelain

D.   aluminum

47

Which example demonstrates body systems working together to maintain homeostasis?

A.   Jessica's tracheotomy opened a breathing obstruction.

B.   Max's muscles, tendons, and ligaments allow his joints to bend.

C.   Kevin's bones thicken from an excessive production of growth hormones.

D.   Stacy shivers from the cold.

48

What is the primary role of amino acids in cells?

A.   break down carbohydrates

B.   break down fats

C.   build proteins

D.   filter waste

49

What part of the atom flows through a circuit to power a lightbulb?

A.   protons

B.   neutrons

C.   electrons

D.   nucleus

50

Which simple machine is shown in the following picture?

Figure 8.1. Simple Machine

A.   inclined plane

B.   pulley

C.   screw

D.   wedge

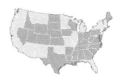

Answer Key

1)

- **A.** **Correct.** A biome is a large ecological community that includes specific plants and animals. Other biomes include rainforests and grasslands.
- B. Incorrect. A cornfield is a part of a prairie biome.
- C. Incorrect. Animals are part of a biome.
- D. Incorrect. A beehive is part of a biome.

2)

- A. Incorrect. Aurora is the phenomenon of colored lights that appear in the sky near the North and South Poles.
- B. Incorrect. The galaxy is a large group of stars held together by gravity.
- C. Incorrect. Black holes are collapsed stars whose gravitational pull is so strong that light cannot escape.
- **D.** **Correct.** Before a star collapses, the star burns brighter for a period of time and then fades from view. This is a supernova.

3)

- A. Incorrect. Inertia is an object's tendency not to change position or direction unless an outside force acts upon it.
- **B.** **Correct.** Friction occurs when motion is impeded because one object is rubbing against another object.
- C. Incorrect. Velocity is the rate at which an object is displaced from its original position.
- D. Incorrect. Gravity is a force that attracts objects to one another.

4)

A. Incorrect. Mercury is the planet closest to the sun. Venus orbits between Mercury and Earth.

B. **Correct.** Venus's orbit is closest to Earth. Venus is the second planet from the sun and Earth is the third planet from the sun.

C. Incorrect. Jupiter is the fifth planet from the sun.

D. Incorrect. Saturn is the sixth planet from the sun.

5)

A. Incorrect. A thermometer measures temperature.

B. Incorrect. A graduated cylinder measures volume.

C. **Correct.** A balance measures mass.

D. Incorrect. An abacus is a tool used to calculate numbers.

6)

A. Incorrect. Mitochondria are found in animal cells.

B. Incorrect. Mitochondria are found in fungi cells.

C. Incorrect. Mitochondria are found in plant cells.

D. **Correct.** Plant, animal, and fungi cells have mitochondria.

7)

A. Incorrect. Blood tests are used to diagnose diabetes.

B. Incorrect. Magnetic Resonance Imaging (MRI) is used to see soft tissue damage, such as torn ligaments.

C. Incorrect. There are a variety of tests that diagnose cancer, such as blood tests, Magnetic Resonance Imaging (MRI), and ultrasounds.

D. **Correct.** Tachycardia is an abnormally fast heartrate, and electrocardiograms show the electrical activity of the heart.

8)

A. Incorrect. Cave formation is an example of chemical weathering. Chemical weathering involves a chemical change.

B. Incorrect. Rusting is an example of chemical weathering.

C. **Correct.** Mechanical weathering involves breaking a substance down without changing the composition of the substance.

D. Incorrect. Bananas turning brown is an example of a chemical change.

9)

    A.   Incorrect. Protons are positively charged particles in the nucleus.

    B.   Incorrect. Neutrons are particles in the nucleus that have no charge.

    C.   **Correct.** Electrons are negatively charged particles in an atom; electrons orbit the nucleus.

    D.   Incorrect. Ions are atoms that have lost or gained electrons and have a charge.

10)

    A.   **Correct.** A kingdom is the largest group of living things. A kingdom is then subdivided into progressively smaller groups in the following order: kingdom, phylum, class, order, family, genus, and species. The order can be remembered using the mnemonic device: *Keep Pots Clean or Family Gets Sick.*

    B.   Incorrect. An order is a smaller group than a class.

    C.   Incorrect. A genus is a smaller group than a class.

    D.   Incorrect. A species is a smaller group than a class.

11)

    A.   **Correct.** Igneous rocks form when liquid rock cools and solidifies.

    B.   Incorrect. Sedimentary rocks form when sediments are cemented together.

    C.   Incorrect. Metamorphic rocks form when igneous or sedimentary rocks are exposed to extreme temperature and/or pressure to the point that the rocks are changed physically or chemically.

    D.   Incorrect. Sandstone is a type of sedimentary rock.

12)

    A.   Incorrect. Length is measured in kilometers.

    B.   Incorrect. Mass is measured in grams.

    C.   Incorrect. Mass flow rate is measured in grams per second.

    D.   **Correct.** Pressure is measured in pounds per square foot.

13)

    A.   **Correct.** The metabolic rate of crustaceans is too low to regulate their temperature. Crustaceans use behavioral techniques, such as moving to shallow water, to maintain body temperature.

    B.   Incorrect. Dolphins are mammals. Mammals are endothermic, meaning they have a mechanism to regulate body temperature internally.

    C.   Incorrect. Whales are mammals.

    D.   Incorrect. Birds are endothermic.

14)

    A.   Incorrect. Plants produce their own food through photosynthesis, making them producers.

    B.   **Correct.** Mushrooms are fungi. Fungi break down organic material left by dead animals and plants, making them decomposers.

    C.   Incorrect. Goats eat producers, such as grass, making them primary consumers.

    D.   Incorrect. Lions are carnivorous animals that feed on primary consumers and secondary consumers, making them secondary or tertiary consumers.

15)

    A.   Incorrect. Acids have a pH between 0 and 7.

    B.   Incorrect. Acids have a pH between 0 and 7.

    C.   Incorrect. Acids have a pH between 0 and 7.

    D.   **Correct.** Bases have a pH between 7 and 14.

16)

    A.   Incorrect. The digestive system turns food into energy.

    B.   **Correct.** The endocrine system releases hormones, including growth hormones.

    C.   Incorrect. The nervous system is a network of communication cells.

    D.   Incorrect. The circulatory system delivers nutrients to cells and removes wastes from the body.

17)

    A.   **Correct.** When water changes form, it does not change the chemical composition of the substance. Once water becomes ice, the ice can easily turn back into water.

    B.   Incorrect. The chemical composition of the substance changes and cannot be reversed. Baking a cake is an example of a chemical change.

    C.   Incorrect. Rusting is an example of a chemical change.

    D.   Incorrect. Setting off fireworks causes a chemical change.

18)

    A.   Incorrect. Water can generate hydropower, which is a renewable energy source.

    B.   Incorrect. Wind is a renewable energy source.

    C.   **Correct.** Coal is nonrenewable because once coal is burned, it cannot be quickly replaced.

    D.   Incorrect. Solar energy is a renewable energy source.

19)

A.   Incorrect. One hour is 1/24 of the time it takes for the earth to rotate on its axis.

B.   Correct. Earth takes approximately 24 hours to rotate on its axis.

C.   Incorrect. The moon takes approximately one month to revolve around the earth.

D.   Incorrect. The earth takes approximately one year to revolve around the sun.

20)

A.   Correct. Reptiles like crocodiles have scaly skin, are hatched from eggs on land, and are cold-blooded.

B.   Incorrect. Amphibians like frogs are hatched from eggs in water, have gills but develop lungs, and become land animals as they mature.

C.   Incorrect. Salamanders are amphibians.

D.   Incorrect. Fish like salmon live in water; they also have a backbone, gills, scales, and fins.

21)

A.   Incorrect. Digestion is the process whereby large food particles are broken down into small particles.

B.   Incorrect. A chloroplast is the part of the cell where photosynthesis takes place.

C.   Incorrect. Decomposition is the process where substances are broken down into smaller parts.

D.   Correct. Photosynthesis describes the process by which plants convert the energy of the sun into stored chemical energy (glucose).

22)

A.   Incorrect. Waves on the surface of the ocean are transverse waves.

B.   Incorrect. Light waves are transverse waves.

C.   Correct. Sound waves are longitudinal waves because the vibrations travel in the same direction as the energy.

D.   Incorrect. Electromagnetic waves are transverse waves.

23)

A.   Correct. The light of the sun hits rain droplets and bends into a band of colors. The bending of waves is refraction.

B.   Incorrect. Echo is an example of sound reflection.

C.   Incorrect. A mirror is used to show light reflection.

D.   Incorrect. A radio is an example of sound waves reflecting off layers in Earth's atmosphere.

24)

A.   Incorrect. Producers are living things, which are biotic factors.

B.   Incorrect. Consumers are biotic factors because they are alive.

C.   Correct. Nonliving things in an ecosystem, like air and water, are abiotic factors.

D.   Incorrect. Living things are biotic factors.

25)

A.   Incorrect. In mutualism, both organisms benefit.

B.   Correct. Parasitism describes a relationship in which one organism benefits from another organism, to the detriment of the host organism.

C.   Incorrect. Commensalism is when one organism benefits from another without causing harm to the host organism.

D.   Incorrect. Predation is killing and consuming other organisms for food.

26)

A.   Incorrect. Mitochondria release chemical energy from glucose to be used by the cell.

B.   Incorrect. Cytoplasm provides support to the cell.

C.   Incorrect. Vacuoles store water.

D.   Correct. Ribosomes are responsible for production of proteins.

27)

A.   Correct. The sun is the only star in our solar system. The sun is about ninety-three million miles from Earth; the next closest star is about twenty-five trillion miles away.

B.   Incorrect. The moon orbits Earth.

C.   Incorrect. Even when Jupiter is closest to the sun and Earth is farthest from the sun, Earth is always closer to the sun than Jupiter is.

D.   Incorrect. Mercury is the closest planet to the sun, and Venus is closer to Earth.

28)

A.   Correct. Magnets readily attract iron.

B.   Incorrect. Not all metals are attracted to magnets; copper is not.

C.   Incorrect. Magnets do not attract all metals; for example, they do not attract silver.

D.   Incorrect. Gold is not attracted to magnets.

29)

A.   Incorrect. Newton's First Law is that *objects in motion stay in motion.*

B.   Incorrect. Tides are affected by the gravitational pull of the moon. Gravitational force is the attraction between two masses.

C.   Incorrect. The moon revolves around Earth because of the gravitational pull between the two masses.

D.   Correct. Electrostatic force is an attraction between charged surfaces.

30)

A.   Incorrect. Roots extract water and minerals from the soil.

B.   Incorrect. The stem transports nutrients to other parts of the plant.

C.   Correct. Through photosynthesis, leaves use the sun's energy to convert carbon dioxide into glucose (food).

D.   Incorrect. The flower is the reproductive part of a plant.

31)

A.   Incorrect. A plane flying through the sky would have kinetic energy because of its mass and velocity.

B.   Correct. Something that is not moving has zero velocity; therefore it has no kinetic energy.

C.   Incorrect. Even though it has a low mass and a low velocity, a ladybug does have a small amount of kinetic energy.

D.   Incorrect. A meteorite falling toward Earth would have a large amount of kinetic energy because of its mass and velocity.

32)

A.   Correct. Geysers are caused by geothermal heating of water underground.

B.   Incorrect. Glaciers are formed when snow and ice do not melt before new layers of snow and ice are added.

C.   Incorrect. Tsunamis are caused by earthquakes on the ocean floor.

D.   Incorrect. Tornadoes are caused by instability of warm, humid air in the lower atmosphere mixing with cool air in the upper atmosphere.

Go on →

33)

A.   Incorrect. A supernova is a huge explosion of the core of a star that marks the end of the life cycle of the star. Since supernovas occur outside our solar system, they are not considered space weather.

B.   Incorrect. Black holes occur outside our solar system, so they are not considered space weather.

C.   Incorrect. Volcanic lightning is a lightning storm that occurs during a volcanic eruption when positively charged lava is launched into the negatively charged atmosphere. This does not occur in space; therefore, volcanic lightning is not considered space weather.

D.   Correct. Solar flares are huge explosions on the sun. Space weather refers to conditions in the solar system that could potentially affect the work of astronauts in space and cause auroras on Earth.

34)

A.   Incorrect. Carbon monoxide is a rare gas.

B.   Incorrect. Bromine is a rare gas.

C.   Correct. Nitrogen makes up 78 percent of Earth's atmosphere.

D.   Incorrect. Fluorine is a rare gas.

35)

A.   Correct. An atom is the smallest unit of an element.

B.   Incorrect. A molecule is the simplest form of a compound, consisting of two or more atoms.

C.   Incorrect. A proton is a positively charged particle in the nucleus of an atom. A proton by itself will not make an element.

D.   Incorrect. An ion is an electrically charged atom or group of atoms.

36)

A.   Incorrect. Mass is the amount of matter in an object. Weight is a measure of the gravitational pull on an object. Weight changes in space, but mass does not.

B.   Incorrect. Weight is affected by gravitational pull, not mass.

C.   Correct. Weight is affected by gravitational pull.

D.   Incorrect. The surface area or size of an object does not indicate the mass of that object.

37)

A. Incorrect. A solar eclipse is when the moon moves between the sun and Earth.

B. Correct. A lunar eclipse is when Earth moves between the moon and the sun.

C. Incorrect. A black hole is a collapsed star with tremendous gravitational pull.

D. Incorrect. A supernova is an explosion of the core of a star.

38)

A. Correct. Carbon is a common element found in every organic compound and in the atmosphere of some planets.

B. Incorrect. Lithium is highly reactive and is found in small amounts in igneous rocks.

C. Incorrect. Potassium is found in Earth's crust and is essential to plant growth.

D. Incorrect. Titanium makes up less than 1 percent of Earth's surface.

39)

A. Incorrect. Hurricanes form over warm ocean water. Depending upon where a hurricane forms, it can also be called a typhoon or a cyclone.

B. Incorrect. A hurricane that forms in the western Pacific Ocean is called a typhoon.

C. Incorrect. A hurricane that forms in the Indian Ocean is called a cyclone.

D. Correct. Tornadoes occur when warm air masses collide with cold air masses over land.

40)

A. Correct. Sodium bicarbonate, which is a base, will neutralize an acid.

B. Incorrect. Citric acid neutralizes a base spill.

C. Incorrect. Once the spill is neutralized, cat litter may be used to absorb it.

D. Incorrect. An acid spill needs to be neutralized before water is used.

41)

A. Incorrect. Helium is found in large quantities on the sun. It is an inert, colorless, tasteless gas.

B. Incorrect. Oxygen makes up about 20 percent of Earth's atmosphere.

C. Incorrect. Seventy-eight percent of Earth's atmosphere is made of nitrogen, and nitrogen is essential for all living organisms.

D. Correct. Carbon dioxide is formed when fossil fuels containing carbon are burned. Excess carbon dioxide is responsible for global warming.

42)

A. **Correct.** A warm front is when a warm air mass moves into a cold air mass.

B. Incorrect. A cold front is when a cold air mass moves into a warm air mass.

C. Incorrect. An isobar is a contour line indicating locations of equal barometric pressures.

D. Incorrect. A tornado is caused by unstable air.

43)

A. Incorrect. Poor reproduction is one of the identified causes of extinction. If a species is not able to reproduce, it will eventually die out.

B. Incorrect. Climate changes, such as the Ice Age and global warming, are responsible for the extinction of a species.

C. **Correct.** Habitat conservation restores the natural habitat of organisms, protecting a species.

D. Incorrect. Overexploitation by humans through hunting for sport, animal testing, and illegal trapping has caused the endangerment of many species.

44)

A. Incorrect. The stratosphere is a layer of the earth's atmosphere.

B. **Correct.** The lithosphere is the top layer of the earth's surface.

C. Incorrect. The atmosphere refers to the layer of gases that surrounds the earth.

D. Incorrect. The biosphere is the part of Earth where life exists; the biosphere includes the atmosphere, the oceans, and the life-supporting areas above and below Earth's surface.

45)

A. **Correct.** Velocity is the speed of an object in a certain direction.

B. Incorrect. Momentum is calculated by multiplying the velocity of an object by its mass.

C. Incorrect. Mass refers to the amount of matter in an object.

D. Incorrect. Energy describes the capacity to do work.

46)

A. Incorrect. Plastic is an insulator. Insulators block the flow of heat from one object to another.

B. Incorrect. Rubber is an insulator.

C. Incorrect. Porcelain is an insulator.

D. **Correct.** Aluminum is a good thermal conductor because heat energy can move easily through it.

47)

A. Incorrect. A tracheotomy is not a body system reaction; it is a medical intervention.

B. Incorrect. Max's muscles, tendons, and ligaments are part of the muscular system. The bending of joints is a normal function, not a way to maintain homeostasis.

C. Incorrect. Excessive production of growth hormones is an example of disease.

D. **Correct.** Homeostasis refers to body systems working together to ensure that temperature, pH, and oxygen levels are optimal for survival. Sensors in Stacy's nervous system trigger her muscular system to shiver in an attempt to warm her body.

48)

A. Incorrect. Amino acids do not break down carbohydrates.

B. Incorrect. Fats (lipids) are insoluble in cells.

C. **Correct.** Ribosomes make proteins by building amino acid chains.

D. Incorrect. Lysosomes in the cytoplasm filter waste from a cell.

49)

A. Incorrect. Protons remain in the nucleus of an atom.

B. Incorrect. Neutrons remain in the nucleus of an atom.

C. **Correct.** Electrons are negatively charged subatomic particles that exist outside the nucleus of an atom. A power source forces moving electrons through a circuit.

D. Incorrect. The nucleus is the part of an atom that contains protons and neutrons.

50)

A. **Correct.** An inclined plane is a flat surface raised to an angle so that loads can be easily lifted.

B. Incorrect. A pulley is a wheel with ropes that change the direction of the force in order to lift an object.

C. Incorrect. A screw is a rod-shaped object with a spiral groove.

D. Incorrect. A wedge is a type of inclined plane, such as an axe, that has both a wide and a thin end.